Religious and Cultural Difference in Modern British Political Cartoons

Also Available from Bloomsbury:

Comics, Culture, and Religion: Faith Imagined, edited by Kees de Groot
The Bloomsbury Handbook of Religion and Heritage in Contemporary Europe,
edited by Todd Weir and Lieke Wijnia
Religious Diversity in Australia: Living Well with Difference, edited by
Douglas Ezzy, Anna Halafoff, Greg Barton, and Rebecca Banham

Religious and Cultural Difference in Modern British Political Cartoons

Tahnia Ahmed

BLOOMSBURY ACADEMIC
LONDON • NEW YORK • OXFORD • NEW DELHI • SYDNEY

BLOOMSBURY ACADEMIC
Bloomsbury Publishing Plc, 50 Bedford Square, London, WC1B 3DP, UK
Bloomsbury Publishing Inc, 1359 Broadway, New York, NY 10018, USA
Bloomsbury Publishing Ireland, 29 Earlsfort Terrace, Dublin 2, D02 AY28, Ireland

BLOOMSBURY, BLOOMSBURY ACADEMIC and the Diana logo are
trademarks of Bloomsbury Publishing Plc

First published in Great Britain 2024
Paperback edition published 2026

Copyright © Tahnia Ahmed, 2024

Tahnia Ahmed has asserted her right under the Copyright,
Designs and Patents Act, 1988, to be identified as Author of this work.

For legal purposes the Acknowledgements on p. xii constitute
an extension of this copyright page.

Cover image: Man and woman read newspaper (© CSA Images/Getty Images)

All rights reserved. No part of this publication may be: i) reproduced or transmitted in
any form, electronic or mechanical, including photocopying, recording or by means of any
information storage or retrieval system without prior permission in writing from the
publishers; or ii) used or reproduced in any way for the training, development or operation
of artificial intelligence (AI) technologies, including generative AI technologies. The rights
holders expressly reserve this publication from the text and data mining exception
as per Article 4(3) of the Digital Single Market Directive (EU) 2019/790.

Bloomsbury Publishing Plc does not have any control over, or responsibility for, any
third-party websites referred to or in this book. All internet addresses given in this book were
correct at the time of going to press. The author and publisher regret any inconvenience caused
if addresses have changed or sites have ceased to exist, but can accept no responsibility
for any such changes.

A catalogue record for this book is available from the British Library.

Library of Congress Cataloging-in-Publication Data
Names: Ahmed, Tahnia, author.
Title: Religious and cultural difference in modern British political cartoons / Tahnia Ahmed.
Description: London ; New York : Bloomsbury Academic, 2024. | Originally presented as the author's
thesis (doctoral)–King's College, London, 2020. | Includes bibliographical references and index.
Identifiers: LCCN 2023046681 (print) | LCCN 2023046682 (ebook) |
ISBN 9781350294103 (hardback) | ISBN 9781350294141 (paperback) |
ISBN 9781350294110 (pdf) | ISBN 9781350294127 (ebook)
Subjects: LCSH: English wit and humor, Pictorial. | Racism–Great Britain. |
Ethnic attitudes–Great Britain–History–20th century–Caricatures and cartoons. |
Ethnic attitudes–Great Britain–History–21st century–Caricatures and cartoons. |
Religious minorities–Great Britain–History–20th century–Caricatures and cartoons. |
Religious minorities–Great Britain–History–21st century–Caricatures and cartoons. |
Great Britain–Politics and government–1945-
Classification: LCC DA125.A1 A69 2024 (print) | LCC DA125.A1 (ebook) |
DDC 305.800941/0904–dc23/eng/20240130
LC record available at https://lccn.loc.gov/2023046681
LC ebook record available at https://lccn.loc.gov/2023046682

ISBN: HB: 978-1-3502-9410-3
PB: 978-1-3502-9414-1
ePDF: 978-1-3502-9411-0
eBook: 978-1-3502-9412-7

Typeset by Integra Software Services Pvt. Ltd.
For product safety related questions contact productsafety@bloomsbury.com.

To find out more about our authors and books visit www.bloomsbury.com
and sign up for our newsletters.

For Nanumoni, Nanubhai, Dada and Dadu.

Contents

List of illustrations	viii
Preface	ix
Foreword *Aaron Rosen*	x
Acknowledgements	xii
Introduction	1
1 Nuns, guns and balaclavas: The Irish in political cartoons	23
2 Noses, Moses and war: Jews in political cartoons	55
3 Turbans, terrorism and transport: Sikhs in political cartoons	81
4 Burqas on the beach: Muslim women in political cartoons	103
5 Beards, bombs and barbarians: Muslim men in political cartoons	127
Conclusion	151
Glossary	166
Notes	167
Bibliography	199
List of images cited	217
Index	232

Illustrations

1	John Leech, 'Cartoon No 1. Substance and Shadow' (*Punch*, 15 July 1843)	7
2	H. Strickland Constable (*Ireland from One or Two Neglected Points of View*, 1888)	27
3	John Tenniel, 'Two Forces' (*Punch*, 29 October 1881)	28
4	Nicholas Garland 'No! No! No!' (*Daily Telegraph*, 26 October 1993)	36
5	Nicholas Garland, 'I find it difficult not to feel sympathy for both sides in these tribal conflicts.' (*Daily Telegraph*, 16 August 1969)	38
6	Michael Cummings, 'How marvellous it would be if they DID knock each other insensible!' (*Daily Express*, 12 August 1970)	40
7	David Low, 'What, he's not anti-semitic? We'll soon alter that' (*Evening Standard*, 22 November 1946)	61
8	David Low, 'Lebensraum for the Conquered' (*Evening Standard*, 20 January 1940)	65
9	Stanley Franklin, 'It makes a change from Z-cars' (*Daily Mirror*, 29 January 1970)	89
10	Michael Cummings, 'The good news is that our next war will be fought in outer space – the bad news is that other people's wars will be fought in the streets of Britain' (*Daily Express*, 13 June 1984)	94
11	Paul Thomas, uncaptioned image (*Daily Express*, 12 November 2001)	110
12	Peter Schrank, 'What am I doing here?' (*Independent on Sunday*, 11 March 2012)	111
13	Christian Adams, 'Trojan horse in niqab' (*Daily Telegraph*, 4 May 2014)	119
14	Peter Brookes, 'New UK Poll … ' (*The Times*, 26 February 2015)	120
15	Peter Schrank's 'Back to the future' (*Independent*, 20 August 2006)	137
16	Paul Thomas, uncaptioned cartoon (*Daily Express*, 27 April 2004)	140

Preface

Whilst studying for my Masters in Jewish Studies, a visiting scholar asked me what my dissertation was on. I told her it was on Jews in cartoons. Thereafter, whenever I would see her she would ask me about the Jews in Sudan. I didn't understand why as I had no idea on the topic. A few years later, I was speaking to my friend on the phone. I told him my PhD was expanding on the Masters research I had done looking at Jews in cartoons. When I met up with him, he asked me to tell him more about my research on 'Jews in Khartoum'. I finally understood why the woman had kept asking me about Sudan and its Jewish community!

Foreword
Aaron Rosen

Tahnia Ahmed's monograph about modern British political cartoons could hardly have appeared at a more fitting time. One could certainly make an argument that contemporary Britain, and especially British politics, have become ever more cartoonish in recent years.

Is there still a role for cartoonists to play when political farce writes (or sketches) itself? Absolutely. The finest political cartoons do not simply settle for cheap laughs, which risk banalizing serious offenses or providing a smokescreen for further malfeasance. At their most incisive – as Ahmed reveals on multiple occasions – political cartoons shrewdly reveal the ironies and hypocrisies which underlie political rhetoric and deeds. And because politicians so often trade in visually saturated symbols and stories, cartoonists are uniquely primed to perforate their soaring imagery with sharpened pencils. In their more self-aware moments, great politicians may even learn to welcome this deflating prick, as Winston Churchill did of David Low, at times his most strident critic as well as champion (see Chapter 2).

While a cartoonist's well-timed fusillade can let the air out of a blimpish politician, just as importantly cartoonists can uplift causes and communities that fly below the radar of social, economic and political privilege. This is where Ahmed's analysis of political cartoons proves especially illuminating. She certainly provides instances of cartoonists missing the mark, dangerously reifying and replicating ethnic and religious prejudices. However, she offers plenty of examples of cartoonists who expose the inequities and indignities facing minority communities in Britain, from extreme immigration hurdles to discriminatory employment practices and social alienation.

Ahmed's method, rooted in close visual study, historical contextualization and comparative analysis, has the effect of disclosing unexpected parallels and resources for contesting prejudice today. By delving into anti-Catholic and anti-Jewish visual tropes in early chapters, for example, she helps reframe representations of Muslim women and men in later chapters. Despite the highly varied experiences of these communities, the villainization of these groups has often been striking similar in syntax and symbolism, drawing upon a common, toxic wellspring of resentment. By treating this material together, Ahmed offers us a fresh chance to study and dissolve old prejudices more effectively and prevent new ones from bubbling up in their place. While this book thus makes a major contribution to the analysis of political cartoons and the study of religion and visual culture, I suspect its impact will – and should be – far wider.

Acknowledgements

I never would have guessed that from a conversation about graphic novels and a suggestion on looking at the portrayal of Jews in political cartoons as a potential Masters dissertation topic, my academic future would be changed forever. For this, I have Professor Aaron Rosen to thank. I will forever be indebted to you for being an incredible supervisor and mentor. This book would not have been possible without you. Thank you so much.

I would also like to thank Professor Ben Quash for his feedback and oversight of the original PhD thesis.

Thank you to the cartoonist Peter Schrank for kindly allowing me to use his images and for taking the time to speak to me as part of my research.

Finally, thank you to Ammu, Abbu, Onik and Almin for believing in me even when I did not.

Introduction

As a child, I lived in a four-storey block of flats in East London. On 9 February 1996, my family and I were visiting my cousins who lived next door. Aged seven, I recall playing with my cousins when suddenly we felt the building shake. We ran out of the bedroom and found all the adults had run out of the sitting room to find out what had just happened. Everyone came out onto their balconies looking at one another in confusion. Later, we found out that the Provisional Irish Republican Army had detonated a bomb in the Docklands, near where we lived. Looking back on the incident, many interlacing questions of identity come to mind. My grandparents lived and grew up in British India. My parents endured life in East Pakistan and the subsequent Bangladesh War of Independence in 1971. Despite all of this, as a second-generation Bangladeshi born and brought up in London, to the perpetrators of the attack none of this mattered; I was a legitimate target.

Therefore, whilst I feel positioned as an Other in some contexts where I am not English/British by virtue of my ethnicity, in other contexts I am considered authentically English/British. An interesting example of this is how Shahara Islam, one of the victims of the 7/7 attacks, was described as 'the embodiment of a modern Muslim woman'.[1] Her profile highlighted how the 7/7 attackers killed indiscriminately and that the Muslim community were also affected by the attack. The IRA bomb incident illustrates the fluidity of identity wherein different criteria are applied in different contexts. In my case, I just happened to be part of the large Bangladeshi diaspora living near one of London's key financial districts. The memory of the attack also serves to highlight the different context in which I now live. In today's world, I am often seen as the Other; rather than being a victim of terror, I am associated with the perpetrators of terror simply because I am Muslim. This was even more striking when I looked at cartoons of other religious communities and how the same messages of Otherness are applied, transferred and shared between communities over the centuries.

Why cartoons?

Several recent controversies have demonstrated the power of political cartoons to provoke debate and action across the globe. In 2005, the Danish newspaper *Morgenavisen Jyllands-Posten* published twelve cartoons of the Prophet Muhammad, including one with a bomb on which the *shahadah*, the Islamic creed, is written on his turban. The backlash against the cartoons was violent in some parts of the world – including Afghanistan and Nigeria.[2] The cartoonists also faced death threats (one survived an axe attack in 2010)[3] and a boycott of Danish products led to a 40 per cent fall in exports to Saudi Arabia and 47 per cent to Iran.[4] In response to the publication of the cartoons by *Jyllands-Posten*, the Iranian newspaper *Hamshahri* hosted the International Holocaust Cartoon Contest in 2006, which was designed to challenge the limits of the freedom of expression.[5] The competition was held 'in the context of official Iranian policy and practice of promoting Holocaust denial', in which the winning entry depicted a wall, with the image of Auschwitz on it, being erected around Jerusalem.[6] The response to the *Jyllands-Posten* cartoons shows how images have the power to affect trade and political relations because of their accessibility: one does not need to learn a new language to read a cartoon, thereby making them easier to understand – and misunderstand – across continents, than a written piece.

Another example occurred in January 2015 where the French satirical magazine, *Charlie Hebdo*, was targeted by two Muslim terrorists who killed twelve of its staff at its Paris headquarters. This was done in retaliation for the magazine's depictions of the Prophet, and Muslims in general, over a number of years. However, it was not the first terror attack the magazine had experienced – in 2011 the headquarters were targeted in an arson attack following the publication of a cartoon featuring the Prophet in a wheelchair being assisted by an Ultra-Orthodox Jew. Both the men in the image say, 'you must not mock' in French.[7] By invoking religious and cultural symbols, a racist dimension can be found. This can be seen in *Hebdo*'s depiction of a Muslim woman in the likeness of a monkey[8] and the way Jews have been depicted for centuries in British cartoons using ethnic stereotypes such as long noses to mark them out as 'the malevolent Jew'.

The image of Serena Williams published in September 2018 in the Australian newspaper the *Herald Sun* attracted global criticism for portraying Williams in a manner that evoked racial stereotypes such as 'lips the size of a baboon, a nose the width of the Mississippi and the tongue of a camel'.[9] This was in contrast to Williams' opponent, Naomi Osaka, who was depicted as slim and blonde and which many saw as an act of whitewashing the Japanese and Haitian tennis player.[10] The use of such iconography is indicative because cartoons feed into debates on how religious, cultural and ethnic identities are constructed. By offering a visual depiction of what is meant by the Other, cartoons have the potential to create, sustain and even resurrect stereotypes of different communities.

In October 2020, Samuel Paty, a schoolteacher in France, was beheaded after showing two cartoons of the Prophet to students. His killing once again sparked debates in France surrounding free speech, secularism and the relationship between the state and its 6 million Muslim citizens. Similar to the 'Je suis Charlie' (I am Charlie) hashtag that trended after the Hebdo attacks in 2015, the hashtag 'Je suis Samuel' (I am Samuel) or 'Je suis prof' (I am a teacher) started trending in France, demonstrating solidarity with the schoolteacher. President Emmanuel Macron paid tribute to Paty at a private ceremony where he emphasized the late teacher's commitment to '[m]aking republicans'.[11] Images of cartoons of the Prophet were also projected onto government buildings.[12] However, the impact of the incident was felt far beyond France as Muslims around the world reacted to Macron's speech. This included the Turkish President, Recep Tayyip Erdogan, questioning Macron's mental health and the then Pakistani Prime Minister, Imran Khan, accusing Macron in a tweet of creating divisions and 'hurt[ing] the sentiments of millions of Muslims in Europe & across the world'.[13] Similar to the fallout of the Danish cartoon controversy, French goods were boycotted in countries such as Qatar and Bangladesh and French flags burnt.[14]

In April 2023, Richard Sharp resigned as the BBC's chairman due to his failure to disclose his links to the former Prime Minister Boris Johnson during the appointments process.[15] On the same day, the *Guardian* published a cartoon on its website by Martin Rowson, 'The Copros Touch' (28 April 2023), depicting Sharp (who is Jewish) and Boris Johnson. Tropes including Sharp's exaggerated features and a squid being held in a box with the words 'Gold' and 'Sac' visible were criticized for 'fall[ing] squarely into an antisemitic tradition of depicting Jews'.[16] The image was swiftly taken down by the *Guardian* which stated that the image 'did not meet our editorial standards […] The Guardian apologises to Mr Sharp, to the Jewish community and to anyone offended'.[17] Rowson published a lengthy apology on his website, where he stated that '[t]here are sensitivities it is our obligation to respect in order to achieve our satirical purposes'.[18] Interestingly, another of the *Guardian's* regular cartoonists,

Steve Bell, responded to the controversy on Twitter by sharing an image he had previously drawn of Sharp 'in solidarity with Martin'.[19] Bell questions what constitutes an antisemitic trope, concluding that '[a]ny trope can be used for antisemitic purposes'.[20] This incident shows how cartoons still ignite discussions over race and religion in Britain today and how cartoonists may have differing opinions on the subject.[21]

However, it is also important to bear in mind that cultural, religious and ethnic difference in cartoons not only lies with the authorship, but the readership too. The examples above highlight the importance of the reader and her reception and response to the images. For example, in their discussion on the *Jyllands-Posten*'s cartoon controversy, Peter Morey and Amina Yaqin make a crucial point in highlighting how the issue became a battleground about free speech in the West and Muslim censorship, rather than the 'more interesting question of conflicting notions of the role of humor'. Morey and Yaqin quote a Muslim comedian's viewpoint on the issue who distances himself from protestors, 'I don't go shouting in the street, I get up on stage and make jokes about it', demonstrating how one person chooses to use humour as a way of expressing their opinions on the topic.[22]

An interesting case study is that of the depiction of the Prophet. David Low's image 'IT' (*The Star*, 18 August 1925) (1.1)[23] depicts Jack Hobbs, a member of the England cricket team. He is flanked by other 'most important historical celebrities' including 'Chaplin' and 'Mahomet'. Whilst some readers of *The Star* lauded the image, others wrote in to criticize it and the offence it had caused to 'many Britishers and millions of fellow subjects of the Empire', for the inclusion of the Prophet. This led to the editor of *The Star* to express his regrets at the offence caused.[24] The reaction to the cartoon in India was much more violent and Muslims were said to have been outraged.[25]

Thus, offence can be felt but it is the way in which the offence is expressed that can differ greatly, where different cultural contexts can provoke different reactions to the same image. This demonstrates how crucial the readership is in negotiating the boundaries of free speech and censorship. As we can see from even this abbreviated list of incidents, political cartoons raise several questions: is there a responsibility on behalf of the artist to be cognisant of what may be deemed as offensive – or does the cartoonist have the right to offend? Secondly, does the readership have a responsibility in the way it reacts to an image that it deems offensive? Thirdly, is it the iconicity that makes an image memorable or is it because of the audience reception – or both?

Historical context

Britain has a uniquely long history of political cartooning, which, coupled with the freedom of the press, has resulted in a wealth of material. The artist William Hogarth (1697–1764) is widely considered to be the forefather of the political cartoon. Hogarth produced five series of paintings, including 'A Harlot's Progress' (1.2) and 'Four Stages of Cruelty' (1.3) which were reproduced as engravings (in 1732 and 1751, respectively), thus allowing them to be printed and circulated to a wider audience. For example, 'A Harlot's Progress' charted the gradual descent of a fictitious innocent country girl (Moll Hackabout) who becomes embroiled into a life of prostitution and eventually dies from venereal disease. Such works would have been displayed in places such as coffeehouses, leading to discussions amongst those in attendance. Hogarth did not consider himself a political cartoonist *per se*.[26] However, as 'readable images' which the reader is expected to decode, Hogarth's work crossed into both journalism and literature, marking 'the defining moment when the prehistory of comics intersected with that of literature and the modern press'.[27]

James Gillray (1756–1815) is often considered Hogarth's most direct successor. He focused on political satires during the 1780s, leading to the artist concentrating solely on caricature from 1786.[28] Gillray's embrace of caricature and satire led to the production of the well-known cartoon, 'The plumb-pudding in danger: – or – state epicures taking un petit souper' (1.4). Much like Hogarth, Gillray uses symbolism for the reader to digest Image 1.4. At the same time, Gillray employs caricature, using this as a device to make the people featured instantly recognizable to the readership. Another famous cartoonist of the time was George Cruikshank (1792–1878) whose images were instrumental in constructing a national identity during the Napoleonic Wars (1803–15), through their visualization of what it meant to be English. During this period, satirical prints were accessible to large parts of the public who could buy them from dealers or pay a fee to peruse them in a shop. When a major news story occurred, crowds would often block the street as they tried to view the caricaturist's image on the topic in the print shop.[29]

Punch; or, The London Charivari was first published in 1841, with a circulation of 50,000–60,000 copies per week by the middle of the Victorian period and a much higher readership.[30] One of the key differences the publication had from its counterparts was the breadth of topics that it dealt with, such as theatre and the fine arts. Moreover, its humour was considered benign enough that *Punch* was able to find 'its way into respectable homes where it could be seen by women without violating increasingly constricting canons of modesty'.[31] One of *Punch*'s most celebrated cartoonists, John Leech (1817–64), was considered by his contemporaries to produce respectable cartoons in contrast to vulgar Georgian caricature.[32] Indeed, Leech's role in the success of *Punch* and the popularity of the cartoon has been described as monumental – both by his contemporaries and more recently.[33]

Leech contributed to periodicals including *The London Magazine, Charivari, and Courier des Dames* (1840), *Bentley's Miscellany* (1840–9) and, in 1841, joined *Punch*, first appearing in the 7 August edition.[34] It was during his time at *Punch* that Leech enjoyed fame and fortune as an artist. *Punch* stepped away from the personal attacks that were so commonplace in cartoons by the likes of Gillray and his fellow artists. In order for politicians to evade the accusation that they had no humour if they did not agree with the way they were portrayed in cartoons, they were often positive in their response to cartoons depicting them.[35]

An example of Leech's work can be seen in 'Cartoon, No 1. Substance and Shadow' (*Punch*, 15 July 1843) (1.5; Figure 1), which comments on the plight of the impoverished as they look on in wonder at the paintings of the wealthy. The cartoon was a satirical remark on the way the government chose to allocate funding for a painting competition rather than spending it on alleviating the suffering of the poor.[36] 'Cartoon, No 1. Substance and Shadow' was the first instance of a *Punch* image referring to itself as a cartoon. This was in order to ridicule the preparatory drawings of paintings depicted in the image, which are commonly known as a 'cartoon' in the art world. Henceforth, the term 'cartoon' was used to label the images in *Punch*, resulting in the modern-day usage of the term. Significantly, *Punch*'s form and style of cartoons dominated the field, with competitors such as *Judy* and *Fun* emulating it, whilst offering diverging political opinions on contemporary issues.[37]

Punch's focus changed from when it first began and from the late 1840s it became less radical; both political extremes were poked fun at from an apolitical viewpoint and there was a shift away from satirizing the perceived injustices caused by the elite:

> Such a focus meant that *Punch* was directing its mild comic satire to an upper-middle and middle-class audience [...] *Punch* depended for its long survival not on a sustained critique of the limitations and injustices of the British economic, social and political system, but rather on a decorous liberal view of the political and social establishment from the point of view of an insider.[38]

Figure 1 John Leech, 'Cartoon No 1. Substance and Shadow' (*Punch*, 15 July 1843). Attribution 4.0 International (CC BY 4.0), Wellcome Collection, London.

This was indeed the case for many of the staff at *Punch* who came from educated backgrounds and had day jobs outside of journalism, such as the contributor Gilbert á Beckett who was a practising lawyer, as well as Leech who had formerly been a medical student.[39] This had an impact on the desire to set limits on cartoons due to notions of respectability in many of the periodicals at the time. Additionally, the editorial process of being published in a periodical like that of *Punch* – which was intent on upholding its respectability – meant that if a cartoon did not conform to editorial standards, it could be cut out.[40] Leech avoided caricature much like Hogarth; John Tenniel (1820–1914), another of *Punch*'s celebrated artists, also claimed his dislike for it.[41] Tenniel was greatly respected in his field, where his work was praised as belonging somewhere 'between journalistic and "high" art'.[42] Alongside working for *Punch*, Tenniel illustrated several books including Lewis Carroll's *Alice's Adventures in Wonderland* (1866) and *Through the Looking Glass* (1872). Taking over as chief cartoonist for *Punch* in 1864 after Leech's death, Tenniel was able to influence the tone of the publication in which he aspired 'to be severe without cruelty'.[43]

However, what is interesting is how such limits were applied subjectively, leading to minority groups such as Jews and the Irish being caricatured and attacked in a derogatory manner. This can be seen in the treatment of the former British Prime Minister, Benjamin Disraeli, who is depicted as anything *but* an Englishman, such as in John Doyle's cartoon 'A scene from Shakspere (compressed!)' (8 August 1844) (1.6)[44] in which a scene from Shakespeare's *The Merchant of Venice* depicts Disraeli as Shylock. Despite the fact that he was baptized at the age of twelve, Disraeli's Jewish heritage indelibly marked him out as an Other.[45] As a consequence of the power and clout that they had over how people and issues could be perceived, cartoonists were able to meet prominent people, rather than because of their financial or familial position.[46]

Thus, as their vocation as cartoonists became an increasingly respected one, the tolerance granted by the state also allowed this tradition to flourish. This was in contrast to the situation of their contemporaries on the continent where the mass media was seen as a powerful tool that posed a potential risk to those in power. This led to suppressive rules and regulations in which journalists and newspapers found themselves being fined and exiled in the nineteenth century.[47] Eventually, what came to replace *Punch* and other cartoon publications was the daily editorial, with Francis Carruthers Gould (1844–1925) becoming the first British cartoonist for a newspaper in 1888, namely the *Pall Mall Gazette*.[48] Gould later edited his own paper, *Picture Politics*, from 1894 to 1914. He also worked at the *Westminster Gazette* from 1893 to 1914 in which his cartoons, significantly, were often on the front page, making Gould 'the first political cartoonist to be given so central a position'.[49] Giving his cartoons such prominence allowed readers to be able to see them almost immediately.

This rich visual culture is still popular to this day, with well-known cartoonists featuring in British national newspapers such as Steve Bell, Dave Brown and Nicholas Garland. This book focuses on the British perspective in the modern age and does not look at how communities choose to portray themselves or how they are portrayed in other countries. I have chosen this as my focus in order to be able to look to Britain's long past and contrast it with how it deals with issues of identity in a postcolonial world, where ideas such as the Commonwealth and freedom of movement in the EU are constantly being challenged. I find patterns and trends in the way communities are depicted – both consciously and unconsciously – by cartoonists in Britain over the centuries. My aim is to show how an image that can often be the size of a thumb, embedded amongst text, contains a multitude of meanings and messages. In this way, the cartoon demands and deserves more than a few seconds of the reader's attention.

The power of the gaze

Therefore, both authorship and the readership play vital roles in the production and reception of images, in which the act of looking is itself a form of power – often referred to as the 'gaze'. David Morgan defines the gaze 'to mean the visual network that constitutes a social act of looking'.[50] The 'visual network' includes the subject, the viewer and the context, making it crucial to take all of these into consideration because they all form the gaze. By taking these into consideration, one can attempt to understand the different meanings of the cartoons examined and the responses to them, thereby highlighting the importance of the relationship between the viewer and the subject. The concept of the gaze has been utilized by scholars in a variety of contexts. Pertinently, in her examination of the *hijab*, Salam Al-Mahadin asks:

> [W]hat exactly is a 'gaze'? It is the anxiety of the subject as s/he seeks meaning and sense. Phenomena must be invested with meaning since nothing is more traumatizing than a signifier that escapes meaning. Gaze is first and foremost one of fear and apprehension; two emotions that construct and weave narratives to allay anxiety.[51]

Thus, in the act of seeing, it is the viewer's experiences, assumptions, limitations and practices that are laid bare. This is relevant to ideas relating to Othering and postcolonial discourse. Edward Said, in his seminal work *Orientalism*, focused on 'the internal consistency of Orientalism and its ideas about the Orient […] despite or beyond any correspondence, or lack thereof, with a "real" Orient'.[52] In this way, what became known as 'the Orient' in the West was what was represented by those not from there, thereby serving the colonialist's vested political interests and demonstrating the dominant power of the West over the Orient.[53] Therefore, it follows that Said's 'Orientalism' 'refers to the ideological construction of a mythical Orient, whose characteristics are treated as immutable traits defined in simple opposition to the characteristics of the Occidental world'.[54]

Homi Bhabha developed Said's theory, uncovering the 'fixity'[55] of the construction of the Other who is unchanging and predictable as it emerges in the stereotype. At the same time, this fixed stereotype coexists with the 'ambivalent' because it is associated with disorder.[56] Bhabha's theory on the importance of ambivalence demonstrates how it plays a key role in the formation of the identity of the Other. In the Other, the colonizer finds the difference it seeks in which 'the question of identification is never the affirmation of a pre-given identity […] it is always the production of an image of identity and the transformation of the subject in assuming that image'.⁵⁷ Crucially, Bhabha argues that the ambivalence lies in the fact that it is not simply a rejection of difference in which Othering occurs; it is also a recognition of that which is both desired and derided by the colonizer.⁵⁸ It is in the stereotype that one finds this ambivalence in which the Other is constructed and by uncovering this ambivalence, it demonstrates how the process of Othering allows the viewer to both take delight in what they have made sense of and yet still fear as an unknowable.⁵⁹ More importantly, Bhabha argues, it is the effect of the stereotype that is crucial, rather than assessing if it is positive or negative. This is because

> to judge the stereotyped image on the basis of a prior political normativity is to dismiss it, not to displace it, which is only possible by engaging with its *effectivity* [...].⁶⁰

Bhabha argues that this then demonstrates the normality constructed by the colonizer which is used to justify its desire to exert control over the Other. Bhabha goes onto talk about the 'colonial mimicry' which relies on ambivalence – as opposed to equivalence – in order to justify colonial rule. Ambivalence, as exposed in the colonial mimicry, 'is the desire for a reformed, recognizable Other, as a subject of a difference that is almost the same, but not quite'.⁶¹ It is the fact that this mimicry is never completely accurate which exposes the flawed nature of the colonialist's discourse.

Bhabha's theory is useful in understanding how the Other emerges in the cartoons examined below and what the Other represents in relation to the subject. It also explains why identity, as uncovered in this book, can often be so fluid. This is because the Other and the subject are able to transform according to what differences the subject seeks and what is both desired and feared by the subject by projecting this onto the Other. The colonialist project is an example of how it at once civilized and Othered at the same time, so that the Other is continually subject to this process. This then informs us of the context, the artist's intentions and the effects of producing such constructions of the Other. This is because as Ania Loomba states, (mis-)representation does not occur in a timeless or unchanging vacuum and therefore needs to be unpacked.⁶² In doing so, I am able to uncover how the artist aims to influence the reader's gaze so that the images are interpreted in a specific way. Applying this to the cartoons examined here, I look at the power of the gaze and the impact the postcolonial optic has had on the portrayal and perception of the communities depicted.

By depicting the mythical Other the cartoons also – by inference – demonstrate the construction of the mythical self. Samir Amin et al. refer to 'the ideological veil through which Europe sees itself' and uses the example of how the West has managed to appropriate Christianity's Oriental origins so that Jesus is imagined to be blonde.[63] This is important because the cartoons seek to portray the Other as what the Self is not. As a result, the cartoons focus on the regressive nature of those who are not English Anglican Christians. This is used as a way to justify and explain why different races and those who follow other faiths pose a threat to the British public. This is similar to the colonial project, which used missionizing as a process to 'whiten' blacks and as a justification for the upheaval they entailed.[64] Through conversion, the colonized was made civilized and good. Therefore, if we were to invert the messages of the cartoons, we can ascertain that in order to no longer be considered the Other, one must change one's race to Caucasian, and religion to Anglican Christianity. It follows, therefore, that Anglican Christianity is superior to all other religions and Christian denominations, and that what underlies the concept of a single unifying British identity is fundamentally based on race. Taking into consideration the fact that immigration and acculturation have occurred for many centuries in the UK, the persistence of such a message is striking.

What do cartoons do and how?

There is a distinct nature to the medium of the political cartoon – this is apparent in the way cartoons are published with the original intent of commenting on a topical news item. Although it is common for museums and galleries to host exhibitions of a cartoonist's works, a painting differs in that it is usually produced with the intention of longevity, being displayed in its original form to be viewed by audiences who do not necessarily need to know the context in which the painting was produced. Therefore, the inherently topical nature of political cartoons makes it impossible to attempt to read the image without first establishing – or having prior knowledge of – the context.

I attempt to establish both a synchronic and diachronic usage of certain visual tropes. This is because cartoons are produced within the parameters of their time, making it important to establish the context in which the cartoons were published, so as to be able to read the image and understand the narratives dominant at the time. Additionally, it is important to understand how such narratives have evolved (if at all) by examining the use of visual tropes over a period of time. As Gamson et al. state:

> What is uncontested now may be difficult or impossible to detect without contrast with a discourse in which such matters were once de-naturalized and matters of contested meaning.[65]

By taking such an approach, the reader is able to understand how the audience at the time would have interpreted the messages of the cartoons and contrast this with how I, as the reader, in a different context with different prevailing narratives, can establish influences or goals that the cartoonist themselves may not have recognized at the time.

Building on Peter Berger and Thomas Luckmann's assertion that reality is a social construction in which our 'commonsense "knowledge" … constitutes the fabric of meanings without which no society could exist',[66] the cartoons I examine reveal the social constructions of what is acceptable, normal – or as Gamson et al. put it – 'as transparent descriptions of reality',[67] for both the cartoonist and the reader. Therefore, the argument does not concern itself with whether reality does indeed exist or not, but how we construct our sense of reality. Instead, Berger and Luckmann argue that this is done through 'a social stock of knowledge […] which is transmitted from generation to generation',[68] and it is this institutionalized knowledge that we encounter as reality. Thus, the political cartoons I examine are published in newspapers which have a target audience in mind which the newspapers presume shares its specific political ideology.

Indeed, British newspapers targeted and appealed to particular social backgrounds and class. In the eighteenth century, newspapers were mainly read by the middle class owing to Government imposed taxes which made them unaffordable for the working class.[69] By 1861, all taxes on newspapers had been abolished and improvements in printing methods allowed newspapers to be available to a wider readership. In today's Britain, tabloids such as the *Sun* and the *Daily Mirror* have a strong focus on entertainment and television, with a smaller focus on politics, in order to appeal to a diverse audience. This has had a huge impact on the broadsheet newspaper which has also had to focus on popular culture somewhat and has also had an impact on the format of publication.[70]

For example, since 2018, the *Guardian* is published in the tabloid format, having previously opted for the 'Berliner' format from 2005. Newspaper publications are largely split along party political lines, in which research has shown how readers have been influenced, or are already predisposed, in their voting behaviours as reflected in the newspaper that they read. For example, 79 per cent of the pro-Conservative *Daily Telegraph* readers voted Conservative, whilst 73 per cent of readers of the pro-Labour *Guardian* voted Labour in the 2017 general election.[71] The choice of newspaper, therefore, filters and leads to a reinforcement of an already existing worldview.

In this way, the views conveyed in the cartoons seek and/or presuppose the reader's agreement which, at the same time, demonstrate the underlying beliefs that are taken for granted and need not be explicitly stated. This is what Antonio Gramsci describes as our '"common sense" or traditional conception of the world',[72] which then dominates media discourse. Consequently, the reader may not be aware of what beliefs they hold and that such beliefs may even be contradictory. Therefore, cartoons expose these different, contradictory beliefs because the reader takes the message of the image to be a representation (in some way) of reality. Furthermore, the publication of cartoons is, of course, dependent on their newsworthiness. The consequence of this is that the image must relate to topical events.

As a result, what I find is a packing of complex ideas and concepts into a single image which may not necessarily be accurate but is intended to be readily accepted by the readership. Cartoons not only record, but shape, the debate on which they comment. I argue that political cartoons play an active part in creating the social reality that it purports to merely describe and visualize. Therefore, the tropes and iconography employed by cartoonists are more than just visual signifiers which help the reader to decode the image; they are signifiers which have been – and are – taken outside the context of the image and applied to the minorities portrayed. In his survey of British cartoons on the Irish, Lewis Perry Curtis, Jr. makes clear that the importance of the cartoon lies on the

> reciprocal relationship between those who create it and those who consume it […] As much as any of their contemporaries [… cartoonists …] live and practice within ideology, drawing literally and figuratively on prejudices that already lurk or inhere in their audiences.[73]

Therefore, a cartoonist's educational, economic and personal background is all crucial in understanding the angle from which they approach certain subjects and the artistic styles that are employed. Consequently, whilst some images are treated as symptomatic of widely held prejudices, others are treated as demonstrating greater critical insight into such prejudices. This is because, as Pierre Bourdieu argues, the 'same dispositions lead to opposite aesthetic or political positions, depending on the state of the field in relation to which they have to express themselves',[74] so that there can only ever be a limited number of such 'dispositions'. This is evinced in the way political cartooning, as examined above, has developed over time with attitudes of respectability, publishing techniques and the changing political discourse having influenced the way topical issues are treated.

By focusing on different communities over several decades, my research sheds light on topical issues that at one time were debated in a certain way and which have now taken on new nuances. This follows the argument that the meaning of an artwork is not limited to what the artist intended, but goes beyond this. Therefore, I do not consider cartoons to have lost their meaning; rather, they have different impacts and effects across time, thereby potentially bringing new meanings and insights. This is a crucial hermeneutic distinction because we are then able to understand *difference* and 'thereby gain a fuller consciousness about how our presuppositions about a subject matter differ from those of the work'.[75] Accepting that the lens through which I view the cartoons is heavily influenced by ideas and concepts that may not have existed at the time of the publication of the cartoons, this book demonstrates the debate over identity – namely, who is deemed British and how the communities examined fail to fit this category.

Methodology

The publications looked at representing a broad range of political views, with high numbers of circulation, and therefore are indicative of the diverse views that were being shared and digested at the time. The full list of publications include: *The Times*, the *Guardian*, the *Sun*, the *Daily Mail*, *The Star*, the *Evening News*, *The Sunday Times*, *Independent*, *Daily Telegraph*, *Sunday Telegraph*, *Observer*, *Daily Star*, *Daily Mirror*, *Daily Sketch*, *Daily Express*, *i News*, *Harper's Weekly* and *Pat*. For example, *The Times* had the highest circulation of all London daily papers in the 1850s.[76] In 1855, after a gradual repeal of various tax duties other newspapers rose in circulation, including the *Daily Telegraph* in London and the *Manchester Guardian* outside of London.[77] I also look at periodicals such as *Punch* and *Tomahawk* as examples of how some of the communities examined here have been the subject of focus for cartoonists for centuries and were also as popular as the newspaper. For example, in 1854, *Punch* sold 40,000 copies, compared to *The Times* which sold between 50,000 and 60,000 in 1854.[78] Moreover, such periodicals were important in creating the popularity of the cartoon amongst the news-reading public and were the forerunners to the inclusion of the cartoon in mainstream newspapers.

Including both tabloids and broadsheets in this research was important in order to reflect the different readerships because, as mentioned above, the different types of newspaper differ in their focus. This has led to tabloids having the largest percentage of readers amongst adults. For example, in a 2021 Ofcom survey, the most read daily title in print was the *Daily Mail* at 35 per cent, followed by *The Sun* at 24 per cent. This contrasts with *The Times* at 17 per cent and the *Guardian* at 16 per cent.[79] Breaking this down further by looking at the most popular tabloid, 48 per cent of *Daily Mail/Mail on Sunday* readers are over the age of sixty-five and overall, 42 per cent white. This compares to *The Times/Sunday Times* at 17 per cent in the '65+' category and overall 20 per cent white.[80]

It is also important to note that traditional newspapers have been challenged by other news sources; 79 per cent of adults in the UK over the age of sixteen accessed the news through television as the main source of news.[81] Only 32 per cent used printed newspapers as their main platform for news, trailing behind the internet (which includes social media, podcasts and websites/apps) at 73 per cent and radio at 46 per cent.[82] Newspapers have tried to adapt to such challenges; their combined online and print readership demonstrates that they are still popular amongst the British public. In 2021, the *Daily Mail/Mail on Sunday* was the most popular title with a combined readership of 9,623,000 per week – the majority of which was in print. This was followed by the *Guardian* at 8,031,000 which in contrast had a majority of online readers.[83] This reflects the different ways news is consumed across different titles. Moreover, the range of publications I look at also covers the changing shifts in the British newspaper industry such as the *i News*; established in 2016, the paper demonstrates how the political cartoon is still considered a key element of the British newspaper.

My primary source is the University of Kent's British Cartoon Archive (BCA), using keywords relevant to each community. To address the possibility that the BCA archival methodology may not be comprehensive, I carried out archival research by hand at the British Library and of the private papers of cartoonist David Low and Carl Giles at the BCA. I also used internet searches, Twitter and Instagram, to find more material which has not yet been archived. Specifically, I searched for cartoons relating to the 2017 terror attacks; the 2017 general election and the Conservative-DUP alliance; the controversy over abortion laws in Northern Ireland following Eire's referendum to amend abortion legislation; and images by Kenneth Mahood on the *Punch* website.

I looked at cartoons based on patterns emerging from a single news event or on patterns unique to the cartoonist (for example, the depiction of IRA members by Michael Cummings). At the same time, if there was a cartoon that gave an alternative narrative, it was important to include this too to highlight the different discourses. In terms of typology, I looked at Elder and Cobb's use of three categories to determine political and non-political symbols:

> 1) symbols of the political community; 2) symbols associated with regime norms, structures and roles; and 3) situational symbols relating to a) current authorities, b) non-governmental political actors, and c) policies and policy issues.[84]

I adapted the criteria to determine which cartoons should be included in my study if they have at least one of the following: symbols of the religious community; symbols associated with religious norms, structures and roles; or symbols ascribed to members of specific religious communities. The third criterion is important since not all of the cartoons display religious symbols. For example, often the cartoon will deal with religious issues through race or the persistent use of a specific trope.

I also use gender as an analytical tool throughout the thesis in order to highlight how ideas relating to belonging/not belonging are impacted by ideas of masculinity and femininity. This provides insight into how the genders are socially constructed around certain concepts in which the male and female are often portrayed in contrast to one another, such as the violent male attacking the helpless female. In my analysis of the number of women and men who appear in the cartoons, I look at the breakdown of how many feature a member of the community of interest. This is in order to understand how the groups are represented in terms of gender and how cartoons can function in perpetuating ideas of gender roles within different religious communities.

A key point to note is that my research does not include Hindus due to the fact that most cartoons deal with Indian – rather than Hindu – identity. The absence of cartoons focusing on Hindus may be due to the fact that it is challenging for the cartoonist to visualize the Hindu male/female without touching on tropes which are used to signify the Indian. To see the image of an Asian woman in a sari or an Asian man in *salwar kameez* would suggest a focus on ethnicity rather than religion. Additionally, whilst the practice of wearing the turban is connected to the Sikh faith and the *burqa/niqab* are contentious veiling practices for Muslim women, the Hindu community does not have religion-specific attire. Thus, amongst the struggles the Hindu community may have endured in postcolonial Britain, they were not connected to the right to be able to wear a specific religious garment.

Structure and key findings

My research focuses on the Irish, Jews, Sikhs, Muslim men and Muslim women precisely because it is both their religious and ostensibly ethnic identities that have been (and still are) points of contention in relation to British identity. In all cases the communities are Othered on both religious and ethnic grounds against the Caucasian Anglo-Saxon Protestant. The first two chapters look at the Irish and Jews in order to understand how, throughout the course of the communities' long history in Britain, they are Othered in a way that makes them racially different to that of the Caucasian Anglo-Saxon Protestant. In today's world, ideas of race have changed considerably so that such ideas of the Irish and Jewish communities would not be accepted by the majority of people. Consequently, this provides a useful foreground for the case of the Sikh and Muslim communities who are also depicted in the cartoons as being racially different. Furthermore, their process of Othering converges in many ways with that of the Irish and Jews, despite the fact that Muslims and Sikhs do not lay claim to such a long and varied history as that of the Irish and Jews in Britain. By structuring the book in this manner, my research demonstrates the commonalities of the portrayals of completely different communities, with widely varying histories spanning hundreds of years.

The first chapter focuses on the impact terrorism has had on the depiction of the Irish. Although the Irish have featured in art and literature since the mediaeval period, this is a useful starting point in understanding how British identity was formed in its capacity as a colonial power over the Irish Other, leading to self-conceptions of Britain as a nation from the early modern period onwards. I find that such ideas of Otherness and who is entitled to belong in this nation cut across the different communities looked at in this thesis. I start off by looking at the Victorian era and move on to the period surrounding the Troubles, up to the immediate impact of the UK's exit from the European Union (commonly referred to as 'Brexit'). Initially, my intention was to focus on the depiction of Irish Catholics. On examining the material, I found that there was indeed a focus during the Victorian period of depicting the Catholic Irishman who was presumed to be racially distinct to that of the Anglo-Saxon Englishman. This is found in the way the Irishman is depicted in a simian-like manner, contrasted against the tall Anglo-Saxon Englishman. Although this stereotype is resurrected by cartoonists such as Mac and Carl Giles in the twentieth century, they are in the minority. Instead, as such racial presumptions fell away, there is more of a focus on attempting to highlight the sectarian nature of the conflict where Irish Catholics appear alongside Irish Protestants. As such, this chapter looks at the shift in focus of the portrayal of the Irish Catholic to that of the Irish irrespective of faith.

However, just prior to the signing of the Good Friday Agreement in 1998 and the period following, cartoons focus less on the religious commitments of the Irish. Instead, they focus on their political commitments and how paramilitary support (rather than religious affiliation) is fuelling the conflict in Northern Ireland. Thus, I find the focus on the inherently violent and flawed nature of the Irishman is shifted to that of the flawed nature of the terrorist fighting for either the republican or the loyalist cause. This demonstrates how the process of Othering has changed and is predicated more on the violent versus the non-violent, whatever side they may be. I end the chapter by looking at the recent debates over Brexit, the result of the UK 2017 general election, and how cartoonists focus on the role of the Northern Irish political party, the Democratic Unionist Party, in Westminster. This has led to questions being raised of what it means to be British and where Northern Ireland fits into it.

I then go on to look at Jews, who much like the Irish, although depicted as Caucasian, are Othered so that neither community could ever achieve the status of the genteel Englishman in Victorian times. From my survey emerges the image of the fictive Jew who is devious by virtue of his Jewishness. The fictive Jew adapts to the context of the time, so that in the Victorian period he is depicted with the Semitic nose to symbolize his cunningness and deception. During the Second World War and the events of the Shoah, cartoons humanize the Jew so that the reader is able to identify with their suffering under the Nazis. However, with the establishment of Israel, I argue that the fictive Jew re-emerges so that he is increasingly seen through the prism of Israel, thus representing both the Jewish nation and the Jewish religion. Consequently, whilst the Jew was depicted as an unidentifiable person during the Shoah and the struggle for the establishment of Israel, this then changes so that Israeli politicians are seen as representative of the Jewish community. I use the concept of 'liquid racism' to argue that despite the fact that a cartoonist's intentions may have been to make a political point against an Israeli politician, the use of symbolism and iconography that harks back to centuries-old stereotypes exposes cartoons to the charge of being antisemitic.

I subsequently look at the Sikh community. The cartoons demonstrate how the British public slowly began to accept the idea of the Sikh transitioning from a temporary immigrant to a permanent citizen. The cartoons also show the struggle Britain was facing with no longer being an empire and instead being confronted by ideas of the Commonwealth. I argue that the images convey a message of 'transactionality' in which the Sikh community is expected to trade in parts of their identity in order to be accepted by wider British society. Within this, I find the turban to be a crucial symbol of the changing demographics which is primarily seen as a sign of cultural and political subversion, rather than of religiosity. Consequently, the turban is taken as an indicator of the inevitable change that is to come in which minority ethnics (Sikh or otherwise) are now a permanent part of the demographic landscape, rather than filling a labour shortage temporarily. Moreover, the absence of Sikh women in the images creates the idea of the Sikh religion as predominantly male, where the Sikh female is voiceless and has no interest or part to play in furthering Sikh rights. Additionally, it has the effect of Othering the Sikh male based on a multiple of factors – his race, religion and gender.

The following chapter looks at Muslim women, where the focus of the cartoons is more on the question of how people who dress in a particular way – namely in the *burqa/niqab* – can possibly be an integrated British citizen. The focus on the *burqa/niqab* is used to emphasize that women who veil as such do not belong in a democratic country because they are likely to hold regressive, anti-liberal views. The *burqa/niqab* is also used as a way of highlighting gender inequality within the Muslim religion by using this trope to symbolize the oppressed Muslim female in need of saving. Therefore, much like the case of the depiction of male Sikhs and the turban, the *burqa/niqab* is used to identify the Other, thereby linking this process of Othering to gender. Another parallel is found in the way the *burqa/niqab* is seen as a political, rather than religious, statement – similar to that of the turban for Sikhs. Interestingly, a trend emerges in which the *burqa/niqab* is shown to be used as a tool for deception, projecting the fears associated with being unable to see a face and identify the person. As a result, the cartoons focus on a particular form of Islam which is conflated with a political ideology intent on subverting the current British democratic system so that the woman in *burqa/niqab* is the norm rather than the exception.

Finally, I look at the depiction of Muslim men. I find the Muslim community (as symbolized by the Muslim male) is depicted as originating from the Asian continent, despite the fact that Muslims are not a race. This is in stark contrast to the Muslim female who is disembodied and dehumanized. Instead, the Muslim male is given attributes that may not be factually true but serve the purpose of enabling cartoonists to contrast the regressive Asian Muslim community to that of progressive Christian Britons. I look at how the changing terror threat has also made cartoonists change their iconography. In the aftermath of 9/11 and 7/7, the perpetrators were the focus of the images. However, as terrorists do not always fit the Asian male stereotype in reality, cartoonists have focused on the nature of the attacks.

This has again changed with the emergence of Daesh and the prominence of Britons such as Mohammed Emwazi (referred to as 'Jihadi John' in the press). The case of Emwazi highlights how someone who was seemingly integrated – having spent much of his life living and being educated in Britain – could end up committing acts of barbarity. The fear then arises: how does one identify what I call the 'Muslim Barbaric'? Within this lies the argument that all Muslim men are innately inclined towards radicalism and violence. The emergence of Daesh and those such as Emwazi confirms the existence of the Muslim Barbaric. The recent terror attacks occurring in Britain in recent years shift focus yet again so that it is more about the response to the attacks as a way to convey messages of solidarity and defiance.

Crucially, I find that there is a sense of fear of the Other integrating and no longer being identifiable as such. Consequently, I use Othering as a concept which is applied to the communities examined, resulting in cartoons presenting a binary of them and us by demarcating who belongs in which category. I find that the peculiarities of the different histories of each community are key in the ways they are Othered. Thus, the process of Othering takes into account not only the different immigrant histories, but also the different cultural contexts in which the cartoonists work(ed). This is still relevant today, with Paul Gilroy commenting on the more recent immigration of Eastern Europeans into Britain who find that '[e]ven if they are "white", they can be held hostage by the racialized specification that they are immigrants'.[85] Thus, one of the key things political cartoons demonstrate is the outcome of the subject's gaze when attempting to interpret and define the Other. In all cases, the communities are portrayed through the postcolonial optic which persistently deems them as inferior to the Caucasian Briton.

The cartoons present assimilation as *the* goal for the minorities portrayed in the cartoons. At the same time, however, such a goal is deemed an impossible one to attain because difference is rendered ontological and unchangeable. Through using stereotypes, the cartoons perpetuate and sustain the ontological Otherness. In doing so, the stereotypes act as visual signifiers of a multitude of negative characteristics including regression, violence and an aversion to liberal values. Such signifiers are important because they are transferable from the Other in cartoons to the Other in reality. As the caricaturist Max Beerbohm argued, 'one soon forgets that caricatures are distortions or exaggerations – they quickly become realities'.[86] In this way, the cartoons convey the message that to be British is to be progressive, civil and liberal-minded. However, this is impossible because the cartoons often conflate race and religion as one and the same – one cannot change one's race and even through religious conversion, one's race signifies Otherness. Central to the cartoons is the idea of identity and who is permitted to identify with 'us', demonstrating the crucial role cartoons play in the stability and enduring power of the archetype. In this way, the cartoons demonstrate how both racial and religious prejudice subtly interface and reinforce one another. This then exposes how racial prejudice is, in fact, religious in disguise and what is conveyed as religious difference is actually a cover for outright racism.

1

Nuns, guns and balaclavas: The Irish in political cartoons

Introduction

This chapter looks at the depiction of terrorism in relation to the Irish issue and the impact this has had on the portrayal of the Irish – both Catholic and Protestant. Although what the divide truly means between the English/British and the Irish is a complex recurring question throughout the centuries, I start off with the popular Victorian belief that the Catholic Irish were racially different from the Protestant English. I look at the way the Irish were perceived as being inherently unstable, violent and unable to self-govern. During the Victorian period, negative attitudes towards the Irish permeated popular culture where the word 'Irish' had many negative connotations; 'to weep Irish' meant to pretend sorrow, for example, and 'to go to an Irish wedding' meant to empty a cesspool.[1] Moreover, in the eyes of the English, the Irish Celt loved to fight. Such themes are found in cartoons during this time, where the Irishman (or Paddy as he was commonly known) was seen to be fighting futilely for self-government.

This chapter focuses on the representation of the Irish in newspapers published in mainland Britain. By taking this approach, I examine how the perceptions of the Irish held by those living on a different island – and yet citizens of the same nation – are reflected. Unsurprisingly, as the colonial power, Britain controlled the Irish presses at the time. Consequently, Britain's long history of caricature and political cartooning has led to the discourse surrounding Ireland being dominated by British cartoonists; it was not until 1870 when Dublin had its first comic published.[2] I go on to examine the impact the formation of Northern Ireland had on ideas of Home Rule and the desires of figures such as Sinn Féin's Eamon De Valera for a completely independent Ireland. Crucially, I argue that the depiction of terrorism in Ireland has evolved from the man in a trench coat, to that of the masked man. Thus, the focus has moved away from depicting the *Irishman* committing acts of terror, to that of the *terrorist*. Instead, rather than referring to the Irishman's ostensibly violent nature, the cartoons look at whether the person depicted is a member or sympathizer of a republican or loyalist paramilitary.

Ireland under Protestant rule

Ireland came under Protestant rule following the Battle of the Boyne in 1690 when the Dutch Protestant, King William of Orange, defeated the Catholic King James II. This led to almost two centuries of rule by the landowning Protestant ascendancy over a population who were 75 per cent Catholic[3] on whom restrictive laws were enforced – the most significant of which was that they could not buy or lease land; neither could they inherit it. This measure reduced Catholic landownership to 14 per cent in 1703, whilst Protestant landownership had risen from 41 per cent to 86 per cent in the period of 1641–1703, thereby increasing poverty amongst the Catholic population.[4]

By the eighteenth century, Ireland's relationship with Britain was akin to a colony in which any legislation in Ireland could not be made without British authority and where Ireland's economy was also strictly regulated by Britain. In 1798, a number of rebellions across Ireland took place, including in Wexford town and County Mayo. Although these failed, the Act of Union was passed in 1800 as a result, in which direct control from Westminster was established and the Irish parliament was abolished. Instead, 100 Protestant MPs would sit in the British House of Commons and 32 peers in the House of Lords, directly from Ireland. It was not until 1829, under the auspices of the then Home Secretary, Robert Peel, that Catholic emancipation was granted, allowing members of the Catholic church to sit as MPs at Westminster. This was largely due to the Irish activist, Daniel O'Connell, who established the Catholic Association in 1823 and campaigned for Catholic emancipation.

O'Connell was the first open Catholic to be elected to Westminster in the County Clare by-election in 1828 against the Protestant, William Vesey Fitzgerald. However, his election caused controversy because he was disbarred from taking up his seat at Westminster due to his Roman Catholic faith. Fearing insurrection and revolt in Ireland, Peel and the then Prime Minister, the Duke of Wellington, guided the passage of the Roman Catholic Relief Act 1829 through parliament. O'Connell subsequently went on to campaign for Home Rule through re-establishing the Irish parliament and repealing the Act of Union.

Although O'Connell failed in this particular aim, his legacy as an Irish politician had a lasting impact on Irish nationalism, demonstrated by his nickname 'the Liberator'.

What is most interesting about the O'Connell case study is how Jewish MPs faced similar difficulties, especially with regard to the oath that MPs had to take in order to take up their seat. For example, one of the key obstacles that prevented O'Connell from sitting at Westminster was the Oath of Supremacy which had been established under King Henry VIII in 1534. This oath had to be taken by all MPs which stated that 'the king's majesty justly and rightfully is and ought to be supreme head of the Church of England'.[5] Such a statement went against O'Connell's Catholic faith. Similarly, Baron Lionel de Rothschild faced such challenges with the Oath of Allegiance, until he was finally able to take up his seat as MP thirty years after O'Connell in 1858. This is examined later in Chapter 2.

The simian Paddy

In 1858, the Fenian Brotherhood was established, named after the legendary Irish warriors, the Fianna Eireann. The Fenians sought an Irish republic through violent means which contrasted with that of O'Connell, who disavowed any violence to achieve his political goals. On 11 September 1867, the Fenian leader, Thomas Kelly, was rescued from a prison van in which a policeman was killed, making this 'the first significant act of Irish revolutionary violence on British soil'.[6] This was followed by the bombing of Clerkenwell prison in London on 13 December. It was during this time that the Irishman was frequently depicted as the simian Paddy, rather than the ignorant Celt. John Leech's 'The "Repeal Farce"' (*Punch*, volume 4, page 37, 1843) (2.1) exemplifies the idea current at the time that there was a clear racial distinction between the Irish and the English (namely the Celts and the Anglo-Saxons, respectively).

This followed the idea that the Anglo-Saxons had 'a peculiar genius for governing themselves – and others by means of a constitutional and legal system that combined the highest degree of efficiency with liberty and justice'.[7] What further reinforced the idea of Them and Us was the sectarian divide between Protestantism and Roman Catholicism. Commenting on the Repeal Association set up by Daniel O'Connell in 1840 to repeal the Acts of Union in 1800, 'The "Repeal Farce"' demonstrates the Celt's inability to self-govern by visualizing the stereotypical Paddy with a projecting jaw, wearing bedraggled clothes. This was in contrast to the faces of Englishmen who had high facial angles and whom Protestant Ulstermen were often made to resemble.[8]

However, Lewis Perry Curtis Jr argues that in the 1860s there was a marked change in the depiction of Paddy from prognathous Celt to a simianized creature who resembled more ape than human.[9] This was no coincidence; during the Victorian period, there were numerous theories regarding race which were accessible and influential to the public. This included the publication of Charles Darwin's *The Origin of Species* in 1859. However, the debate on this had started well before Darwin's book, such as with the popular theorist Robert Chambers.[10] Such theories of scientific racism relied on physiognomy where different races inherited both physical features and characteristics. Although not a cartoon, the image of the Irish Iberian, Negro and the Anglo-Teutonic by H. Strickland Constable (2.2; Figure 2) is indicative of the way the Irish were viewed by the English. Originally appearing in Constable's book, *Ireland from One or Two Neglected Points of View*, a review of the book by *The Spectator* at the time of publication reads:

> According to the author, the Southern Irish are a low-type race, and are quite incapable of governing themselves. This, indeed, is a fact that does not need very much demonstration.[11]

Furthermore, the image was reproduced in other publications including the American magazine *Harper's Weekly*, illustrating how such beliefs regarding race were so popular at the time. The accompanying caption comments on the belief that the Iberians were 'originally an African race, who thousands of years ago spread themselves through Spain over Western Europe', thereby connecting the Irish to a lower species of race.

This hierarchy of the different races saw the Teutons (which the Anglo-Saxons were) at the top, the 'Negro' was placed at the bottom with Celts and Jews sitting somewhere slightly above them. Thus, cartoonists drew inspiration from the debates surrounding the origins of man and evolution. Crucially, this meant that such simianization of the Irish in cartoons was given scientific backing. Moreover, the Irish were not only simianized, but they were also shown to be monsters, especially at times when Fenian activities were on the rise. The trope of Hibernia, the oft-depicted suffering woman used to symbolize Ireland, was used to contrast against these ape-like male monsters. This approach to the idea of an innate male bestiality compared to an innate feminine civility is also found in the visualization of the Sikh and Muslim male, where violence is inextricably linked to gender, which I explore in Chapters 3 and 5, respectively.

IRISH IBERIAN.   ANGLO-TEUTONIC.   NEGRO.

The Iberians are believed to have been originally an African race, who thousands of years ago spread themselves through Spain over Western Europe. Their remains are found in the barrows, or burying places, in sundry parts of these countries. The skulls are of low, prognathous type. They came to Ireland, and mixed with the natives of the South and West, who themselves are supposed to have been of low type and descendants of savages of the Stone Age, who, in consequence of isolation from the rest of the world, had never been out-competed in the healthy struggle of life, and thus made way, according to the laws of nature, for superior races.

Figure 2 H. Strickland Constable (*Ireland from One or Two Neglected Points of View*, 1888). CC0, Wikimedia Commons.

Attributing this visual change to John Tenniel, Curtis Jr argues that the rise of Fenianism and the idea that British rule had to be brought to an end through violent means meant that '[i]n Tenniel's hands those who dared to defy British authority in Ireland were made to look like denizens of the jungle: Paddy thus passed from prognathism into simianism'.[12] This can be seen in Tenniel's 'Two Forces' (*Punch*, 29 October 1881) (2.3; Figure 3), where Britannia is shown to be protecting Hibernia and standing defiantly in the face of an Irishman threatening to hit her with a rock. The image reinforces the idea of Ireland in need of Britain's help and generosity in order to ensure the country does not fall into disorder, separating the Irish people from the land.

Thus, the image shows how Britain perceived itself literally protecting Ireland from her own people. The Irishman stands hunched, wearing a hat with the word 'anarchy' across it. However, the key thing to note is his facial features including fangs, long facial hair, snub nose and his shallow jaw, making him resemble an ape:

> Since the very integrity of English civilization seemed to be menaced by Darwinism, democracy [… and …] Fenianism, one convenient way of epitomizing those fears was to shift the burden of proximity to the gorillas onto the burly shoulders of those Irish agitators who wanted nothing better than to strike terror into the hearts of their oppressors.[13]

Figure 3 John Tenniel, 'Two Forces' (*Punch*, 29 October 1881). Rogers Fund, 1966, courtesy of the Metropolitan Museum of Art.

Another key cartoon demonstrating the link between the Irish simian nature and violence is Matt Morgan's 'The Irish Frankenstein' (*Tomahawk*, 1869) (2.4). The cartoon juxtaposes the ape-like Irishman who has the word 'Fenianism' across his torso against the Englishman who stands tall, fully clothed and looks on at the Fenian beast in bemusement. This is an example of the category of cartoon known as 'Irish Bulls' during the nineteenth century, 'where the joke lay in pointing out a rather endearing contrariness in the Irish character'.[14] This, coupled with the simian nature of the Irishman, confirmed for the British public the ineptitude of the Irish to be able to look after themselves. Thus, the resulting impact of growing Irish agitation was a change in attitude by the Victorians in which the simian Paddy emerged. Scientific theories about the origins of man gave backing to the idea of the Irish propensity towards violence and his inner bestial nature.

In contrast, whilst British cartoons during the Victorian period showed the Irishman as prognathous and simian, cartoonists in Dublin reversed these tropes 'into Pat the honest farmer, a man of noble features as well as behaviour'.[15] Published in the Irish magazine *Pat* in 1881, an unnamed Irish cartoonist depicts a genteel Irishman well dressed and groomed modelling for a British cartoonist, whose final output is a monstrous beast who is armed and dangerous (2.5). The image demonstrates a sense of frustration at the way British cartoonists intentionally depicted the Irishman in a negative way. By 1914, the simianized Paddy was no longer being used by cartoonists because 'the "gorilla controversy" had lost […] its ability to wound the *amour propre* of God-fearing Englishmen'. Instead, traditional symbols such as Hibernia and Erin were used as visual tropes in connection to the Irish.[16]

Ireland divided

In December 1920, the Government of Ireland Act was passed, separating Ireland in two: Northern Ireland comprised of the predominantly Protestant six counties of Ulster, with the remaining twenty-six counties making up Southern Ireland. As Douglas et al. comment on the Act:

> This Act, the most momentous piece of British legislation to affect Ireland in 120 years, was a compromise solution which failed to satisfy any of the competing strands of Irish political opinion. It was, in effect, a British solution to an Irish problem.[17]

The famous cartoon 'The Kindest Cut of All' (*Punch*, 10 March 1920) (2.6) depicts the then Prime Minister Lloyd George about to perform a magic trick by cutting a map of Ireland and putting it in a magician's hat. The hat is labelled 'Irish Council' in reference to the proposal to establish a body which would bring 'about harmonious action between the parliaments and governments of Southern Ireland and Northern Ireland, and to the promotion of mutual intercourse and uniformity in relation to matters affecting the whole of Ireland'.[18] The accompanying text suggests that George himself is unsure that his trick of getting the two parts to 'come together of their own accord' will work, whilst the caption of the image strongly hints at the irony of splitting something in two in order to create unity.

British cartoonists focused on the reaction of the nationalists over the status of Ireland. Eamon de Valera, the head of Sinn Féin and President of the Republic, objected to the new 'Irish Free State' being granted dominion status rather than a fully independent republic. Bernard Partridge's 'A Forgotten Patriotism' (*Punch*, 24 August 1921) (2.7) shows the ghost of Charles Stewart Parnell, a prominent Home Rule campaigner and politician, telling de Valera to be content with the offer of Home Rule and dominion status. The image demonstrates how British cartoonists perceived the situation of the British acting in a generous way, whilst the Irish were ungrateful. The caption also reinforces the idea that de Valera was working for his own selfish gains, rather than for the Irish nation.

Following the approval of the Anglo-Irish Treaty on 7 January 1922 by the Dáil, the Irish Civil War broke out between those who were for the Treaty and those who were opposed to it. Sinn Féin's anti-Treaty stance meant that the party, including de Valera, did not take up its seats in the Dáil. Leonard Raven-Hill's 'Ireland's Evil Genius' (*Punch*, 6 June 1923) (2.8) conveys *Punch*'s relief at de Valera's non-participation in parliamentary politics. The cartoon depicts Ireland, as Erin, being left by de Valera who is 'compelled by circumstances to leave'. Erin seems unfazed and urges de Valera to make his absence 'as long as you can'. Eventually, however, de Valera called for a ceasefire in May 1923, instructing the IRA to momentarily lay down their weapons: 'Military victory must be allowed to rest for the moment with those who have destroyed the Republic'.[19] This led to the elections on 16 June 1922 which demonstrated strong pro-Treaty support amongst the electorate: less than 22 per cent voted for anti-Treaty candidates on first-preference votes,[20] thus showing how Sinn Féin had not managed to influence nor capture public opinion on the issue.

Northern Ireland's Catholics

The first elections for the Parliament of Northern Ireland were held in May 1921, where forty out of the fifty-two seats were won by the Ulster Unionist Party

(UUP) and headed by the Prime Minister James Craig. The UUP won successive elections, with the Nationalist Party being the second largest party. However, they abstained from participating in the parliament on the basis that they did not accept a divided Ireland. It was not until 1965 that the Nationalist Party accepted to become the official opposition to the Northern Ireland government. In 1967, the Northern Irish Civil Rights Association was formed. It was borne out of a desire by many of the younger generation of Catholics living in Northern Ireland for reform of the state which they considered their home. As Alvin Jackson states, one of 'the most remarkable of the many astonishing features of Northern Irish politics in the 1960s was the comprehensive mobilisation of Catholic political opinion that had occurred by 1968–9'.[21]

One of the key indicators for this change in attitude towards the issue was the way in which the IRA campaign against the British in Northern Ireland during 1956–62, known as Operation Harvest, failed. This was because the Catholics from the north no longer identified with the aims of the IRA who, in turn, blamed them for its failure by not supporting the cause.[22] On 5 October 1968, a banned civil rights march went ahead in Londonderry leading to violent clashes with the police. The scenes of violence were broadcast across the globe; this was crucial because not only did the images ignite sectarian flames once more, it led to Catholics supporting the civil rights movement who, prior to the event, were unsure of where they stood. The violence and coverage of the event also demanded attention from the British government:

> It was apparent that a new version of the Irish question was emerging, successive British governments having for too long neglected their responsibilities.[23]

There followed two further days of violence in the city. JAK's 'Owing to a spot of bother in Ireland, we're recruiting again for the Black and Tan' (*Evening Standard*, 8 October 1968) (2.9)[24] depicts a parade of ageing men in uniform. JAK views the violence following the civil rights march as a slight disturbance when referring to it as 'a spot of bother', rather than as a serious incident requiring serious action and thought.

JAK (Raymond Allen Jackson, 1927–97) often portrayed the Irish in a negative manner (interestingly, JAK's mother was Irish[25]). Another of his cartoons, 'The Ultimate in Psychopathic Horror – The Irish' (*Evening Standard*, 29 October 1982),[26] proved controversial and led to the then leader of the Greater London Council, Ken Livingstone, to withdraw all advertising from the paper.[27] Another cartoon commenting on the incident is Keith Waite's second of the trio of frames, 'I don't understand the police violence – all we did was throw a few petrol bombs at them' (*Sun*, 9 October 1968) (2.10).[28] The image depicts two men discussing the Londonderry incident in a pub (as indicated by the sign on the door, 'Minney's Irish House'). Their casual reference to throwing petrol bombs at the police indicates how such violent acts for them are a part of everyday life. The two cartoons convey an attitude of indifference and apathy at the situation where violence in Ireland is taken for granted, and is almost expected to occur. Consequently, both Waite and JAK exemplify the idea of the British cartoonist not fully understanding the Irish situation by explaining the violence away as something that is intrinsic and inevitable, rather than acknowledging and highlighting the underlying issues of the situation.

The Troubles

Commonly referred to as 'The Troubles', the period from 1969 to 2000 saw Northern Ireland's sectarian conflict deteriorate to 'unprecedented'[29] levels. This began in large part due to the deployment of the British army in Belfast and Londonderry in August 1969, eventually leading to Direct Rule from Westminster in March 1972. John Darby argues that the presence of the British army in Northern Ireland became the catalyst for focusing the attention of British cartoonists, rather than the violence that was occurring. Moreover, it changed their perception of the situation in Northern Ireland.[30] Both JAK's 'In Christ's name' (*Evening Standard*, 16 August 1969) (2.11)[31] and Bernard Cookson's uncaptioned image (*Evening News*, 18 August 1969) (2.12)[32] refer to the sectarian nature of the conflict through JAK's reference to Christ in the caption and Cookson's nailing of the clover to the cross. Both images depict a scene of devastation – the focus being on the loss of human life due to religious differences. Jon's 'It's all this wanton destruction, sir' (*Daily Mail*, 18 August 1969) (2.13)[33] attempts to view the destruction from a humorous angle where a soldier (presumably British) opines at the damage sustained by a bar.

'Bloody Sunday' was a catalyst event during The Troubles. It occurred on 30 January 1972 where, during a civil rights march, thirteen unarmed people were killed by British paratroopers in Londonderry, which led to the British embassy in Dublin being burnt down on 2 February. According to Darby, British cartoonists in 'popular papers were reluctant to contradict the supportive stance which they had taken previously by criticising the army, and played the incident down. It was left to those in more serious publications to express concern',[34] such as Leslie Gibbard's 'Under Orders' (*Guardian*, 5 February 1972)

(2.14).³⁵ Gibbard depicts a man with a petrol bomb in his hand with his back to a British soldier holding a rifle in his hand. On either side stand the then Taoiseach, Jack Lynch and the then British Prime Minister Edward Heath. All four stand in obstinate defiance, refusing to look at one another. Beneath them is the word 'NEWRY' – a reference to the city in Northern Ireland which witnessed many violent incidents throughout the Troubles.

JAK's 'He fired first!' (*Evening Standard*, 31 January 1972) (2.15)³⁶ takes a similar approach, depicting a British soldier and a member of the IRA both pointing the finger at one another, separated by a pile of corpses. Both images 2.14 and 2.15 focus on the violence committed by either side of the conflict, with Gibbard focusing on the underlying political causes of the violence. By depicting Lynch and Heath in the same image as the republican and the British soldier, Gibbard draws comparisons between the politicians and the men on the ground, highlighting Lynch's and Heath's culpability in the tragedy.

JAK's 'I wonder how the British Press will distort this!' (*Evening Standard*, 26 October 1971) (2.16)³⁷ interestingly picks up on the criticism aimed at the British press for its coverage of Northern Ireland at the time. A soldier lies dead on the ground, shot by two IRA gunmen, one of whom poses the question in the caption. Here, JAK resists the criticism aimed at the British press by presenting a simplistic scenario – the IRA gunmen shooting a lone British soldier in cold blood. There is no question who is good and who is bad in this image, and therefore by extension, in the conflict. Although it is fair to criticize the IRA for their violent actions, there is no recognition by JAK of the wrongdoings committed by the British army, nor the other issues that compounded the situation. Such themes can also be found in Paul Rigby's 'Look at this – how could anyone stoop to such brutality?' (*Sun*, 20 October 1971) (2.17),³⁸ relating to the controversy over the torture of detainees. Here, the IRA are presented as hypocrites – enraged over the issue and at the same time watching a funeral parade pass by – presumably the deaths having been at their hands.

Nicholas Garland's uncaptioned image (*Daily Telegraph*, 4 February 1972) (2.18)³⁹ portrays the situation as clearly being instigated by the IRA; a bedraggled man with a placard in one hand is ordered to 'MARCH!' by a member of the IRA who stands in the shadows, whilst the British army soldiers order the man to 'HALT!' as they approach him. The ground is strewn with broken glass, rocks and barbed wire; homes have broken windows and a bus burns in the background. In this image, the civil rights marcher is a reluctant pawn in the IRA's battle against the British army, where the issue of civil rights is a literal smokescreen for the IRA's violent motives. The British Army, on the other hand, is absolved of any blame in the Bloody Sunday tragedy. The image shows them to be on the defensive with their rifles pointing in the air – rather than at the civil rights marcher – instructing him to halt his attack as they stand behind the barbed wire.

Image 2.18 follows Darby's theory on the supportive stance many British cartoonists took with the British army in relation to the Bloody Sunday incident. The issue of civil rights for Catholics in Northern Ireland is called into question with the presence of the IRA – was there really a grievance or was it just a front for political antagonism? Furthermore, in both 2.18 and 2.15, the cartoonists employ the iconography of the IRA man in a trench coat. It was this iconography that became synonymous once again with the IRA during The Troubles for British readers – despite the fact that this 'image had been left gathering dust'[40] since the 1920s. For example, Bernard Partridge's 'Out of the Ashes' (*Punch*, 12 July 1922) (2.19) depicts a man in a trench coat and hat, holding a gun in his hand. The very fact that the man has no insignia demonstrates how powerful the image of the man in a trench coat had become, making him instantly recognizable to readers that he was undoubtedly a member of the IRA. Furthermore, that this visual trope was used many decades later indicates an intentional use of the man in the trench coat to symbolize the IRA member, demonstrating the enduring power of the visual stereotype for both readers and cartoonists alike. This is a recurring theme throughout my research, where older stereotypes which are no longer part of the common visual language are powerfully resurrected and sustained by cartoonists.

Mad dogs: The IRA

Mac's 'I've killed a soldier, Dad – now can I go and play football?' (*Daily Sketch*, 9 February 1971) (2.20)[41] and Bernard Cookson's 'He said his first word today, Paddy … "Kill!"' (*Evening News*, 9 February 1971) (2.21)[42] demonstrate the outrage of the killing of 'the first British soldier on active service' in Belfast during riots.[43] The depiction of children refers to the fact that they had been throwing stones at the soldiers and had taken part in the violent clashes which had led to the death of the soldier. Figure 2.21 features the man in the trench coat, indicating his IRA membership, whilst Figure 2.20 shows a little boy posing the question in the caption to his dad. Crucially, however, in both images the fathers hold a rifle in their hands, seemingly pleased that their sons have murderous inclinations.

Both images convey the idea of violence as something instilled and normalized by both the IRA and those who more generally sympathized with the nationalist cause. This idea is also seen in relation to the Muslim male, in Chapter 5, where the propensity towards violence is predicated on being un-British and alien in contradistinction to the white Caucasian Briton who is both civilized and civilizing. Whilst Cookson explicitly criticizes the IRA, Mac delegitimizes any sympathy to the nationalist cause. The use of children serves to undermine the humanity of the IRA and those who sympathized with their cause and, at the same time, highlight their barbarity.

Nicholas Garland's 'Mad dogs and Englishmen … ' (*Daily Telegraph*, 15 July 1971) (2.22)[44] was published following a similar incident to that referenced in images 2.20 and 2.21, published a few months earlier. The incident took place on 14 July by the Provisional IRA (PIRA) in retaliation for the deaths of two Catholics who had died in riots two years earlier.[45] The PIRA was formed in 1969 after splitting from the IRA following their decision to allow Sinn Féin candidates to the Dublin, Belfast and London parliaments:

> The basic ideology of PIRA is fairly similar to that of the pre-1960s IRA. The 'treachery' of the IRA Army Council in 1969 in recognising the illegitimate parliaments in Dublin and Belfast meant that the mantle of the legitimate government of Ireland passed to the PIRA Army Council.[46]

Therefore, although the PIRA was separate to the IRA, the wider public identified the splinter group with that of the IRA as demonstrated in image 2.22, where the dog collar reads 'IRA'.[47] By portraying the IRA as being tantamount to a mad dog, Garland seeks to dehumanize members of the paramilitary group precisely because of their inhumane actions. This strikes a chord with that of the image of the Daesh fighter examined in Chapter 5 under whose guise the suspicion of the 'Muslim Barbaric' is confirmed. Moreover, the image is meant to be provocative – by portraying the IRA as a mad dog, it seeks to undermine and debase their actions and ideology as bestial and irrational, contrasting the IRA against the 'Englishman': namely the soldier who hides behind the riot shield.[48]

The perceived barbarity of the IRA was a theme that continued into the next decades. Stanley Franklin's uncaptioned image (*Sun*, 16 November 1981) (2.23)[49] depicts the group's acronym, with the 'A' being formed by human skulls. Nicholas Garland's 'Remember – squeeze don't pull' (*Daily Telegraph*, 15 November 1991) (2.24)[50] and Mac's 'Hero of Auld Ireland' (*Daily Mail*, 22 March 1993) (2.25)[51] both focus on the child victims of the IRA attacks. Importantly, these images were published in the wake of the aftermath of several different attacks perpetrated by the IRA. Most poignantly, image 2.24 refers to the shooting of a six-week-old baby in Belfast,[52] whilst image 2.25 refers to the litter bombing tactic widely used by the IRA in which a four-year-old girl was killed as a result.[53] Garland's equally provocative 'No! No! No!' (*Daily Telegraph*, 26 October 1993) (2.26; Figure 4)[54] shows a woman, labelled 'Northern Ireland', attempting to resist being raped by a man labelled 'IRA'. Published nearly two decades later from image 2.22, image 2.26 demonstrates the persistence of the strength of feeling against the IRA in Britain. The cartoon was published following a bombing of a fish shop on Belfast's Shankhill Road – a Protestant part of the city. The bombing caused outrage, threatening ongoing peace talks at the time.[55] These images emphasize the innocent victims of the attacks through demonstrating a sense of revulsion, rather than resistance, as a form of response. This is comparable to that of the immediate response to the 7/7 attacks examined in Chapter 5 and the way Al Qaeda were identified as being akin to death such as in Images 6.9 and 6.10. Thus, parallels can be found between the different terrorist groups and the response to their violent activities.

Darby argues that '[f]or most cartoonists […] it was impossible to find any humour in the IRA'.[56] However, the archival material demonstrates that this is not necessarily true; Keith Waite's 'Look here, we ordered guns, not nuns' (*Daily Mirror*, 25 August 1970) (2.27)[57] is an example of how the IRA are mocked and

Figure 4 Nicholas Garland 'No! No! No!' (*Daily Telegraph*, 26 October 1993). © Nicholas Garland/Telegraph Media Group Limited (1993).

belittled through satire. Image 2.27 depicts a crateful of nuns being incorrectly shipped to members of the IRA who, as the caption makes explicit, were expecting arms. It is also important that Waite chooses to illustrate nuns to convey his point through referring back to the sectarian nature of the conflict. The image uses humour and satire as a way of undermining the IRA cause, insinuating that they are incapable of waging a war because they lack the basic mental faculties and common sense. Waite pokes fun at the IRA's attempts at Northern Ireland's independence, sharing the same ideas as that of the lovable – but violent – Paddy as featured in 2.4 examined above.

Ireland vis-à-vis other conflicts

Unlike the War of Independence in 1919–21, when the British government refused to deal with the situation as a military effort, the presence of the army in Belfast and Londonderry in 1969 meant that both the British government and cartoonists had to acknowledge the military aspect of the situation. However, this presented challenges to British cartoonists when dealing with the Northern Ireland issue; events such as Bloody Sunday, internment and allegations of torture against detainees 'demonstrate the difficulties facing British newspapers and their cartoonists in covering a story which, while taking place in the United Kingdom, was treated more like a foreign war'.[58] This emerges in one of the key themes of comparing the Irish situation to that of other conflicts around the world.

Cartoons such as Garland's 'I find it difficult not to feel sympathy for both sides in these tribal conflicts' (*Daily Telegraph*, 16 August 1969) (2.28; Figure 5)[59] approaches the conflict by looking at events abroad. The image depicts two Kenyan men, sitting in a luxurious setting, discussing the events in Northern Ireland as indicated by the headlines on the newspaper 'RIOTING SPREADS SHOTS FIRED IN ULSTER'. Here, Garland highlights the irony of the two men's sadness at events taking place thousands of miles away, whilst in Kenya tribal conflict was being spearheaded by the then President Jomo Kenyatta, against those who did not belong to the Kikuyu tribe.[60] In the same vein, Garland is also drawing parallels between events taking place in a former British colony (Kenya having gained independence only six years ago in 1963), with that of the riots in Northern Ireland, and how the two did not differ greatly in terms of cause and circumstance. Thus, Garland seeks to demonstrate the absurdity of such divisions and the violence that leads from them.

Figure 5 Nicholas Garland, 'I find it difficult not to feel sympathy for both sides in these tribal conflicts' (*Daily Telegraph*, 16 August 1969). © Nicholas Garland/Telegraph Media Group Limited (1969).

Trog's 'Heathen Bloody Savages!' (*Punch*, 27 September 1972) (2.29) focuses on the violent actions of the IRA. A man in dark glasses and a hat responds to the 'Belfast Telegraph' headline: 'UGANDA – civil strife continues'. His rifle rests behind him, whilst his comrade in a balaclava holds another rifle in his hands. The two men are hiding behind a fence where in the background a house stands dilapidated and destroyed. The cartoon also features fighters from the Protestant paramilitary organization, the Ulster Defence Association (UDA), who look on at the IRA gunmen from behind the house. One holds a flag with the initials UDA whilst another holds a rifle. The cartoon insinuates that the caption applies to both sides of the conflict, although perhaps with more emphasis on the IRA, since they are so prominent in the cartoon.

Similarly, Jon's 'Glory be, Mrs Murphy, isn't it terrible what the Arabs and Israelis are up to?' (*Daily Mail*, 11 September 1969) (2.30)[61] compares the Northern Irish situation to that of events abroad. The image of two women discussing the Arab-Israeli conflict over barbed wire, whilst a soldier and houses with broken windows loom in the background, highlights the irony of the caption. By drawing attention to the Arab-Israeli conflict, Jon seeks to demonstrate the commonality Northern Ireland shares by way of the religious dimension of the two conflicts. This is examined in greater detail in Chapter 2, where religion is focused on as being fundamental to the Arab-Israeli conflict. The cartoon at 2.30 takes a similar approach where the conflict is approached as a primarily religious one in which the Irish are criticized (albeit indirectly) in their capacity as Protestants and Catholics fighting against one other.

Therefore, although the conflict is primarily sectarian in nature, the cartoon emphasizes that it is the two women's mutual Irish nature that has led the two communities becoming violent and primitive, rather than their religion – in much the same way as the Victorians perceived this flaw in the Irish character.

Michael Cummings' 'We're pagan missionaries come to try to make peace among the bloodthirsty Christians' (*Daily Express*, 12 September 1969) (2.31)[62] depicts three African tribesmen arriving by boat to the shores of Ireland in a quest, as suggested by the caption, to stop the sectarian violence. Douglas et al. comment on how the cartoon demonstrates the lack of understanding of the situation by the British through depicting

> primitive tribesmen arriving to reconcile the barbarous Irish, who seem intent on tearing each other apart. The racist implication is that black, presumably African, tribesmen are more civilised than the Christian Northern Irish, who have now slipped below even primitive pagans in their innate barbarity. The cartoon thus reinforces stereotypical notions of the Irish as violent and blacks as primitive, making no attempt to convey any understanding of the underlying causes of conflict other than bigotry.[63]

The image suggests that Cummings sympathizes with the idea of the colonization of other countries in order to make them more sophisticated. It is also noteworthy that he refers to 'pagan missionaries' in order to emphasize the religious dimension of the conflict. Thus, in his attempt to be ironic, Cummings fails by demeaning those who were colonized and subject to missionizing under different colonial powers, including Britain.

Another Cummings cartoon, 'How marvellous it would be if they DID knock each other insensible!' (*Daily Express*, 12 August 1970) (2.32; Figure 6)[64] conveys the sense of frustration and impatience at the ongoing situation in Northern Ireland and the desire for the British army to pull out from there. The image shows a British soldier expressing his exasperation at being unable to carry out his orders to 'STOP THE RIVALS FROM KNOCKING EACH OTHER INSENSIBLE' (indicated by the placard in front), as the 'Ulster Catholics' and the 'Ulster Protestants' pelt one other with rocks and bricks.

"How marvellous it would be if they DID knock each other insensible!"

Figure 6 Michael Cummings, 'How marvellous it would be if they DID knock each other insensible!' (*Daily Express*, 12 August 1970). © Cummings/Daily Express/Mirrorpix.

Carl Giles' 'I don't think it's a stupid question. I simply asked how throwing a little brick through someone's window and knocking a policeman's hat off helped the Irish cause' (*Daily Express*, 19 August 1969) (2.33)[65] is situated in a café where a young Caucasian woman (possibly English) poses the question in the caption to a remarkably ape-like man who smiles knowingly. In the background a bearded man sits at the window with a placard: 'KICK THE WELSH OUT OF SCOTLAND'. Both the caption and the placard imply the futility of both the Irish cause (to kick the Brits out of Ireland) and the Scottish cause sought by the Welshman. The Welshman's cause in reality did not exist, further emphasizing the absurdity of the Irish cause.

Crucially, in both images the Irishmen have simian features, akin to the Paddy published nearly a hundred years ago in Tenniel's 'Two Forces' at 2.3, examined above. By portraying them in such a manner, Cummings and Giles ignore the valid reasons for the conflict and suggest that the Irishmen – regardless of whether one is Catholic or Protestant – is by nature bestial and barbaric and therefore is the root cause of the conflict. The Irishman's apelike nature is further emphasized against the beauty of the young woman in 2.33 and the humanity of the small, bruised British soldier in 2.32, who is caught in the crossfire attempting in vain to stop such barbarity. As Douglas et al. explain:

> The implication underlying both cartoons [2.31 and 2.32] is that the irrational nature of the Irish question can only be explained through some form of racial madness. Far from helping British readers to understand the complexities of the Northern Irish situation, such cartoons reinforced the growing anti-Irish prejudice among sections of British opinion and so exacerbated the hostile public mood.[66]

Thus, although religion was a cause of the conflict, the fact that British cartoonists like Cummings, Mac and Franklin focus on this issue suggests the ignorance of both the cartoonists and the readers. The focus on sectarian divisions in these cartoons indicates a sense of confusion and bemusement that the same faith could engender such violence. A common visual trope to emphasize this is the use of barbed wire in many of the cartoons looked at in this chapter, a reference to the peace lines between Catholic and Protestant neighbourhoods in different parts of Northern Ireland. Mac's 'Ye lying ol' devil, Paddy. Ye know mother's the same faith as us!' (*Daily Sketch*, 11 September 1969) (2.34)[67] and Stanley Franklin's '"'Tis a strange thing that among us people can't agree the whole week because they go different ways on Sundays" Irish dramatist Farquhar 1700' (*Daily Mirror*, 11 September 1969) (2.35)[68] both focus on the announcement of the erection of a peace line by the army between Falls Road, a Catholic area, and Shankhill Road, a Protestant area.[69] The images emphasize the fact that such barricades were being erected in order to quell violence committed by members of the same religion.

This is all the more pertinent since the cartoonists came from an Anglo-Christian background and it is most likely that they took the assumption that the majority of their readers did too. This is similar to the other communities examined, where there is an assumption that the Jew/Sikh/Muslim is the Other in relation to the reader who is most likely connected to the 'Anglosphere' that I discuss in Chapter 3. Cartoons 2.34 and 2.35 evoke the sentiments of the cartoon at 4.10, examined in Chapter 3, where the division of 'us' vs 'them' lies along civility and barbarity. There is an implication in these images that violence is alien to the very nature of the Anglo-Caucasian male and it is due to this reason that battle scenes do not and should not take place on British soil.

The referencing of conflicts involving races other than Caucasians, such as Uganda, Kenya and the Middle East crisis, conveys a sense of failed expectation on behalf of the Irish white male who has fallen into the trap of barbarity which other races are so prone to. Significantly, this shows the gradual acceptance of the Irish as being white and therefore being the same race as that of the Englishman. This is in contrast to the views conveyed in earlier cartoons such as 2.3 and 2.4, in which the Irish as a non-Caucasian is pitted against the Caucasian Anglo-Saxon. Thus, by situating and paralleling the Irish conflict to international conflicts, the cartoonists convey a sense of aloofness and bemusement at the situation despite the fact that Britain's role is so fundamental to understanding the causes of the conflict.

A notable exception to this is David Low's 'Progress to Liberty – Amritsar style' (*The Star*, 16 December 1919) (2.36),[70] which explicitly connects British imperialism to Ireland (Low was known for his critical stance towards the British government on the Irish issue).[71] The powerful image shows a British soldier looking on in glee as two men crawl away from him. One wears a turban with the word 'INDIA' and the other wears a hat with the word 'IRELAND'. 'Progress to Liberty' was originally published following the Amritsar massacre which took place earlier that year on 13 April, where hundreds of mainly Sikh unarmed pilgrims were shot dead by the British Indian Army. This took place under the orders of Colonel Reginald Edward Harry Dyer and was condemned across government and shocked the Indian public.[72] The cartoon shows how the often-cruel actions of the British authorities were inhibiting both India and Ireland's progress towards independence; not only was this goal being achieved at a snail's pace, but the cartoon refers to the crawling order instituted by Colonel Dyer in India. This was put in place on a street in British India where a Briton was assaulted following the shooting of protestors on 10 April 1919, forcing Indians who wished to walk that street to crawl on all fours.[73] The image emphasizes the cruelty of the British at the expense of human suffering.

Who is the Other?

During the early 1970s, the conflict came to mainland Britain with the Republican bombing campaign, making it difficult for cartoonists to ignore the violence, but also creating a sense of resentment amongst the British. In turn, those who had come over from Eire and had settled in Britain found the situation challenging because it presented them with the dilemma of being seen to be sympathetic to the republican cause, resulting in hostility against the Irish as a consequence. One interesting parallel can be drawn between the situation of the 35 Irish

Labour MPs (out of 363) and the Jewish Labour MPs during the Suez Crisis in 1956.[74] For both groups their mixed heritage, at times, presented difficulties in navigating domestic politics.

Another interesting case study is that of the cartoonist Kenneth Mahood (1930–2021) who was born in Belfast[75] and moved to London in 1955.[76] The cartoons examined here depict the challenges faced by the Irish living in Britain. For example, 'I hope you're not Irish or coloured?' (*Punch*, 29 October 1969) (2.37) depicts the owner of a boarding house, a Caucasian woman, asking a man whose face is obscured by his long hair, the question in the caption. The clothing and hairstyle of the Caucasian male indicate a bohemian lifestyle, suggesting that the woman would prefer someone from that lifestyle over that of the Irish or ethnic minorities. Furthermore, the casual manner in which the woman poses the question indicates how prevalent and accepted negative attitudes were towards ethnic minorities and the Irish at the time. Mahood makes it unclear if the man is indeed Irish, suggesting how prejudices based on race are flawed, where one's outward appearance is not an indicator of one's character.

'I think this chap's call should have priority – he has an Irish accent!' (*Punch*, 29 May 1974) (2.38) takes a humorous approach to the IRA bombing campaign in Britain in the early 1970s and the tactic used by them to call the police and warn them of a bomb attack. The reaction of the (presumably English) gentleman to the Irishman's accent encapsulates the mood of fear amongst the general public of a possible terrorist attack carried out by Republicans. This is similar to the way Garland uses humour to show how one minority can instil such fear in the cartoon at 6.16. Both images also illustrate the knee-jerk reaction of the wider public towards innocent members of the same ethnic or religious community to which terrorists belong.

Another interesting theme that emerges from cartoons relating to the Irish is the way they are juxtaposed against Indians as Others in Britain. Both JAK's 'Bloody foreigners!' (*Evening Standard*, 29 August 1969) (2.39)[77] and 'As far as I can make out, we Irish are two-and-a-half per cent more sexy than the rest of you!' (*Evening Standard*, 12 March 1970) (2.40)[78] comment on the way the Irish, who themselves were Othered, did the same to Indian immigrants based on similar racial prejudices that the Irish were exposed to by the English. At the same time, the cartoons also show a sense of camaraderie between the two different communities at their shared sense of Otherness and being able to joke about it amongst themselves. These cartoons were published in a context of debate surrounding immigration, preceding the introduction of the Immigration Act 1971 which sought to limit immigration by taking away the automatic right to remain for Commonwealth citizens.

Moreover, the then Conservative MP Enoch Powell's 'Rivers of Blood' speech in 1968 resonated with much of the British public in which he voiced his fears of '[w]hole areas, towns and parts of towns across England will be occupied by sections of the immigrant and immigrant-descended population'.[79] This fear is echoed in Michael Cummings' 'Please, Mr. Whitelaw! When the Irish have fought to the very last man, can we go and live in the unoccupied space?' (*Daily Express*, 21 October 1972) (2.41).[80] The cartoon depicts William Whitelaw, the then Secretary of State for Northern Ireland, with a deeply worried expression on his face as he is overwhelmed by men in turbans posing the question in the caption. The insinuation in JAK's and Cummings' cartoons is that there is an invasion of Commonwealth citizens in Britain and, furthermore, that this is an intentional move by such opportunistic immigrants to overrun the country and profit off a troubled Caucasian population.

The turban is used as a visual trope to emphasize Otherness in relation to Indians in general, rather than to Sikhs specifically. This is similar to the image at 4.14, examined further in Chapter 3. By using the trope of the Indian man in a turban, JAK and Cummings seek to emphasize both the religious and ethnic differences between Indians and that of the Caucasian population living in Britain. Thus, as discussed in Chapter 3 the cartoons reflect the growing unease of the wider public at the changing face of the Briton. Therefore, although cartoons such as 2.37 and 2.33 examined above depict the Irish as an Other, Images 2.39 and 2.41 demonstrate that in juxtaposition to the Indian, the Irishman resembles the Englishman more because they are both Caucasian and they both come from a shared Christian heritage.

Published a few years later, Mahood's 'There is no need for a Nationality Bill, says MAHOOD – all that is required is a few simple tests' (*Punch*, 18 February 1981) (2.42) comments on the British Nationality Act 1981 which categorized Citizenship of the UK and Colonies into three: British citizenship; British Dependent Territories citizenship; and British Overseas citizenship. This meant that those who fell under British citizenship had the automatic right to live in the UK, whilst those who came under the other two categories did not. Mahood pokes fun at widely held stereotypes of the British, such as the propensity to talk about the weather and the perception that all Irishmen are lazy. Again, this cartoon uses the man in a turban to illustrate the different Others in British society and how prejudices are applied across communities.

The face of terror: The IRA

Reminiscent of the way Daesh dress – masked in black so that they are unidentifiable[81] – paramilitary organizations in Ireland also wear balaclavas as part of their uniform. These include both the IRA and the loyalist UDA. The next two images are by [Arthur Stuart] Michael Cummings (1919–97). Cummings directs vehement criticism towards the IRA, through using the trope of a short and stout man wearing a mask with the word 'IRA' covering half of his face. 'Can't you British see straight – you've imprisoned another innocent!' (*Sunday Express*, 21 June 1981) (2.43)[82] is one of the many images featuring this trope. Darby describes Cummings' visualization of the IRA having 'vaguely simian jaws'[83] vindicated by a comment Cummings made that the IRA's violence led them to 'look like apes – though that's rather hard luck on the apes'.[84]

This thought is further exemplified in Cummings' 'We mustn't keep him out of the Club on grounds of his species! After all, it's not his fault that the human race is descended from him!' (*Daily Express*, 22 December 1971) (2.44),[85] in which a gorilla looks perplexed at a poster of humans committing violence. The humans portrayed include an 'Ulster man' who has 'IRA' written across his sleeve as he shoots from a gun and throws a bomb. The 'Club' includes predatory animals such as a cobra and vulture and yet they are hesitant at admitting the gorilla because of his link to man – specifically members of the IRA – even though he has no direct involvement in such actions. Thus, Cummings marks Northern Irish members of the IRA as a distinct group of people, singled out for their violence. Cummings was not the only cartoonist to draw comparisons between the IRA and gorillas – Sidney William Martin's uncaptioned image (*Sunday Express*, 27 February 1972) (2.45)[86] is another example of how the IRA's violence was visualized in such a manner. By visualizing the IRA in this way, both Cummings and Martin sought to belittle the IRA and highlight their cowardice by depicting an animal that is frequently associated with comic humour and jest.

The Good Friday Agreement was made on 10 April 1998 between the British and Irish governments, as well as the Northern Irish political parties including Sinn Féin and the Ulster Unionist Party. The Democratic Unionist Party (DUP) was the only major party who did not sign up to it. The Agreement stated a 'commitment to the total disarmament of all paramilitary organisations,'[87] but it was not a pre-condition to the implementation of the peace process. Following the Agreement, the IRA released a statement in which it outlined that the Agreement fell 'short of presenting a solid basis for a lasting settlement' and declared 'that there will be no decommissioning by the IRA.'[88]

Chris Priestley's uncaptioned image (*Independent*, 1 May 1998) (2.46)[89] comments on the IRA's refusal to give up its arms, following an IRA car bomb in Lisburn, a mainly Protestant town. The IRA member is masked under a balaclava, dressed all in black. He speaks through gritted teeth, 'Decommission? ... Not on your life!' The portrayal of the IRA member in such a manner emphasizes the organization's aim to strike terror and discord for the sake of it, despite the chance for real peace. On 7 May, a few weeks ahead of the referendum on the Good Friday Agreement, the Real IRA (RIRA) was formed in opposition to the Agreement and the principle of decommissioning. This was based on their perception that such measures would not lead to the formation of a united Ireland.

An overwhelming majority on both sides of the border in Ireland voted in favour of the Agreement: 71.1 per cent in Northern Ireland and 94.4 per cent in Eire,[90] with the first Northern Ireland Assembly being elected on 25 June 1998. On 15 August 1998, a car bomb exploded in the Northern Irish town of Omagh, leading to the loss of twenty-nine lives and two unborn children.[91] The attack, carried out by the RIRA, was widely condemned – most notably by Sinn Féin's leader Gerry Adams, who refused to condemn such attacks in the past.[92] Published in a context of escalating tension between both sides of the conflict, Chris Riddell's 'Hero of Omagh' (*Observer*, 7 February 1999) (2.47)[93] demonstrates the impact of the Omagh tragedy months later. Riddell's image resurrects the IRA man in the trench coat that was so widely used during the Victorian period and then later during the Troubles, as examined above. The right lapel of the coat reads 'The Real IRA', with the man wearing it seeming to be almost consumed by it – a metaphor for the violence the garment represents.

The function of the trench coat is similar to that of the way the *burqa*, the *salwar kameez* and the turban are imbued with negative ideas as seen in later chapters. This demonstrates how the same message of Otherness is conveyed through different tropes, moulding itself to fit the community in question. The balaclava over the man's face leaves nothing but two angry eyes visible and the rifle in his hands conveys an air of menace towards the reader. The caption is ironic, insinuating that the man depicted is most likely behind the Omagh attack which led to so many lives being lost and jeopardizing the peace process. David Haldane's 'Where did you get the cash to buy that fancy balaclava?' (*The Times*, 19 February 2005) (2.48)[94] takes a more humorous approach to the way the balaclava-clad man was synonymous with the IRA. The cartoon illustrates an IRA member being posed the question in the caption by a member of the Eire police, the Garda. Crucially, the balaclava is more akin to a bobbled winter hat being pulled down over the man's face and holes being cut out for the eyes.

Harking back to the idea of the British Army being an impeccable force and one that British cartoonists were reluctant to criticize, Mac's 'Spot the difference' (*Daily Mail*, 10 March 2009) (2.49)[95] draws parallels between the British Army in Iraq and Afghanistan and that of the RIRA in Ireland. The British soldiers are at ease, with only one of them wearing a rifle hanging off his shoulder. In contrast, the members of the RIRA wear balaclavas and seem ready to engage in battle, with all three of them armed. The image links gender – specifically masculinity – to being 'real': the actions of the British soldiers affirm their manhood, whilst those of the RIRA do the opposite. Mac valorizes the work of the British armed forces in the Iraq and Afghanistan wars, referring to the soldiers as 'real men', whilst belittling the actions of the 'Real IRA'.

Additionally, Mac legitimizes the wars in Iraq and Afghanistan as being worth the fight for the liberation of the two countries. On the other hand, the war for a united and independent Ireland as acted out by the RIRA in Ireland is futile – especially in light of the progress of the peace process since the 1998 Good Friday Agreement. In this there is a suggestion that warfare and violence when carried out by British soldiers are legitimate and moral because it is for a worthwhile cause – even if this is at the expense of civilian lives (the UN recorded just over 5,000 civilian casualties between 1 January and 30 June 2021 in Afghanistan).[96] However, when conducted by others such as the RIRA, the opposite is deemed true.

Unionists and the UDA

Although the IRA and the republican movements are fiercely criticized by the British press, the same is also true for members of the opposite end of the spectrum, namely the Ulster Unionists and members of the UDA. Stanley Franklin's 'Patriotism is the last refuge of a scoundrel – Samuel Johnson' (*Daily Mirror*, 14 October 1969) (2.50)[97] highlights the hardliner loyalist factions. Symbolizing 'Belfast Extremists', an angry man runs with a flag of the Union Jack in his hand that reads 'God save the Queen (and attack her troops)'. The cartoon was published in the wake of clashes with Protestant crowds against British troops. Franklin here shows the irony of the two sides fighting against one another when they are both loyal to the Crown.

Emmwood's 'Faceless, senseless – brainless' (*Daily Mail*, 12 July 1972) (2.51)[98] and Andrzej Krauze's uncaptioned image (*Observer*, 14 July 1996) (2.52)[99] both pit the IRA and the UDA against one another. Despite the fact that Krauze's image was published over twenty years later, the images show the persistence of the violence perpetrated by both sides of the conflict. Image 2.51 shows both members of the paramilitary organizations masked and unidentifiable as they stand over the female body of Ulster and two ripped pieces of paper reading 'cease' and 'fire'. In 2.52, Krauze uses the balaclava and a rifle to symbolize the IRA, whilst a bowler hat is pulled down over the UDA member, wearing a sash and white gloves – a reference to the traditional uniform worn by members of the Orange Order. A Protestant organization, the Order was founded in 1795, named after William of Orange. The Orange Order is known for its marches, especially that of 12 July, commemorating the victory of William of Orange at the Battle of the Boyne in 1690. Image 2.52 was published in light of a march held by the Orangemen on the predominantly Catholic Garvaghy Road, Drumcree, inflaming sectarian tensions. In between the two men sits John Bull (symbolized by the Union Jack bowler hat) looking on worriedly at a crack forming in the table in front of him. Here, Krauze highlights the extremities of both sides of the conflict – the violence of the IRA and the marches of the Orangemen. At the same time, the masking of both the loyalists and the republicans in the two images points towards the violence and terror for which they are culpable.

Decades later, in the hope that it would help progress the peace process, the then Northern Ireland Secretary of State, Mo Mowlam, took the unprecedented step of meeting with loyalist prisoners at Prison Maze in Northern Ireland. Steve Bell's '1049-9-1-98_MORETEAMADDOG' (*Guardian*, 9 January 1998) (2.53)[100] imagines Mowlam having tea with the UDA in her meeting. The juxtaposition of a UK government Cabinet Minister having tea in a genteel manner with terrorists is highlighted by her casually posing the question, 'More tea, mad dog?' Published on the same day, Chris Priestley's uncaptioned image (*Independent*, 9 January 1998) (2.54)[101] focuses on the violence and prejudice of these men which resulted in their imprisonment. Priestley depicts a more sterile setting of the Maze to emphasize the fact that Mowlam, a democratically elected politician, was meeting people convicted of heinous crimes and yet were so key to unlocking peace in Ireland. In both images, the men are masked in balaclavas to symbolize their status as terrorists. Mowlam's gamble paid off, with the visit resulting in the prisoners no longer opposing the peace process and the Ulster Democratic Party participating in the talks.

A precarious peace

In the years since the Good Friday Agreement, the political situation in Northern Ireland has remained a fragile one. A common trope utilized by cartoonists to convey this fragility is the iconic dove carrying an olive branch. Dave Gaskill's uncaptioned image (*Sun*, 15 February 1999) (2.55),[102] published less than a year after both sides of the border voted in favour of the Agreement, depicts a dove unable to fly under the weight of a rifle symbolizing 'IRA weapons'. The cartoon comments on the controversy that was sparked when the then Irish Taoiseach, Bertie Ahern, was quoted as saying that decommissioning by the IRA had to take place as it was 'not compatible with being part of a government, and part of an executive', thus suggesting that Sinn Féin should not be part of the Northern Ireland Assembly.[103]

Dave Brown's uncaptioned image (*Independent*, 9 October 2002) (2.56)[104] is another example of the numerous images featuring the dove of peace. The cartoon was published in response to David Trimble, the then Ulster Unionist Party leader and Northern Ireland's First Minister, threatening to withdraw from the Executive over allegations that Sinn Féin workers had stolen confidential parliamentary papers and had passed them onto the IRA.[105] Trimble is shown nailing a coffin on which a plaque reads 'Good Friday Agreement RIP'. The dove is shown to be attempting to escape the coffin, as three weeping crocodile standard bearers (in reference to the common phrase of crying crocodile tears) carry it. Two of the crocodiles wear sashes and bowler hats, implying that they are Orangemen, whilst the third crocodile wears a police uniform. Here, Brown criticizes members of the loyalist population as being insincere about desiring peace.

Both JAS's uncaptioned image (*Daily Telegraph*, 29 January 2007) (2.57)[106] and Jonathan Pugh's 'Oh no, not another repeat' (*The Times*, 11 March 2009) (2.58) reflect the frustrations shared by many at the slow pace of the peace progress. Image 2.57 comments on both the then Prime Minister, Tony Blair, confirming that he would be leaving in the summer and Sinn Féin finally supporting the role of the Police Services Northern Ireland (PSNI).[107] This was momentous – for the first time Sinn Féin declared its support for policing and the criminal justice system in Northern Ireland. After the Assembly's suspension in 2003, Sinn Féin's decision paved the way for devolution to return to Stormont ahead of a third election which was eventually held in March 2007. Image 2.58 was published following a spate of attacks against British soldiers and the police in Northern

Ireland by breakaway factions of the IRA. The cartoon shows a middle-aged couple watching television and complaining about 'Northern Ireland Crisis' being aired again. The couple's indifference and resignation show how the cycle of violence was still the norm for Northern Irelanders, despite it having been twelve years since members of the British armed forces had been killed by paramilitaries.[108]

Gender

Interestingly, women are shown either as passive participants in the conflict or as victims of it. The former can be seen in Images 2.21 and 2.30 for example, where the women are shown to be aware of the conflict and yet both images contain armed men, conveying the idea that the conflict is being fought by men. Garland takes the long-suffering trope of Hibernia/Erin (as in 2.3 and 2.8) and takes this further by transforming her into a victim of rape in 2.26. By depicting Northern Ireland in such a manner, the image portrays a sense of brutal suffering being inflicted against an innocent and helpless victim. Out of the fifty-seven cartoons examined in this chapter, thirty-five (61 per cent) are men-only, nineteen (33 per cent) are women-mixed and none are women-only.[109] There were three (5 per cent) cartoons where no people featured in the image. The absence of women in the majority of the cartoons shows how violence and conflict are understood in masculine terms so that men are considered the sole and primary agents of terror in contrast to women who are not innately capable of such deeds. This feeds into ideas of Irish masculinity and how it is perceived to be predicated on savagery and barbarity.

Conclusion: Ireland post-Brexit

Although the political situation in Northern Ireland is still contentious and challenging, much of the context has moved on from terrorism perpetrated by both republicans and loyalists to the different parties being able to govern as part of a power-sharing Executive. Thus, the focus has shifted away from the actions of terrorists (which fortunately are minimal) to those of politicians attempting to make the Good Friday Agreement work. Indeed, at the time of writing, Stormont does not have an Executive since February 2022 and significantly, the twenty-fifth anniversary of the Agreement had been recently commemorated amongst a raised terror level due to 'an increase in levels of activity relating to Northern Ireland Related Terrorism'.[110] Recent events, including Brexit and the implications of the Northern Ireland Protocol, the Conservative-DUP coalition (formed in the wake of the hung parliament in June 2017), and the varying abortion laws across the UK, have highlighted how intrinsic a part of the UK Northern Ireland is.

Consequently, there is a re-examination of the question of what it means to be British in relation to the Irish issue – does it go along purely geographical lines, or does it take a more inclusive approach – especially in today's global context? For example, image 2.31 views the situation from an aloof perspective, suggesting that there is no shared history between Northern Ireland and Britain. This is in contrast to the portrayal of the Conservative-DUP coalition and the ridiculing of the then minority Tory government having to be propped up by a small Northern Irish party which only had ten seats in parliament.[111] The Republic of Ireland's decision to amend its strict abortion laws, following a referendum in May 2018, led to calls for the same to be considered in Northern Ireland. This resulted in cartoonists focusing on the DUP's strong anti-abortion views, coupled with the perceived clout they held at Westminster.[112] As of 22 October 2019, abortion was decriminalized, with legislation introduced in 2020.[113]

Such images demonstrate how Ireland has moved on since the violence of The Troubles. Cartoons no longer focus on rioting, the IRA or the UDA but on more nuanced political issues such as the impact of the UK's exit from the EU[114] or US President Joe Biden's visit to Ireland, commemorating the twenty-fifth anniversary of the Good Friday Agreement.[115] Crucially, these images do not take a fatalistic approach, foreseeing an Ireland that is yet again mixed up in violence, but one that needs disentangling from important political questions. This is perhaps in part because of key events such as the Conservative-DUP 'Confidence and Supply Agreement'[116] following the 2017 general election and the impacts of the UK leaving the EU. The EU negotiations pushed the Republic of Ireland-Northern Ireland border issue further up the agenda viz. the Northern Ireland Protocol, thereby making it an explicitly UK problem that must be given serious consideration. Indeed, the so-called Windsor Framework which seeks to address disputes regarding the Northern Ireland Protocol was agreed by the UK and EU after two years of negotiations in 2023. Announcing the agreement, PM Rishi Sunak stated how it showed 'our Union, that has lasted for centuries, can and will endure', emphasizing Northern Ireland as a key part of the UK.[117] Thus, the move away from comparing the situation to that of a foreign conflict feeds into the move away from depicting the Irish as an Other. Within this there is an acknowledgement that violence is not isolated to one particular group, with the cause of it being much more complex than simply one's religion or ethnicity. Consequently, there is less emphasis on the inherent negative characteristics of the Irishman and his simian features being reflective of his inferior status as seen in 2.33 and 2.4.

Interestingly, there are no parallels (visually or otherwise) made between the Daesh fighter and that of members of Irish paramilitary organizations who dress in a similar fashion – such as in 2.53 and 2.55. This may be intentional, despite the fact that the similarities are so striking. One reason could be that although the acts of terror committed by Irish paramilitaries are shocking and saddening, there is a reluctance, on behalf of cartoonists and the wider news media, to compare Daesh to any other terrorist group in order to underscore Daesh's heinous activities. Another parallel between the way the Islamist terror threat and the Northern Ireland conflict are treated in cartoons is that in both contexts, the images demonstrate a more nuanced understanding of the situation as time has gone on.

For example, earlier cartoons on the Irish issue, such as 2.3, reflect the dominant colonial attitude as well as a refusal to understand the reasons behind why the Irish did not welcome imperialism. Published ninety-nine years apart from one another, 2.4 and 2.9 exemplify how British attitudes of patronizing the Irish and the belittlement of the impact of colonialism in the country have endured. The key difference between the Irish conflict and the Islamist terror threat is that the former has been ongoing for centuries and therefore, both republicans and loyalists have become more entrenched in their views. Images 2.14, 2.52 and 2.53 are examples of the recognition, made over the decades as the conflict has gone on, of how it is not one-sided. These cartoons are critical of the violence that both sides perpetrate and represent. This is in contrast to cartoons such as 2.16 and 2.9, where the republicans were made mostly (if not wholly) responsible for fuelling the conflict further. Crucially, the image of the masked man as the terrorist serves to move away from the prognathous and simianized Irishman – who most likely, for today's audience, would not be easily recognizable as the violent Celt as it would have been for Victorian audiences. If a cartoonist were to use such visual tropes, it would most certainly open them up to accusations of racism.

Similarly, the image of the masked man feeds into Western popular culture of the villainous figure and is therefore easily identifiable by readers today (in much the same way as Daesh figures in Chapter 5). In a way the trench coat could never do, the mask allows the typical Caucasian reader to forget that they are of the same race as that of the republican/loyalist terrorist. Thus, the mask makes the process of Othering much easier for the reader. By predicating difference on violent versus non-violent, the masking of men in balaclavas and bowler hats such as in 2.53 and 2.55 is used as a visual trope to draw attention to their activities in the capacity as *terrorists* rather than as Irishmen.

2

Noses, Moses and war: Jews in political cartoons

Introduction

The depiction of 'the Jew' has a long history in British art, with the earliest images dating back as far as mediaeval times.[1] A caricature from 1233 shows Isaac of Norwich (3.1),[2] a Jewish moneylender and one of the richest men in England at the time. Isaac, his wife and employee (who are all Jews) are vilified in the cartoon by association with the devil:

> The fierce horned devil, called Colbif ... has his index finger upon the pronounced nose of each, as if he were both identifying their ethnic origin and claiming them as his own.[3]

Images such as this one, as Frank Felsenstein points out, portray the negative attitudes Christians held towards Jews, rather than giving an accurate portrayal of Jews of that period.[4]

A few decades after the creation of the Norwich cartoon, Edward I expelled the Jews of England in 1290. It was not until 1655 that Jews were officially readmitted to England by Oliver Cromwell. However, the fictive Jew as visualized in the 1233 cartoon remained during this prolonged period. Thus, the Jew who existed in reality and the fictive Jew that existed in the Christian mind were two entirely separate, but conflated beings. This process has continued in the modern period. While the stereotype of 'the Jew' has taken on different, at times more subtle inflections, there nonetheless remains the idea of the fictive Jew in the British imagination, divorced from the realities of Jewish life in Britain.

This chapter covers the depiction of Jews, using the admittance of the first Jewish Member of Parliament as a starting point. I subsequently look at the seismic events of the Second World War and the fight against the British for a Jewish homeland. Following the establishment of Israel in May 1948, I look at how this led to a transformation of the Jew as militaristic, combative and no longer a victim of persecution. Both the Shoah and the establishment of Israel have shaped British perceptions of *all* Jews – whether or not they were directly involved or affected by either event. Therefore, although many of the cartoons examined in this chapter show Jews in a foreign context, I argue that the perception of Jews in Britain has been increasingly seen through the prism of foreign Jews from the 1930s onwards. Therefore, the point at which Jews were able to participate in their capacity as politicians at Westminster serves as a useful basis with which to compare their treatment in their capacity as politicians in Israel.

This is because the cartoons demonstrate views and attitudes towards the fictive Jew as an individual, without a fixed geographical location, who is imagined to exist in every society where there is a Jewish community. In many ways, this is similar to the 'rootless cosmopolitanism' of Stalinist Russia, an antisemitic term denouncing Jews who were perceived to be against the Soviet regime.[5] I use the concept of 'liquid racism' where the use of different symbols and imagery lends an ambiguity to cartoons which is essential in being able to provoke both racist and non-racist readings of the same image. Thus, cartoons relating to Jews examined below hark back to what Simon Weaver terms 'older racisms', demonstrating the persistence of the fictive Jew in the public imagination.

The first Jewish MP

On 28 July 1858, Baron Lionel de Rothschild became the 'first professing Jewish Member of Parliament'.[6] This was a significant moment for Anglo-Jewry; for eleven years, Baron Rothschild had attempted to take his seat as MP for the City of London. He had been unable to do so because he refused to say the words 'on the true faith of a Christian' which formed part of the Oath of Allegiance MPs had to swear. After several unsuccessful attempts, the Commons was able to pass legislation allowing Jewish members of both the Commons and the Lords to be able to omit the words if they wished.[7] As the *Manchester Guardian* describes, the passage of the 'Jew Bill' 'was received with great cheering'[8] in the Commons, as well as being covered positively by the British press.[9]

Importantly, Jewish MPs were perceived as authorities on Jewish issues by their Gentile colleagues thanks to the popular imagination of Jewish solidarity. As Michael Clark argues:

> This representative nature meant that the politicians served the community as useful indicators of tolerance. That gentiles elected them as Jews, and did so increasingly over the period [1858–87], suggested to both the *JC* [*Jewish Chronicle*] and *Jewish World* a growing integration [...].[10]

Thus, the election of Jews to Parliament served as an indication of how well they were being accepted in British society.

At the same time, however, the treatment of Benjamin Disraeli (who served as prime minister in 1868 and 1874–80) in political cartoons was indicative of the stigma associated with being Jewish or of a Jewish background. Despite being a baptized Christian since the age of thirteen,[11] Disraeli's Jewishness was focused on and emphasized in many cartoons – indicating the way in which there was a commonly held perception of the 'Otherness' of British Jews in Victorian times. John Tenniel's 'New crowns for old ones!' (*Punch*, 15 April 1876) (3.2) is one example of the prolific number of cartoons focusing on Disraeli's Jewish heritage in a negative manner. Published in response to the addition of India to the British Empire and the title of 'Empress of India' to Queen Victoria's Royal title, image 3.2 casts Disraeli as Aladdin, persuading Queen Victoria to surrender her English crown for a much more ornate one, engraved with the word 'INDIA'.

In this image the fictive Jew attempts to deceive the very heart of the nation by forging a link with the Queen. The fictive Jew does this as if trying to legitimize and ingratiate himself by presenting himself as the charming English gentleman. However, Tenniel's cartoon indicates Disraeli's failure to deceive the 'real' Englishman through such 'obvious' obsequiousness. The markings on Disraeli's clothes and box, as well as the devious expression on his face, all point to someone being aided by magic and spurred on by ulterior motives. Furthermore, Disraeli clothed in a dress indicates an oriental effeminacy about him, demonstrating a link between the image of 'the sodomitical schemer and the evil Jew'.[12] Thus, by making Queen Victoria Empress of India, Disraeli is shown to be doing 'an "oriental" and specifically Jewish, certainly un-English act'.[13]

Reminiscent of the imagery of Isaac of Norwich in 3.1, one of the key visual indicators of their Otherness in Victorian cartoons was the Semitic nose, which was seen as 'an indication of a tribal oneness that separated Jews from the native citizens among whom they dwelt. It marked them as alien'.[14] John Tenniel's 'Mosé in Egitto!!!' (*Punch*, 11 December 1875) (3.3) is another key example of the use of the Semitic nose and the Othering of Disraeli. Published in response to the purchase of shares in the Suez Canal by the British government, Disraeli is shown holding 'the key of India' (as the Suez was commonly referred to). The shares were purchased without parliamentary approval using a loan of £4m from N M Rothschild & Sons in order to do so.[15] This caused much controversy with the Leader of the Opposition, William Gladstone, accusing the Government of 'deviat[ing] widely from the usual paths of the Constitution'.[16]

In image 3.3, both Disraeli and the sphinx share a conspiratorial wink, with Disraeli touching his Semitic nose. In both 3.2 and 3.3, Disraeli wears a turban and garish clothing. The visual imagery, as well as the caption for image 3.3 (referring to an 1818 Italian opera based on the Exodus), serves to emphasize Disraeli's Jewishness and Otherness as a way to explain his actions as being intentionally detrimental to the nation whilst he stands to gain. This was an abiding critique of Jews from the Enlightenment and the discourse regarding emancipation; Jews will always pursue what is best for their group, rather than for the nation. By portraying the Jew as an Other in this manner, it also shows how the community was perceived to be racially distinct from that of the Caucasian Anglo-Saxon, in much the same way as the Irish.

Moreover, Wohl argues that Disraeli became a symbol of *all* Jews – not simply Anglo-Jews.[17] Thus, the portrayal of Disraeli was in effect a comment on the entire Jewish community and their innate negative qualities. This was done by using caricature as a vehicle to 'degrade the subject. In effect […] de-humanize the individual',[18] in such a way as to allow the expression of such prejudice 'with an easy conscience ("Don't be so po-faced! it is, after all, just a joke!")'.[19] Thus, images 3.2 and 3.3 reflect Victorian popular opinion and how mediaeval stereotypes of the 'Jew' still persisted centuries later in the guise of harmless humour, rather than an overtly antisemitic cartoon as that of Isaac of Norwich looked at above.[20]

Jewish terrorism or Jewish resistance?

Concurrent with the increasing suffering of Jews under the Nazis in Europe, there were members of the Zionist movement who were actively trying to establish a Jewish state in Palestine. One of the motivating factors for this movement was the issue of Jewish persecution and the need to prevent this from happening; the events occurring in Europe vindicated this conviction. Importantly, Palestine was under the control of Britain from 1920–48 during which there was an often violent struggle for the establishment of the State of Israel. Following the upheaval of the First World War, the 1917 Balfour Declaration announced the British government's positive attitudes towards 'the establishment in Palestine of a national home for the Jewish people'. This was a significant moment in Anglo-Jewish history, one which, as quoted in the *Manchester Guardian*, the *Jewish Chronicle* described as 'a triumph for civilisation and for humanity'.[21]

However, during the years of Mandatory Palestine, Jewish terrorist movements led several campaigns against mostly Palestinian civilians and the British military. Two of the most famous groups were the Irgun (otherwise known as the Etzel) and the Stern Gang (otherwise know as Lohamei Herut Israel Lehi) who were once a unified group. The cause of the split occurred during the Second World War, where although the British Army were trying to suppress the Zionist movement in Palestine, at the same time they were also fighting the Nazis. This resulted in the Irgun suspending its attacks against the British Army – some of its members even joined the British Army in its fight against the Nazis. Those who did not support this avenue formed the Stern Gang under the leadership of Avraham Stern. The group,

> which splintered off from the Etzel in June 1940, considered the use of violence and terrorism a crucial component in the evolution of the Jewish nation. Its objective was to enable the Jewish people to liberate themselves from the defeatist disposition that typified Jewish communities in the Diaspora.[22]

Although it was a complicated situation for the Jews who were situated in Mandatory Palestine at the time, Anglo-Jews were not immune to events that took place there, nor to the Zionist cause. Indeed, it is estimated that 3,000 British Jews emigrated to Mandatory Palestine.[23] Since the Jews in Palestine were technically British, questions over whether Jews really could be patriotic to the country in which they lived, or whether their loyalties lay elsewhere, were raised. For those Anglo-Jews who did not support the political Zionist movement, the assumption of the Mandate allowed them to contribute financially to the revival of Palestinian Jewish life, which they foresaw as being under British control.[24]

Thus, by supporting the Mandate, there was a perception that this facilitated a convergence of being a patriot as well as creating a safe haven for persecuted Jews. British policy at the time was to oppose the political Zionist movement, which meant that those Jews who were British citizens and supportive of the Zionist cause found themselves in a dilemma, often being asked to fund Jewish terrorist groups who were involved in an armed resistance against British soldiers. Such events had a direct impact on Anglo-Jews:

> Anti-Jewish feeling in Britain manifested itself in 1947 following the killing of the two sergeants by *Etzel*, (one of whom, Martin, was Jewish). Although

community leaders condemned the 'murderous' act, it did not stop the looting of Jewish shops, property, and the vandalizing of synagogues and graves.[25]

The influential *Jewish Chronicle* is a key indicator of the attitudes and views of the Anglo-Jewish community. Whilst the Jewish underground movement in Mandatory Palestine was labelled as 'terrorists' in the mainstream media, the *Jewish Chronicle* 'accused the British forces in Palestine of a "terrorism of their own" and called Jewish terrorist acts "Jewish Resistance Operations"'.[26] The use of the term 'resistance' was provocative in the aftermath of the Second World War for the wider British public who did not see the attacks against the British in Mandatory Palestine as being justified. At the same time, however, the paper condemned attacks against British soldiers in its editorials and argued 'that the "resistance movement" was "not anti-British" but simply seeking justice for the Jews [… giving …] the appearance of condoning the violence'.[27] Exemplifying the divisions within the Anglo-Jewish community towards the Zionist cause, the ambivalent and confusing approach of the paper led to the eventual dismissal of its editor of ten years, Ivan Greenberg, in July 1946. Under its new editor, John Shaftesley, the *Jewish Chronicle* changed its approach to the situation in Mandatory Palestine completely. This can be seen in the condemnatory response to the King David hotel attack that took place on 22 July 1946, as well as its attitude towards the Jewish terrorist groups operating in Mandatory Palestine.

The next three images demonstrate the impact of the activities of Jewish terrorist groups in Mandatory Palestine in relation to the Zionist cause, but also on the wider Jewish community. Leslie Gilbert Illingworth's uncaptioned cartoon (*Daily Mail*, 23 July 1946) (3.4)[28] comments on the attack carried out by the Irgun on the King David Hotel. The attack killed ninety-one people including Britons, Jews and Arabs.[29] The hotel had been the headquarters of the Mandate administration since the 1930s and therefore it was a significant attack against the British authorities. Image 3.4 illustrates two British soldiers carrying a person on a stretcher covered with a white shroud on which is written 'WORLD SYMPATHY ZIONISM'. Illingworth uses stark symbolism of the 'death' of sympathy towards the Zionist cause due to the attack.

The next image is by David Low, a contemporary of Illingworth. 'What, he's not anti-semitic? We'll soon alter that' (*Evening Standard*, 22 November 1946) (3.5; Figure 7)[30] was in response to a separate spate of violent attacks against the British by Jewish terrorists a few months later.[31] The caption indicates how the attacks were working against the Jewish community – so much so that it seemed to the British public as if the main objective behind the attacks against the British

Figure 7 David Low, 'What, he's not anti-semitic? We'll soon alter that' (*Evening Standard*, 22 November 1946). Courtesy dmg media licensing.

Army was to ensure that Jews were hated by the British. Members of the Anglo-Jewish community were well aware of the potential impact events in Mandatory Palestine could have on them in Britain and the sentiments echoed in images 3.4 and 3.5 were a cause for concern. One of the key reasons behind Greenberg's dismissal from the *Jewish Chronicle* discussed above was that the paper's editorial stance on the attacks carried out by Jewish terrorists was having an adverse impact on the perception of the Anglo-Jewish community by both the government and the wider British public. David Kessler, one of the Directors of the *Jewish Chronicle*, 'feared one false move could trigger an outbreak of anti-Semitism'[32] – vindicating the thoughts expressed in image 3.5.

The defiant Jew

As demonstrated by 3.4 and 3.5, there is a marked difference between the Jews depicted in the cartoons during the years of the Second World War, with the

Jews depicted in the post-war period. Whilst the plight of the Jews under the Nazis was the main focus of the cartoons during the Second World War, the focus shifts away from the persecuted Jew to the persistent Jew, ready to fight for a homeland. David Low's 'Unhappy partners in Palestine' (*Evening Standard*, 7 August 1947) (3.6)[33] encapsulates the difficulty of the situation. The male represents the violent side of the struggle for Israel, whilst the female represents the stateless Jew who has no home to go to. The image shows that, despite the attacks on the British, there was still some sympathy for the Zionist cause amongst Britons. The cartoon (perhaps unintentionally) also captures the sentiment of the Anglo-Jewish community towards the Zionist cause; whilst many Jews in Britain supported the cause, others did not. The establishment of the state of Israel in 1948 did not resolve the divisions within the Jewish community – both internationally and within the Anglo-Jewish community. Interestingly, few Anglo-Jews emigrated to Israel after it was established and questions as to who was a Zionist and who was not were hotly debated.[34]

David Low's 'New Chapter of Tribulation' (*Evening Standard*, 2 January 1948) (3.7)[35] comments on the Zionist movement with less of a focus on the Jewish terrorist movement and more about the Zionist cause in general. The caption seems to be raising the question of how much more suffering the Jewish people need to go through before attaining the goal of having a homeland. The cartoon overtly refers to the Exodus and the crossing of the Red Sea. However, in this instance, the waters do not part and in fact is a 'river of blood' the male and female must wade through. The blood may be that of the Jews who died under Nazi persecution, but also of Palestinian Arabs caught up in the struggle of Mandatory Palestine. Here, Low is warning that bloodshed will be inevitable if any 'Short Cut' is taken in establishing the state of 'Zion' (i.e. Israel). Low uses the Biblical name of 'Zion', emphasizing the ancient ties that the Jewish people have in connection to the land. The image features the male Jew as having thrown off the garb of victimhood and leading the 'long afflicted Jewish people' (as emblazoned on the woman's dress) headstrong into their 'new chapter of tribulation'. The distressed female looks reluctant to walk through the 'river of blood' to 'Zion'.

The image of Jewish defiance is a huge leap from the cartoons looked at below; here the Jewish man is empowered, being neither a victim nor a villain. The cartoon corresponds to the Stern Gang's ideals looked at above of the Jew no longer being a passive victim. In image 3.7, he is taking destiny into his own hands by establishing the State of Israel and refusing to be subjected to persecution. In light of the fact that there was an 'all-out civil war'[36] between the Jews and the Arabs, when the termination of the British Mandate in Palestine was set for 14 May 1948, Low is most probably commenting on the rising tensions that led to this war. This cartoon displays obvious Zionist sympathies, suggesting that the Jews do need a national homeland to finally bring an end to their afflictions. It is possible that Low is trying to communicate to the British public a new, more positive image of 'the Jew' post-Shoah, in order to elicit sympathy for the Zionist cause. At the same time, however, Low is also issuing a warning by asking at what cost this homeland will be established. Four months after the publication of the cartoon, the State of Israel was declared on 14 May.

The Second World War

By the 1930s, most of the Jewish community had moved out of the East End of London as they climbed up the social and economic ladder and the number of Jews coming from Eastern Europe had stopped. This was in part due to rising fears of 'aliens' overwhelming the country. The consequent legislative measures, including the 1920 Aliens Order, were designed to mitigate the numbers:

> The label 'undesirable' immigrants thus extended well beyond the category of former enemy aliens and included east European Jews, also embracing Afro-Caribbeans and Asians who, though often subjects of the British Empire, were debarred from entry by legislative means.[37]

During this time, the British Union of Fascists rose in popularity. Openly sympathetic to Nazi anti-Jewish ideology, Blackshirt members violently clashed with Jews. This led to a dilemma for Anglo-Jewish community leaders when it came to the issue of Jews coming to Britain to escape Nazi persecution; whilst many Anglo-Jews worked to help the refugees settle in Britain, they also feared that their presence would further fuel antisemitic. In many ways, these fears materialized as the Second World War took its toll on the population:

> The hardships of the war years – especially the rationing, the blitz, and the absence of loved ones – created a climate that worked against the moderation of old fears and hatreds [...] Above all, as before the war, the chief complaint was that Jews were not English. They were alien, exclusive, clannish, and unassimilable. Indeed, they themselves were to blame for creating antisemitism by maintaining their distinctiveness and refusing integration into English society.[38]

Despite the rise of domestic antisemitism, the British press seemed to be perceptive enough to correctly conclude that Hitler's ultimate aim was to exterminate the entire German Jewish population, some months before the Nazis had given solid evidence of this.[39] The next two images demonstrate attempts to highlight the suffering of the Jews under the Nazis. 'Lebensraum for the Conquered' (*Evening Standard*, 20 January 1940) (3.8; Figure 8)[40] and 'I've settled the fate of Jews' – 'And of Germans' (*Evening Standard*, 14 December 1942) (3.9)[41] – both by David Low – depict train carriages full of bodies. The bodies in 3.8 lie lifeless in the carriage as well as on the platform, whilst in 3.9 arms and heads stick out of the carriage. There is no escaping the message Low is conveying here: millions of lives are being lost under Hitler's regime.

With two years between their dates of publication, the cartoons refer to different events unfolding in Europe. Image 3.8 was in response to Hitler's plan to transport 3 million Polish Jews to a 'Jewish State' in Lublin, Poland.[42] By this time, Britain had been at war with Germany for just over four months.[43] Despite there not being any official statement on the purpose of the establishment of the 'Jewish State', this idea of Hitler's had been known for quite a while, with 'most sections of the Press [… having …] no illusions about the probable results', such as the *Spectator* calling the plan 'A Stony Road to Extermination'.[44] Low's cartoons echoes the views of the editorial articles of what the outcome would be with such a plan of action being carried through.

Andrew Sharf comments on image 3.8 that '[i]t was not atrocities alone which were being stressed here, but a system – an integral part of Nazi policy'.[45] It was considered of 'prime importance' to 'free space for Baltic Germans'[46] in Poland, explaining the reason behind the mass evacuation of Polish Jews. Emphasizing the de-humanization of the Jews by the Nazis, the image depicts the Jews neatly piled in the cart as well as on the platform. They are bundled with rope around them, suggesting that the bodies are simply goods being transported from one place to another. The plan to transport these Jews to a state of their own seems a welcome idea in light of the Zionist revival at the time. However, the embedded text 'To Living Hell' makes it clear what the fate is of the Jews who are being transported and where they are being transported to. Described as a 'medieval ghetto',[47] the irony of the caption of the cartoon that 'the conquered' are being given a place to live in of their own is not lost.[48]

Image 3.9 depicts Hitler crouching in a bestial manner, with a look of extreme anger and fury as he walks over to a cloaked figure labelled 'Nemesis' who is writing on a piece of paper on which is written, 'The horrors to be repaid'. Presumably, this is Hitler's nemesis, taking account of the terrible deeds he has perpetrated against the Jews who, in this cartoon, are being taken to 'the slaughter house' – in reference to the systematic murder of the Jews as part of

Figure 8 David Low, 'Lebensraum for the Conquered' (*Evening Standard*, 20 January 1940). Courtesy dmg media licensing.

official Nazi policy.⁴⁹ The title suggests that although the Jews are being taken to a horrific end, there will also be justice for those perpetrating such crimes. The cartoon was published three days before the United Nations Declaration on 17th December confirming that the

> ghettoes established by the German invaders are being systematically emptied of all Jews [...]. None of those taken away are ever heard of again. The number of victims of these bloody cruelties is reckoned in many hundreds of thousands of entirely innocent men, women and children.⁵⁰

Low, 'concerned with the ability of Nazi propaganda to pervert the commonly accepted meanings of words into their opposites',⁵¹ has been lauded as an early critic of Nazi Germany, with his cartoons being considered by many to be very influential in the public consciousness. So much so in fact that, immediately following a cartoon commenting on the burning of the Reichstag, 'It worked at the Reichstag – Why not here?' (*Evening Standard*, 18 October 1933) (3.10),⁵² the paper was banned in Germany. In 1937, Hitler's government protested against Low's works to the then Foreign Secretary, Lord Halifax, who later told Low that Hitler would spread his cartoons in front of him weekly.⁵³ Clearly, the Nazis were worried about the influence Low's depictions were having on the British public's perceptions of Hitler. Demonstrating how powerful his cartoons were, Low was also implored by the *Evening Standard*'s editor, Percy Cudlipp, to be cognisant to the fragile political situation in Europe:

> There are people whose tempers are inflamed more by a cartoon than by any letterpress. So will you please, when you are planning your cartoons, bear in mind my [Cudlipp's] anxiety on this score?⁵⁴

What makes Low's cartoons so significant during his time at the paper is the fact that although he worked under the auspices of Lord Beaverbrook (1879–1964), owner of the *Evening Standard* and a renowned advocate for Appeasement, Low was given the freedom to express his own thoughts in his cartoons. Commenting on Lord Beaverbrook in his autobiography, Low relates that Beaverbrook's 'attitude to my personal character of freedom remained impeccable [...] Often he disagreed with me profoundly and did not fail to say so', but on such occasions the cartoon in question 'went into the paper without a word, except after publication'.⁵⁵ During the 1930s, the attention the British press gave to the violence directed against the Jews was more because of its news value.⁵⁶ However, the focus of images 3.8 and 3.9 is a moral one; by emphasizing the Jews' humanity juxtaposed against the bestiality of Hitler, there is no suggestion of the Otherness of the Jew, but a commonality that is shared with the Briton. By breaking down the prejudices against Jews as an Other and stating their destination in both cartoons, Low's cartoons are an attempt to mobilize the public through empathy and a call for the British government to act.

The establishment of Israel

Britain did not recognize Israel following its withdrawal from Mandated Palestine, whilst America did.[57] There were several reasons behind the refusal to recognize Israel, including fears that the newly established Israeli leadership was prone to Communist ideology, the 'insistence that the whole of Israel was "occupied territory" and that Israel's borders remained unsettled'.[58] Britain also wanted to ensure that the Transjordan was recognized by the United States, which included annexation of the West Bank.[59] The images published in the decade following the establishment of Israel present the tumultuous situation. A key event occurred on 7 January 1949 when

> Britain suffered the most humiliating military loss since World War II when an Israeli dilapidated air force shot down five RAF aircraft reconnaissance over the Sinai border sent to ascertain whether the IDF was still on Egyptian territory.[60]

This resulted in two British pilots being killed and another two being taken prisoner by Israel. The fifth pilot managed to escape to Egypt. This 'humiliating' event led to both the press and an increasing number of politicians to be critical of the British Government's policy of the non-recognition of Israel.[61] Eventually, Britain officially recognized Israel on 24 January 1949. Commenting on the establishment of the new state causing aggression in the region, Low's 'And now to snatch the triumph from *HIM*' (*Evening Standard*, 4 February 1949) (3.11)[62] takes pride in Israel's victory that despite all odds, it emerged triumphant. At the same time, however, Low also acknowledges the cost of this victory; a note at the foot of the flag pole bearing the Israeli flag reads 'WITH ALL ITS ATTENDANT INJUSTICES'. In the corner, the 'UN' is personified as a woman (as in all Low cartoons), with a set of scales in her hands – a reference to justice. She looks on at 'BRUTE FORCE' who, notably, is personified as a man with a rifle in one hand and half dressed, with no military uniform. It conveys the idea of the common man fighting the battle without any sophisticated and expensive military equipment.

In a way, this was true – during the war in May 1948, 'the Arabs initially exhibited an overwhelming superiority in aircraft and heavy weaponry'.[63] Interestingly, in the Low cartoons examined in this chapter, the female is always shown as the restrained character vis-à-vis the male who is more violent and headstrong. Low's imagery contrasts to the Jew who was often seen as the feminized male in other images, such as image 3.2. This was connected to the widespread belief that the act of circumcision was the cause of this occurrence. Moreover, he was seen as representing disease such as syphilis which was connected to the idea that it was brought about by hysteria:

> If the idea of the hysteric is tied to the idea of the feminization of the healthy, Aryan male or his 'Jewification' […] then the representation of the disease must be in terms of models of illness which are convertible into the images of the feminized male.[64]

Image 3.11 epitomizes the reversal of the effete Jew; telegraphing the emergence of an image of Jews that is not simply defiant but now has the upper hand. Whilst the Jew in the previous images were engaged in acts of resistance, here the Jew is victorious: he holds a rifle instead of a pistol, he is muscular rather than of average build, and he leans against the Israeli flag flying above him at full mast. In many ways, the man's lack of clothing is a metaphor of the transition taking place from plain clothed terrorist to uniformed soldier. On the other hand, the image seems to cast the UN in an unfavourable light – indeed Low was often critical of the UN in his cartoons.[65]

The caption suggests that the UN does not share the same enthusiasm for the newly empowered Jew (as embodied by the man); her pensive face indicating, however, that she has not yet decided how she will achieve her goal. The image indicates the UN's lukewarm reception to this transformation. It also showcases a desire to prevent it from happening any further by bringing back the persecuted Jew who is the complete antithesis to the male depicted in the image. The UN had brokered armistice agreements, with the first one being signed twenty days after the cartoon's publication, between Egypt and Israel on 24 February 1949. The cartoon is hopeful of the potential for peace in the region following the end of the first Arab-Israeli war in 1948.

The Arab-Israeli wars

Published a few weeks later, Low's 'There, yesterday, were we' (*Evening Standard*, 23 March 1949) (3.12)[66] takes a more critical look at the nascent state and the impact it had on the Palestinian people. During 'the period between April and

June 1948, the military campaign of the Zionists created the flight of 200,000–300,000 Palestinian Arabs'.[67] Following the departure of the British from Mandatory Palestine and the declaration of the State of Israel in May 1948, the first Arab-Israeli war began. Arab states including Egypt, Syria and Jordan invaded, resulting in another 300,000 Palestinian Arabs fleeing the region:

> There was resentment that so soon after the Holocaust another attempt was being made to decimate the Jews. All this accentuated the desire to maximize the exodus which had commenced before the establishment of the state and to reduce the Arab population of Israel to a politically and militarily impotent minimum.[68]

Image 3.12 comments on the lasting impacts the war had on the region. Both Moshe Sharett (the then Israeli foreign minister) and David Ben-Gurion (the then Israeli prime minister) are labelled as 'ISRAELI GOVT', looking on at the Palestinians behind them. It is possible that 3.12 is intentionally reminiscent of Low's 'Verdict' (*Evening Standard*, 1 October 1946) (3.13),[69] which comments on the verdict of the Nuremberg trials in 1946. 'Verdict' depicts emaciated men, women and children looming hauntingly in front of the witness box where Alfred Rosenberg and Hermann Goering amongst other high-ranking Nazi officials sit with their heads hanging in shame (except for Goering who shook his head or laughed throughout the trial).

Image 3.12 places Sharett and Ben-Gurion in almost the same position as the Nazi officials – as politicians whose actions have real consequences for ordinary, innocent civilians – and is perhaps a warning to the two men not to allow such suffering to be repeated. Instead, the image calls for empathy from the Israeli government in order to deal with the displaced Palestinians and the need to act. The caption, along with the document in Sharett's hands with the words 'Generous compensation for Arab refugees from Palestine????', explicitly links the Jewish suffering of the Shoah to that of the Palestinian refugees. Whilst many Jews and indeed Low were supporters of Israel, at the same time they were critical of many of its actions – such as that of the treatment of Palestinians, as shown here. Thus, the image shows the diversity of opinion on this issue, rather than perpetuate the myth held by many antisemites that Jews tacitly support Israel whatever its actions.

Although Israel had its part to play in the situation, 3.12 ignores the role of Arab, American and British leaders in the way they handled the Palestinian refugee problem. With specific regard to Britain, there was a reluctance to get involved in the issue because, as looked at above, Britain's time spent in

Mandatory Palestine had cost many British lives. At the same time, however, Britain had vested interests in the area due to its involvement in the creation of the Greater Transjordan[70] and, as Ilan Pappé states, the Foreign Office 'even admitted British responsibility for the creation of the problem'.[71] Despite the fact that the Palestinian refugee problem was not being tackled convincingly by all sides involved,[72] I argue that 'there, yesterday, were we' marks a departure from the cartoons examined above.

This is because the focus of 3.12 is the modern version of the fictive Jew: a composite character who represents both the Jewish nation *as well as* the Jewish religion. At the same, today's fictive Jew also has to pay regard to his home country and therefore also represents the Anglo-Jew. By referring to the experiences of the Shoah, the cartoon demonstrates that by virtue of their experiences of persecution, today's fictive Jew should maintain a higher moral standard than that of any other religion or political state actor. Notably, what differentiates the depiction of the Jew today to the one of the past is that whilst the former is either always a member of the Israeli Defence Forces (IDF) or a politician, the latter was unidentifiable. This demonstrates how the Jewish community started to be increasingly seen through the prism of Israel and how events of conflict and war have inevitably impacted the evolution of the fictive Jew.

Following the Suez Crisis from 26 July to 7 November 1956, Israel had managed to capture large parts of Egypt, including the Sinai and Gaza (which was then under Egyptian control and later returned to Egypt under pressure from America). David Low's 'Repairs at Mount Sinai' (*Manchester Guardian*, 16 November 1956) (3.14)[73] depicts the then Egyptian President Abdel Nasser righteously looking on as politicians, including the then British Prime Minister, Anthony Eden, and a man (whose face is obscured) labelled 'USA', attempt to fix the 'U.N. Tablet of the Law'. The image marks the beginning of the use of overtly religious iconography in relation to political incidents involving Israel. Commenting on the ill-judged British- and French-backed Israeli invasion of Egypt, the Biblical reference is impossible to miss, indicating that by virtue of its religious significance, Israel and the other involved parties have failed a higher moral standard expected of them. Ben-Gurion is easily identifiable, thus showing how the non-specific Jew has now been replaced with the name-specific Jew. The familiar UN female looks on in shock at the broken tablet with a vial of ink in her hands, suggesting that it was broken by others (unlike Moses who breaks the first Tablets of Stone in Exodus 32.19 in anger). Low is critical of her apparent incompetence at handling the political situation.

What is most interesting about the Suez Crisis is how it impacted British politics. Whilst the Conservative Government supported Israel during the Suez Crisis, the opposition Labour Party supported Egypt. This seemed to put the seventeen Jewish Labour MPs in a difficult position – so much so that they did not vote in the 30 October parliamentary debate on Suez.[74] Many Anglo-Jews were discontent with this course of (non-)action. Demonstrating the difficulty of the situation in which the Anglo-Jewish community and Jewish MPs found themselves in, Natan Aridan describes this event as 'a watershed in British politics'.[75] The Suez Crisis raised questions of where loyalties lay for the Jewish MPs – both from within parliament and from the Anglo-Jewish community. Aridan argues that the saving grace for the Anglo-Jewish community during this fragile and tense time was 'its tolerance for free discussion and self-confidence'.[76] I now go on to look at cartoons relating to Israel and the Arab world and the impact this has had on perceptions of the Jewish community.

Israel 1967 onwards

The Six Day War (otherwise known as the third Arab-Israeli war) started on 5 June and ended on 10 June 1967. Importantly, the war became 'central to what it meant to be a Jew in Britain'.[77] This was due to the war engendering a strong feeling of solidarity with Israel, evoking memories of the Shoah and another attempt to eradicate Jews. In addition to this, '[f]or those Jews who "felt" Jewish but lacked religious belief, identification with and support for Israel provided a means of and rationale for being Jewish'.[78] Thus, Zionism had become a key component of Jewish identity amongst the Anglo-Jewish community. Published a few days before the onset of the war, JAK's 'So, who's minding the shop?' (*Evening Standard*, 31 May 1967) (3.15)[79] comments on Israel's preparations for a military attack from its surrounding Arab neighbours.

The image of a truckload of soldiers is in stark contrast to the cartoons looked at previously; uniformed and polished, the stateless Jew involved in terrorist activities has been transformed into the militaristic Israeli, as evidenced by the flag. Furthermore, there are both men *and* women in uniform, showcasing a national unity against the enemy threat. The truck reads 'COHEN'S KOSHER BUTCHER Tel Aviv 5710' (which incidentally is incorrect – the Jewish year was 5727 showing that JAK did not even check the date). The cartoon's use of the words 'kosher' and 'Cohen', as well using the Jewish calendar to date the event, clearly link the Jewish religion with the military action taking place. With such overt religious language, JAK seems to be suggesting that the Jewish people in Israel are using religion for, what he considers, illegitimate military actions.

Moreover, the depiction of the Israelis mounted on a butcher's truck conjures up the horrific image that they are on their way to slaughter people as if they were animals, reminiscent of the idea of the bloodthirsty Jew who desires non-Jewish blood. The cartoon indicates that the muscular Jew as visualized by Low in image 3.11 has indeed become the brute that was so feared in the image. The caption, 'So, who's minding the shop?', also reinforces the idea that it is not just a few Israelis/Jews that are out to war but the entire population of Israel. Thus, the cartoon vilifies the entire country, as well as Jews in general, for 'abusing' their religion to justify their actions.

The next cartoon, also by JAK, 'You were in Beirut, and you couldn't find the time to send a card to your mother?' (3.16),[80] was published in response to the Israeli raid in Beirut that occurred the day before. The raid involved the assassination of three Palestinian leaders – Kamal Nasser, Yusif Najar and Kamal Edwan. It was widely considered to be in retaliation against those whom Israel believed were responsible for the killings of eleven Israeli athletes at the Olympic Games in Munich in 1972. Here, the parents of the soldier symbolize Israel, suggesting indifference at the loss of life; this is indicated by the absurd question posed by the mother to her bedraggled son, as well as the father, with both feet up, reading the 'Jerusalem Post' (demonstrating an awareness of current affairs and the events that took place in Lebanon).

The scene depicts the parents carrying on with life as normal, with the mother carrying food to the table on which is a box of 'Matzos'. This serves as a crucial visual indicator of both the family's nationality and religion – suggesting a link with their identity to their apathy. Here, JAK is criticizing the IDF for carrying out an attack in which four of their soldiers had been injured,[81] raising the question: at what price was revenge served? Much like the UN in 3.11, both 3.15 and 3.16 are indicative of a certain discomfort with the way Israel, as a nation-state with its own army, has become a military power.

Peace makers and peace breakers

The Oslo Peace Accords in 1993 was a major event in Israeli-Arab relations which saw Yasser Arafat of the Palestine Liberation Organisation (PLO) renounce terrorism and recognize Israel's right to exist. In return, Yitzhak Rabin (the then

Israeli prime minister) recognized the PLO as representatives of the Palestinian people. As Avi Shlaim asserts:

> The historic reconciliation was based on a historic compromise: acceptance of the principle of the partition of Palestine. At the same time, both sides accepted the principle of territorial compromise as the basis for the settlement of their long and bitter conflict, as the basis for peaceful coexistence between themselves.[82]

Nicholas Garland's uncaptioned cartoon (*Daily Telegraph*, 10 September 1993) (3.17)[83] illustrates the huge step it took for Rabin and Arafat to go ahead with the Oslo Accords. Published a few days earlier, Garland's 'David and Goliath' (*Daily Telegraph*, 2 September 1993) (3.18)[84] depicts Israel as David (signified by the Star of David on his clothes) and the Arab world as Goliath. Both 3.17 and 3.18 are prescient of the handshake that took place on the White House lawn between Arafat and Rabin on 13 September 1993. Rather than Goliath being killed by David as in 1 Samuel 17.49, Garland re-imagines the Biblical story in 3.18 and has the two of them with their hands outstretched towards each other. It could be interpreted that David (Israel), by choosing to make peace with Goliath (the Arab world), has achieved the moral high ground. The reference to the Biblical story serves to emphasize the historic nature of the agreement between the two parties and a hope that real peace will ensue as a result. In contrast, 3.17 uses humour to highlight how the many years of conflict between Palestinians and Israelis has now been so quickly put aside with a simple shake of the hands.

However, Rabin was assassinated two years later on 4 November 1995. In the general election following Rabin's death on 29 May 1996, Benjamin Netanyahu was elected as prime minister. This was partly due to the Israeli public's belief that the 'Oslo process had brought neither peace nor security. The peace process [...] needed to be slowed down, but not extinguished'.[85] The mood in Israel had changed since the signing of the Oslo Accords only two years earlier. Thus, whilst Netanyahu's predecessor, Yitzhak Rabin, was seen as a peacemaker thanks largely due to the signing of the Oslo Peace Accords in 1993, Netanyahu is seen as a peace breaker. Under Netanyahu's leadership, relations with the Palestinians and the rest of the Arab world deteriorated. A key example was a controversial tunnel road constructed near the Temple Mount which was the cause of violent clashes between Israelis and Arabs. There was a perception that Netanyahu 'who directly authorised [the tunnel's] completion, [wanted] to wreck the peace process'.[86]

Steve Bell's '0831-27-9-96_PEACEPROCESSOR' (*Guardian*, 27 September 1996) (3.19)[87] illustrates this perception showing a dove with an olive branch in its beak about to be pureed in 'NETANYAHU'S PATENT PEACE PROCESSOR'. The blade of the machine is in the shape of the Star of David, symbolizing Israel. Published on the same day, Peter Brookes' 'They shall beat their swords into ploughshares ... (Isaiah Ch. 2, v.4)' (*The Times*, 27 September 1996) (3.20)[88] also comments on the worsening situation in Israel. The context of the verse, which is not quoted but appears implied, speaks about God who 'will judge between the nations and will settle disputes for many peoples'.[89] Instead of following the quoted scripture, Netanyahu turns a ploughshare into a sword. Furthermore, by depicting Netanyahu in a kippah (where in reality he does not usually wear one since he considers himself a secular Jew[90]) and an apron with a star of David alongside the Biblical text, Brookes emphasizes Netanyahu's Jewishness.

At face value, image 3.20 reads as a critical comment on the Jewish religion. However, the cartoon criticizes Netanyahu's (mis)understanding of the religion, suggesting that he is intentionally going contrary to the text by choosing to cause discord and strife. The cartoon demonstrates how Netanyahu is quite literally using religion as a tool for his own gains. The blame for the deteriorating situation in Israel is placed squarely on Netanyahu in 3.19 and 3.20. Whilst the images of Rabin are cautiously hopeful, they stand in direct contrast to the portrayal of Netanyahu. Garland's re-imagining of David and Goliath in 3.18 is a positive outcome, where Israel is cast as a Biblical prophet and not as a politician. On the other hand, Brookes in 3.20 re-imagines the Biblical text with a negative outcome precisely because it is Netanyahu that is the main protagonist.

Another prominent Israeli politician who was seen as undermining the peace process was Ariel Sharon, prime minister from 7 March 2001 to 16 April 2006. In a 2019 article, Brown commented on the issue of fellow cartoonist Michael de Adder's contract being cancelled with a publishing company, allegedly for causing offence to Donald Trump. In the article, Brown states that a cartoonist's job is to cause the reader to think more deeply on the issue – including making them feel uncomfortable if necessary. He goes onto comment on the controversies that he has endured,

> The people who complain about my cartoons almost invariably hold a contrary perspective, but what they choose to criticise is the manner in which I make my point. The cartoons, they say, are vile, obscene, grossly offensive – all cries to suggest they have infringed some law of common decency, and all really designed to close down debate.[91]

Brown's point shows how the normative is constructed and that when this is perceived to be transgressed, it inspires debate around cartoons and the issue of free speech. Brown's use of words shows how the discussion incites strong emotions for both the reader and the cartoonist.

It is very likely that when writing this, Brown had in mind his uncaptioned image (*Independent*, 27 January 2003) (3.21),[92] which depicts Sharon about to eat a baby after the likeness of Francisco de Goya's *Saturn Devouring His Son*. The cartoon was published in response to the 'deepest Israeli army incursion into Gaza since the [second] intifada began' in 2000, which Sharon was accused of using as a ploy, days before the general election to gain votes.[93] The cartoon caused much controversy, accused of being 'anti-Semitic, in a fantastically irresponsible way, at a particularly volatile time'[94] because of the way it placed Sharon in rubble, in Gaza, whilst eating the body of a child. Many held the opinion that, in light of where Sharon was placed in the cartoon, he was devouring a Palestinian child.

One of the fundamental aspects of mediaeval Christian antisemitism was rooted in the idea of the Jew as the Christ killer – a charge that every Jew was responsible for – both past and present. Consequently, the deicide charge led to the blood libel in which Jews were accused of killing Christian children at Passover to use their blood to bake matzah bread. Britain shares a long history with the accusation; the first recorded case of its kind in Europe was in 1144 involving William of Norwich, where Jews were accused of the ritual murder of the young boy.[95] Since then, there have been many recorded incidents of the blood libel around the world throughout history.[96] Both Sharon and the Embassy of Israel submitted a complaint to the Press Complaints Commission (PCC) in relation to the cartoon, arguing that it was 'prejudicial'[97] because of its allusions to the blood libel.

The editor of the *Independent* argued that the lack of any Jewish or Israeli symbols meant that the cartoon was not antisemitic, and neither was there a reference to the blood libel in the cartoon, since the baby that was being eaten was representative of the Israeli electorate. In his defence, Brown argued that the Goya painting had been used before to criticize other politicians for policies that seemed to go against their electorate. Thus, the ground on which the complaint was rejected was that Brown's cartoon was criticizing a political figure and therefore, the cartoon was not anti-Semitic, but anti-Sharon.

Similarly, Gerald Scarfe's 'Will cementing the peace continue?' (*Sunday Times*, 27 January 2013) (3.22) caused controversy both for being published on Holocaust Memorial Day and for its overtones of antisemitism. Scarfe (1936–) was first published in 1957 in the *Daily Sketch* and soon appeared in other publications including *Punch* and the *Evening Standard*. In 1961, Scarfe first appeared in *Private Eye*, and from 1967, Scarfe started his fifty-year relationship with the *Sunday Times*.[98] Depicting Netanyahu using blood as cement for a wall, Scarfe's image was accused of evoking the blood libel. At first, the newspaper rejected allegations that the cartoon was antisemitic as it was 'aimed squarely at Mr Netanyahu and his policies, not at Israel, let alone at Jewish people'.[99] Many commentators also pointed out that Scarfe regularly uses blood as a visual tool to criticize politicians.[100] However, the paper and the proprietor (Rupert Murdoch) subsequently tweeted an apology for the 'grotesque, offensive cartoon'.[101]

The parallels between 3.21 and 3.22 are difficult to ignore: both cartoons were accused of evoking the blood libel, and both publications argued that the cartoon criticized the politician and not the Jewish community. In response to 3.22 and referencing 3.21, Mark Gardner of the Community Security Trust (a British charity protecting Jews from antisemitism) wrote:

> It is a harsh fact that blood has long played a profoundly disturbing part in the history of antisemitism, and this has obvious consequences for Jews and antisemites today. The actual intentions of Gerald Scarfe and the *Sunday Times* count for very little within this broader context of history, and its contemporary emotional and racist impacts.[102]

Another cartoon which sparked widespread criticism for being antisemitic was Steve Bell's '421-161112_VOTELIKUD' (*Guardian*, 16 November 2012) (3.23).[103] The cartoon depicts Netanyahu as a puppet master, with miniature puppets of Tony Blair (in his capacity as Middle East envoy) and William Hague (the then British foreign secretary). The image, it was argued, echoed stereotypes of Jews controlling international political powers behind the scenes. Furthermore, in the background, several Israeli flags in the shape of missiles loom behind Netanyahu, a few of which have already been launched, trailing plumes of smoke. Bell refuted the antisemitic allegations, arguing that the cartoon was a comment on Netanyahu and the 'cynical manipulation of a situation by a specific politician'.[104] In this context, it was not just the evocative imagery, but the use of the symbols that caused widespread concern that Bell was explicitly linking the Jewish religion to the idea of a global conspiracy.

Joel Kotek argues that the allegation of 3.21 referring to the blood libel was valid because, regardless of whether or not the child's body in the cartoon is Palestinian or Israeli, it still connects 'the Jew' to infanticide. Rather than accusing Brown of being an antisemite, however, the issue is that the cartoon 'carries an antisemitic charge'.[105] Therefore, although Brown did not intend to convey any antisemitic messages, it is very hard to ignore how his image can be linked to the blood libel. I would also argue that the same applies to Scarfe and

Bell who are both known for their scathing visual attacks on politicians around the world.

In his analysis of the controversy sparked by the Danish cartoons of the Prophet Muhammed, Weaver uses the concept of 'liquid racism' where 'cultural signs can contain the ability to produce simultaneous and ambiguous racist and non-racist readings', in which 'older racisms' are combined with issues that may not be racist.[106] Therefore, regardless of whether Brown, Scarfe or Bell intended to make a political point, rather than directing criticism towards Jews in any way, it can be argued that by employing imagery in such a manner as to evoke 'older racisms' – such as the blood libel and the idea of a Jewish world conspiracy – this opened the cartoons up to the charge of antisemitism. Given the long-standing history of antisemitism within British cartoons – such as that of Tenniel's and Swain's examined above – Brown, Scarfe and Bell should have been cognisant as artists of the possible implications their images might have.

Gender

Of the twenty-two cartoons examined in this chapter,[107] ten (45 per cent) are men-only and twelve (55 per cent) are women-mixed – eight (36 per cent) of which feature Jewish women. There were no women-only cartoons or where the gender was none/not clear. I find that whilst the Jew was feminized – such as Disraeli in 3.2 – the advent of the Second World War marked a shift in the way the Jew was portrayed. For example, 3.6 and 3.7 depict the Jewish man and the Jewish woman as contrasting characters. In both images, the woman displays restraint, whilst the man is headstrong and, in 3.6, is shown to be dangerous as he wields a gun. Low's choice to portray the UN as a woman in 3.11 and 3.14 perhaps mirrors the Jewish woman in 3.6 and 3.7 to convey the idea that women are more level-headed than their male counterparts.

Similar to the Irish case study, the majority of the cartoons depict men, such as in 3.16–3.18, in which it is the Jewish male that plays an active role in the Arab-Israeli conflict (except 3.15 which includes the depiction of a female IDF soldier). This may partly be due to the fact that with the exception of Golda Meir, all the prime ministers of Israel have been male. However, it is also because of the changing perception of Jews being conflated with Israel and the idea of Israel as an aggressive nation state. This then feeds into the idea of the macho Jew – be he a politician or a member of the IDF – who by virtue of his gender is prone to such aggression.

Conclusion: Who is the fictive Jew?

My examination of the portrayal of Jews over the centuries charts how cartoonists from different periods in history chose to focus on specific characteristics of Jews. For example, the overt antisemitic message of the image of Isaac of Norwich (3.1) reflects how openly prejudiced English society was towards Jews at the time. The image employs caricature as a tool to make a serious point for its readers, whilst Tenniel (in Images 3.2 and 3.3) uses caricature as a way of making malignant comments regarding Jews under the guise of benign humour. In the past, the fictive Jew was a moneylender or a politician, and his wealth and success were attributed to his Jewishness. Different visual tropes were used to indicate this, such as the ostentatious clothing of Disraeli in 3.2 and the use of the Semitic nose in 3.3. The shift in emphasis of the Jew becoming an Other to an Us by Low was, in part, a conscious reaction against the Othering of Jews by the Nazis. This led to an absence of the fictive Jew in cartoons during this period, allowing the Briton to identify the Jew as an Us, such as in 3.9.

Moreover, the fictive Jew is still absent during the struggle for the establishment of Israel, in which he is typified as the ordinary man in everyday clothing simply armed with a revolver in his hands, such as in 3.6. However, with the establishment of Israel, a conflation occurs where Israel has become the fictive Jew. Thus, 3.11 demonstrates a discomfort at how the world was forced to change its perception of the fictive Jew. Israel as a military power meant that no longer was it possible to emasculate the fictive Jew. Instead, he was armed and dangerous. Images 3.2 and 3.11 demonstrate how the fictive Jew is always depicted and perceived as the epitome of the nemesis in question so as to indict him. He is either the effeminate male – his masculinity never reaching full potential; or as the establishment of Israel has facilitated – he is the aggressive male who cannot and will not make peace – both of which are attributed to the fictive Jew's intrinsic devious nature by virtue of his Jewishness. This shows how cartoons are instrumental in cementing old stereotypes in new ways.

Interestingly, whilst an apology was given for image 3.22 in the *Sunday Times* (a centre-right broadsheet newspaper), neither the *Independent* nor the *Guardian* (both of which are more to the left) accepted that 3.21 and 3.23, respectively, were offensive. This seems to reflect a more critical stance towards Israel from those towards the left and a resistance to the idea that such criticism may at times be offensive. The debates surrounding images 3.21–3.23 highlight the change in tone in cartoons relating to Israel in the mainstream British press. This showcases the strength of opinion the cartoonists have in relation to the instability in the Middle East and how they see Sharon and Netanyahu as instrumental in exacerbating the situation in their capacity as politicians.

At the same time, the cartoons exemplify the situation of the fictive Jew today – frequently characterized through the prism of Israel, where prominent politicians or the actions of the state are taken to reflect those of the wider Jewish community. The conflation of the fictive Jew with Israel has meant that wherever the fictive Jew may be in the world and whatever his personal beliefs are, he is connected to and represents Israel, disregarding the diversity of opinion that exists. In this way, the cartoons examined above are more indicative of how the cartoonists themselves see Jews – rather than how Jews see themselves. This is demonstrated through employing symbols and indicators such as the matzos on the table in 3.16 or the use of Biblical imagery or quotations such as in images 3.18 and 3.20, as a means by which to connect Israel's actions to the Jewish religion. In this way, the reader sees how liquid racism comes into play; whilst images 3.21–3.23 were criticizing Netanyahu and Sharon in their capacity as politicians, the fact that the cartoons evoked age-old stereotypes (even if unintended) of the fictive Jew led many to read the cartoons as if they were criticizing Netanyahu and Sharon *as Jews*.

3

Turbans, terrorism and transport: Sikhs in political cartoons

Introduction

This chapter looks at the portrayal in political cartoons of the Sikh community in post-war Britain as a lens through which to examine changing attitudes towards religious diversity. I look at how Anglo-Saxon Britons reacted to the growing immigrant population and calls for more rights from the Sikh community from the 1960s to the 1980s, in which the depiction of the turban in cartoons is used as a recurring trope to highlight the Otherness of the Sikh community in Britain. Due to the history of the Sikh community with the British Armed Forces in colonial India, the turban was already freighted with significance for many Britons, making it a crucial symbolic register for changing conceptions of national loyalty.

These have been tested as the Anglo-Sikh community has become more established and called for greater rights. I find that the cartoons ignore this history which was a key theme in Sikh arguments for their status as loyal Britons. I argue that there is an evolution in the way they present Sikhs in relation to the wider British public, depicting the turban as a barrier to integration, a symbol of cultural and political subversion, and finally, as a tool to convey power in post-colonial India. I also look at how the iconography of the turban is used in a wider context of immigration and integration in British society as a tool to convey an Otherness which is not strictly confined to Sikhs, but to 'the immigrant' in general.

After partition between India and Pakistan in 1947, many Sikh men migrated to Britain, with the primary aim of seeking employment in order to save up income and return to India in a better financial position.[1] Most were single males who found that they had to forgo the traditional turban and beard in order to secure employment. For many, to cut their hair and beards was an agonizing decision, since both hair and the turban are connected to ideas of masculinity and strength. However, many Sikh men chose to shave their hair and abandon the turban rather than face the prospect of being unemployed and unable financially to support themselves and their families in India.[2] There was already a strong Sikh community in Britain before the publications of the cartoons looked at below. However, as the Sikh community grew in size from the 1960s onwards, their perceptions of home and identity changed. With an increased sense of permanency, many reclaimed the beard and turban, leading to a series of struggles for Sikh transport workers in London and other English cities to be able to wear the turban to work.

The significance of the turban in Sikhism and under empire rule

The establishment of the Khalsa by the final living Guru, Guru Gobind Singh, at the end of the seventeenth century, summoned Sikhs to join the order through taking *amrit* – sweetened water stirred with a double-edged sword. One of the requirements of Sikhs on joining the Khalsa is to promise to observe five things, commonly known as the 'Five Ks'. The Five Ks include unshorn hair *(kesh)*, a wooden comb *(kangha)*, a sword *(kirpan)*, a steel bangle *(kara)* and undergarments *(kachha)*. It is a personal choice whether a Sikh wishes to join the Khalsa and those that do not may still observe any or all of the Five Ks; often, unshorn hair and wearing the bangle are observed.

Though it is not a religious requirement, the wearing of the turban has gained a prominent position (especially for males), deriving from the observance of unshorn hair, because it manages to cover the hair in a tidy fashion. The turban also acts as a way to distinguish Sikhism from Hinduism, avoiding syncretism.[3] It is important to appreciate the significance of the turban for Sikhs in order to understand why the community sought to fight for the right to wear it to work or on motorcycles, the source of two crucial disputes for the Anglo-Sikh community. As W. H. McLeod states:

> For the orthodox male the turban is compulsory, and for another to try to remove it forcibly is treated as an insult. An assailant should be careful not to lay deliberate hands on either the uncut hair of a Sikh or his turban. Sikhs can act very directly when their own honour or the honour of the turban is impugned.[4]

Therefore, the turban and uncut hair are closely protected because they are deemed essential to male Sikh identity. As we shall see below, the debate on whether the turban is a religious requirement, or a custom, formed part of the discussions in the struggle to be able to wear it without being subject to discrimination. Such discussions were often informed by the history of the Sikh contribution to the British Armed Forces under imperial India. An important point to bear in mind is how colonialism has also played a role in informing Sikh identity, where Sikh soldiers had to observe the Five Ks if they were to serve in the Indian Army, under British rule.[5] As Jasbir K. Puar states:

> British colonial incorporation of turbaned Sikhs (a masculinity narrated against an effeminate Hindu masculinity) into military units, made possible through the oscillation of the turban as 'a mark of discipline and obedience' and also as a trace of savagery and wildness, double significations delicately bound up in each other. British colonialism is therefore complicit with the fusing of the turban in the late nineteenth century with an emergent Sikh identity [...].[6]

Thus, the turban was used as one of *the* defining markers of Sikh manhood under British colonial rule in India, which was then used as an object of contrast to Hindu manhood. Moreover, it is interesting that often the turban is considered more than just attire; perhaps because it is so bound up in ideas of masculinity the turban can be read as a 'phallic extension'.[7] 'As a result, the act of taking the turban off forcibly or under coercion seems to suggest that it may be considered tantamount to castration.

Turbans and masculinity

It is worth noting at the outset that the cartoons commenting on the Sikh community only depict Sikh males – with just one exception. Part of the reason for this is the fact that the cartoons depict specific individuals who campaigned for greater rights to wear the turban. Furthermore, although Sikh women may (and do) wear the turban, it is not as common a practice as it is for male Sikhs. A practising female Sikh may keep her hair untrimmed but the image of an Indian woman with long, black hair is commonly associated with the general female Indian population, rather than being specific to the Sikh female community. It is easier to depict a male Sikh but the consequences of this (unintended or not) present Sikhism as a macho religion, allowing the religion to be associated with ideas of aggression and violence. This is similar to the way the Irish, Jewish and Muslim male are depicted, in which certain characteristics are gendered and associated primarily with men.

The depiction of male Sikhs in such a way is problematic because it seems to imply the existence of the archetypal Sikh man who is bearded and turbaned, ignoring the diverse understandings of what it means to be a male Sikh. As Santokh Singh Gill states, 'the turbaned Sikh male could be seen to represent a form of Othered masculinity, which is regarded as traditionalist, patriarchal and backwards'.[8] The dominance of men with beards and turbans in the cartoons conveys an implicit message that to be Sikh means to be one that observes *kesh*, ignoring the many different ways one may choose to express one's Sikh identity without having to wear the turban or beard. Furthermore, even if they do not observe all of the Five Ks, it is more common for Sikhs to wear the *kara*.[9] In none of the cartoons do any of the Sikhs depicted feature wearing the *kara* nor any of the other Five Ks.

The lack of female Sikhs in all but one of the cartoons examined below lends credence to Gill's opinion in which Sikh men are made into an Other in two respects: their masculinity and their faith. By combining the two it suggests an Otherness that is impossible to overcome with the implication that Sikh men are (more of) a threat than Sikh women. Conducting interviews with young British Sikh men, Gill found that the turbaned Sikh was always male:

> Discussion around the authentic Sikh identity revolves around men and appropriate/respectable masculine behaviours. The hegemony that Khalsa masculinities hold is then not easily transferable to women's bodies or femininities.[10]

Therefore, there is also a very masculine view of what it means to be Sikh that dominates discourses both within and without the British Sikh community. This is further showcased by the fact that only one of the cartoons examined below features a Sikh woman (4.8). Of the nineteen cartoons examined in this chapter, nine (47 percent) are men-only.[11] There were no cartoons which were women-only or where the gender was none/not clear. Taking the gender imbalance into consideration, I contend that the cartoons considered here are intended to reflect the wider Sikh community – regardless of gender, class or age – by virtue of the attitudes conveyed that display ignorance of the Sikh community and its diversity.

First turban campaign

Unavoidably, those who do choose to wear the turban are visible, drawing attention to a part of their identity where the turban has become inextricably linked to the Sikh faith. The issue of the beard and turban for Sikh transport employees first came to national attention in 1959, when a Sikh bus conductor, Mr G. S. S. Sagar, was not allowed to work wearing the turban by Manchester City Council because it 'did not conform to existing conditions of service'.[12] It was only when Sant Fateh Singh, a Sikh spiritual and political leader, visited Britain in 1966 that this particular case was resolved. He appealed for the ban on beards and turbans to be lifted:

> He reminded British politicians of the services that Sikhs had rendered to the British in India and abroad: 83,000 Sikhs 'in beards and turbans' had died for Britain in the Second World War. More pertinently, he argued that if Sikhs in beards and turbans could operate a tank they could certainly drive a bus or ring a bell without endangering the safety of passengers or causing an offence.[13]

Singh's efforts resulted in the Manchester Transport Committee allowing Sikhs to wear the turban at work so long as it matched the colour of the uniform. However, the issue had not been resolved nationally, and the following year a similar case appeared in Wolverhampton. The incident saw Tarsem Singh Sandhu being suspended after refusing to remove the beard and turban while performing his role as a bus conductor. By 1969, the case was followed both nationally and internationally, with Sikhs marching to the British Embassy in New Delhi on 6 April to protest against the council's decision. Eventually, the government intervened and persuaded the local council to lift the ban on 9 April 1969. Sandhu's case has been described as 'more acrimonious and caused more widespread soul-searching among Sikhs in general than the episode in Manchester'.[14] This is because though many Sikhs supported Sandhu's cause, they had become accustomed to cutting their hair and beards, with only a small minority of Sikh men observing *kesh* and wearing the turban.[15]

Much like the Irishmen who look on menacingly at the Indian men as they walk by in image 2.39, the cases of the transport employees demonstrate how a segment of the wider British public were resistant to the changing definition of what it meant to be British: no longer did Britons necessarily fit the model of Caucasians with a shared Christian faith and cultural traditions. Instead, there was a strong Sikh community who wanted to be visible and were proud of their distinctive Sikh heritage. Whilst there was resistance to accepting the Sikh community as part of British society, the obverse was occurring within the Sikh community: many were proud to be working and living in Britain and saw no conflict between their faith and the country in which they lived.[16]

Changing demographics and legislation

Owing to its large South Asian population, Southall in West London is often referred to as 'Little India'. Southall received immigrants from diverse backgrounds including many Sikh men from the Punjab from 1948 onwards who found work at Woolf's Rubber Company.[17] Heathrow Airport and the surrounding areas of Southall were also areas where immigrants found employment.[18] As Brian Keith Axel states, with 'the movement of "Asian" men from Punjab to Southall came the transformation of those men from "immigrant" to "settler"',[19] thus demonstrating the centrality of employment in the identity of the Sikh immigrant. In this way, not only were the Sikh men primarily viewed as potential employees who were plugging the labour shortage in Britain at the time, but self-perception changed as employment engendered a sense of permanency and stability in their lives.

However, the large numbers of immigrants entering Britain, especially from the Commonwealth, caused growing concern about the changing demographics within the country. One of the ways these concerns were reflected was in the changes in parliamentary legislation regarding immigrants. The 1948 British Nationality Act, which for the first time defined British citizenship,[20] stipulated that '[e]very person who under this Act is a citizen of the British United Kingdom and Colonies [...] shall by virtue of that citizenship have the status of a British subject'.[21] Significantly, this meant that any British subject – including those from former colonies – had the right to enter Britain, to vote in elections and even stand for Parliament. However, by 1962 the Commonwealth Immigrants Act put in place restrictions for those coming from the Commonwealth seeking to live in the UK. Immigrants would now be issued job vouchers providing they met certain provisions, such as already having secured employment before entering the country.

The alteration from automatic subject to one who now had to vie for such status illustrates the changing attitudes to Commonwealth citizens after the end of the Empire. The Sikh tensions looked at here were part of a much larger discourse on immigration. With imminent restrictions on immigration coming into force in the 1962 Commonwealth Immigration Act, many wives of Sikh immigrants came to Britain to join their husbands and established their families here.[22] Consequently, many of the men felt a renewed connection to their Sikh faith and identity, leading them to grow their beards and don the turban once more.[23]

Turbans and transport

However, this posed problems between the men and their employers as illustrated in David Myers' uncaptioned cartoon (*Evening News*, 4 July 1968) (4.1).[24] This image is one of a number from the 1960s specifically commenting on the plight of male Sikh transport workers who wanted to be able to wear the turban and the beard as part of their uniform. Myers' cartoon shows a lone protestor holding a placard which reads 'LONDON TRANSPORT WORKERS UNITE! BAN SIKH TURBANS!' In this image, Myers seems to be challenging the reader to question what it means to be 'British' and more specifically, how Londoners should react to a more diverse capital. It is ironic that the protester wears a bobbly hat on his head as well as his work uniform. There are placards behind the protester referencing deaths in Biafra and Vietnam, highlighting the triviality of the protestor's call to ban turbans. Myers seems to imply that pursuing such a cause is futile, lending support to Sikh London transport workers who desire to wear the turban at work. Published in a tabloid, the cartoon illustrates how the issue of turbans on public transport had become controversial on a national scale.

Keith Waite's 'Actually I'm wearing my turban underneath it' (*Sun*, 4 July 1968) (4.2)[25] illustrates how eager the bus driver is to impress upon the wider British public and his colleagues that he is committed to both his British and Sikh identities in equal measure. The image depicts two recognizable London red buses, with the drivers at the wheel. It is ironic that the Sikh bus driver is wearing a bearskin – an iconic British symbol – whilst the other bus driver is wearing a cowboy hat; however, he is Caucasian and therefore ostensibly has no need to prove his commitment to his British identity. The cowboy hat seems to make a wider point that, though this is an American symbol, it is acceptable because being British or American is contained within the generic 'Anglosphere' – so long as one is not 'coloured'. Implicit in the cartoons is the idea of a social contract which I call 'transactionality': the Sikh community must abide by the rules of trading in parts of their identity in order to be accepted by the wider community. Consequently, the turban is turned into a litmus test for belonging and integration and if Sikhs wish not to observe the rules, they cannot *expect* to belong nor be *considered* to belong.

Again, the London red bus is portrayed as a battleground between Sikh employees and their Caucasian colleagues in Stanley Franklin's 'I told you one thing would lead to another' (*Daily Mirror*, 11 April 1969) (4.3).[26] The image depicts a red bus with a domed roof and two Sikhs on the bus wearing turbans – one is driving the vehicle and the other is a bus conductor. Two Caucasian men in the corner of the image watch as the bus drives past them. The caption implies that the Caucasian men in the cartoon (whose uniforms and caps suggest that they are bus drivers) had the foresight to see that once Sikh transport workers were given the right to wear the turban and beard to work, they would soon demand more rights and privileges, culminating in the demise of British values, symbolized by a domed double-decker bus, echoing the architecture of a Sikh gurdwara.

This idea is repeated in another cartoon by Stanley Franklin, 'It makes a change from Z-cars' (*Daily Mirror*, 29 January 1970) (4.4; Figure 9),[27] which depicts a turbaned Sikh police officer riding an elephant. Both the elephant and the domed bus convey a sense of the familiar giving way to something alien. An iconic British symbol, the red bus imaginatively undergoes a radical change in which it loses its British character. The iconography of a turbaned police officer riding an elephant rather than driving a car reinforces the point that the police force (considered a core part of a developed society) is being trampled on. I would argue that Franklin's images go further than simply presenting the turban as a barrier to integration, as in the images above. They may indicate a reluctant acceptance of the turban as a new cultural reality, yet they also give voice to an underlying fear that this acceptance will lead the Sikh community or other minority groups, to demand more rights, indelibly altering the cultural landscape.[28] The turban is presented as an icon of *subversion* denoting a defiant, culturally and politically charged, statement of difference that is not 'merely' a sign of personal religious devotion. The turban is read in an increasing number of cartoons as an external statement subverting British society at its most fundamental level, and threatening to transform it into something foreign and not British at all.

Both Keith Waite's 'It's all right, big boy – we're allowed to wear turbans now' (*Sun*, 11 April 1969) (4.5)[29] and Franklin's 'I told you one thing would lead to another' were published on the same day. Waite again takes a satirical approach to the issue of allowing Sikh bus drivers to wear the turban to work. The cartoon shows a female bus conductor (identified by the ticket machine hanging around her neck) speaking to a male colleague who looks at her in bemusement. Her head is bound in cloth which can be presumed to be what she is referring to in the caption. Published simultaneously, Images 4.3 and 4.5 view the issue from

Figure 9 Stanley Franklin, 'It Makes a Change from Z-Cars' (*Daily Mirror*, 29 January 1970). Copyright Franklin/Daily Mirror/1970.

different angles. What both images share is a common sense of dread about what the consequences will be now that Sikh transport workers have been allowed to wear the turban to work. According to Franklin in 4.3, the potential erosion of British values is a real one, making a wider point about the dangers of making concessions to minorities. In 4.5, Waite concentrates on the erosion of the respect for the uniform itself, and in turn, the observance of rules and regulations that any employee would be expected to follow. Waite seems to highlight how granting the turban as part of the uniform means a watershed moment for others to test how far they can abuse this right for their own gain.

Turban vs British identity

The key theme in the images of this period seems to be how the turban in and of itself is perceived as *the* barrier to integration for Sikh men. Significantly, these images were published in a context of high racial tension. Writer Dilip Hiro speaks about the racial conflict between white and Asian youth gangs existing since the mid-1960s. Antagonizing the situation further was the Commonwealth Immigration Act 1968 which was legislated in response to the thousands of British Asians who were fleeing East Africa and attempting to enter Britain. Enoch Powell's infamous 'Rivers of Blood' speech was delivered in April 1968 leading to racial clashes in many parts of the country.[30]

In fact, days before Powell delivered this speech, the Indian Workers' Association sought his support for Sandhu's case. However, he 'dismissed it as an industrial dispute, a foretaste of "things to come"'.[31] Powell was Conservative MP for Wolverhampton South West at the time, but there was shared consensus across the political parties on immigration and the way some ethnic communities were viewed. In his speech, Powell referenced Labour MP John Stonehouse's views on the way Sikh communities specifically were trying to 'maintain customs inappropriate in Britain'[32] because of their efforts to wear the turban to work.

Thus, as hostilities between the Sikh community and the (Anglo-Saxon) British community grew in tandem, the turban and beard became symbolic of those tensions. Indeed, cartoons from the 1960s and 1970s convey a sense of hostility towards Sikh men wearing beards and, especially, the turban, with the issue posed as a battle of Sikh vs British identity. This can be seen in Michael Cummings' 'If this is the "Mother" Country, cobber, I think I'd rather take the next flight back to Australia ... ' (*Daily Express*, 20 November 1972) (4.6).[33] Set in 'London Airport Immigration', two Caucasian men look aghast as they are faced with several distinctively foreign-looking men, including one who is presented as a Sikh due to his turban and facial hair (in contrast to the man to his left who wears a Jinnah cap and so appears to be Muslim).

Significantly, the cartoon only features the two Caucasian arrivals, with everyone else depicted being a member of an ethnic minority. Furthermore, different landmarks in London are given a radical makeover, including St Paul's Cathedral where one can 'Hear the "Muezzin" from St. Paul's Mosque'. The sign written in German prohibiting the flying of the Union Jack 'By order of the Common Market Commission' belies misgivings over Britain's imminent entry into the European Economic Community (EEC). Everything in this image screams of a 'foreign' takeover of London, where Caucasians cease to live and where British sovereignty has been eroded because of its membership in the EEC. This image demonstrates that whilst Jews and the Irish slowly became accepted as being 'white', Sikhs have always been Othered on the basis of their ethnicity, as well as their religion.

On 1 April 1984, a new Code of Practice for the Elimination of Racial Discrimination and the Promotion of Equality of Opportunity in Employment came into force. It was issued by the Commission for Racial Equality (CRE) in 1984 under the Race Relations Act 1976. The code specifically referenced Sikhs and the fact that employers 'should not refuse employment to a turbaned Sikh because he could not comply with unjustifiable uniform requirements'.[34] The case of *Mandela v Dowell Lee* was brought under the 1976 Act which involved a Sikh boy being refused admission to a private school on the basis that he was not allowed to wear the turban to school. In discussing the case, the House of Lords determined that Sikhs are a racial group and were therefore covered by the Act.[35] This demonstrates the irony of how the Sikh community obtained legal protection on the basis of race for a primarily *religious* issue. It was not until 2003 that religious discrimination was recognized in law in *The Employment Equality (Religion or Belief) Regulations 2003*.[36]

Motorcycles and the turban

Another major event in Anglo-Sikh history was the demand for Sikh motor cycle riders to be allowed to ride without a helmet. In 1973, the Conservative Minister for Transport, John Peyton, received requests from the Sikh community to exempt Sikhs from wearing a helmet on motor cycles. Peyton did not acquiesce because he feared that such exemptions would make legislation difficult to enforce and because of the strong public support for the legislation.[37] Keith Waite's 'No, I'm not a Sikh – it's just that I wasn't wearing a crash helmet' (*Daily Mirror*, 11 September 1973) (4.7)[38] shows why there was such support: the public saw the issue primarily as one about safety and not as a tug of war between religion and the law. The image portrays two men lying in hospital beds: one has a beard and turban on, whilst the other has a bandage wrapped round his head in the style of a turban. Despite the safety risks that Waite was attempting to highlight, many Sikh motor cycle riders still rode without a helmet after the law came into effect.[39]

Mac's 'And we can't do a damned thing – the driver's wearing a crash helmet!' (*Daily Mail*, 11 September 1973) (4.8)[40] shows a police car chasing a motor cycle on which a female-helmeted rider carries eleven turbaned male Sikhs in a circus-style act. Although the driver is not wearing a turban, she is dressed in a garment that covers her hair underneath the helmet, suggesting that she is also of Indian heritage and, given the context, most likely Sikh. This is significant because it is the only cartoon examined in this chapter to feature a Sikh female and in which she is shown to be a cunning character. The cartoon comments on the situation the police were facing with those Sikh men who were determined to ride motor cycles without a helmet, demonstrating a sense of frustration at the situation.

Leslie Gibbard's 'No thanks – it's against my religion … ' (*Guardian*, 11 September 1973) (4.9)[41] features the then Prime Minister, Edward Heath, and the Leader of the Opposition, Harold Wilson. Gibbard's cartoon seemingly comments on Heath's decision to join the EEC in 1973, in which the prime minister is labelled with the word 'EXPANSION' on his turban and Wilson holding out a safety helmet with the word 'PRICE RESTRAINT', which Heath refuses. This ostensibly benign picture not only makes a political point about Britain entering the Common Market in 1973 and the potential risks to this measure, but uses this as vehicle for making a point against the calls for exemption to wearing a helmet from the Sikh community.

The day before the publication of image 4.9, a protest was held by the Sikh community in Trafalgar Square against the wearing of helmets. The caption implies that Heath's decision to enter the EEC was not well-considered, in the same way that the Sikh community refused to think about the helmet issue from a safety perspective. What is problematic about this image is that it draws parallels between a sensitive religious topic and a controversial political one, leading to a strong sense of sarcasm and belittlement of the turban. In doing so, Gibbard seems to suggest that there is no real difference between the two issues, downplaying the significance of the turban and, as a result, mocking the Sikh religion.

These cartoons suggest that the fears conveyed in image 4.3 were not completely unfounded: having acquired the right to be able to wear the turban to work, the Sikh community were demanding further rights. When the issue of a helmet exemption for Sikhs was presented to Parliament, one of the key questions asked was whether the turban is an essential part of Sikh faith.[42] Furthermore, a key point raised in both the Commons and the Lords debates was the long-standing history of service of Sikhs in the British Armed Forces.[43] In much the same way that the issue of Sikh military contributions was used to make the case for Sikh transport workers to wear the turban, the same case was made here: 'In battle time, the Sikh has never been called upon to discard his turban in favour of the war hat or tin helmet worn by other soldiers under battle fire.'[44]

The matter of exempting turbaned motorcycle riders from wearing a helmet raised a number of other issues, including the idea that if Parliament insisted on the use of helmets, it would 'undermine the progress made in persuading employers in government and industry to dispense them from the normal requirements of caps, uniforms, hard-hats, etc provided they wore turbans'.[45] Sebastian Poulter also points out that this raised the issue of whether religious freedom overrules equal treatment under the law, as well as the cost implications to the National Health Service for those sustaining injuries which could be prevented from wearing a helmet.[46]

The Motor-Cycle Crash Helmets (Religious Exemption) Act was enacted in November 1976, exempting Sikhs who wear the turban from having to wear a helmet. A critical message to take from these cartoons is how immigration does not end as soon as someone arrives at their destination; transactionality is a two-way process involving the 'host society,' as well as the immigrants themselves. Both the Sikh community and Anglo-Saxon British society were rediscovering and reinterpreting their ideas of identity. Under Empire rule, Sikhs were associated with loyalty and respect, especially in dangerous situations, where the Sikh soldier could be expected to sacrifice his life for Britain.[47]

The fact that the Sikh community had played such a critical role in British India through their military service was used as a powerful tool in recognizing the contribution the community had made, well before there was a sizeable contingent living in Britain. However, this changed when this contribution was brought into the domestic sphere where ethnic pride was no longer encouraged or accepted by British society. Perhaps because their contribution was largely outside of mainland Britain before Sikhs immigrated in large numbers, Britons had to keep being reminded that Sikhs had played a prominent role in British history.

Turbans and terrorism

During the 1980s, the perception of Sikhs changed dramatically. The assassination of India's Prime Minister, Indira Gandhi, by a Sikh bodyguard projected an image of violence and terrorism. There was political agitation in India for an independent Punjab, known as Khalistan, which resulted in the attack on the Golden Temple in 1984 by the Indian army, codenamed Operation Blue Star. Magnified by the media, the events of 1984 led to ideas of Sikhs taking their martial background to extremism and terrorism.[48] The fact that Sikh military recruits were encouraged to join the Khalsa through taking Amrit during the colonial period demonstrates how this understanding of what it means to be Sikh was influenced by the British.[49]

Michael Cummings' 'The good news is that our next war will be fought in outer space – the bad news is that other people's wars will be fought in the streets of Britain' (*Daily Express*, 13 June 1984) (4.10; Figure 10)[50] is a satirical take on the inter-communal violence in Britain as a result of the events that were taking place in India. The caption implies an 'us' and 'them' division in which the events of India belongs to 'them' (Indians in India) and not 'us' (Britons, whatever their ethnic background). Margaret Thatcher and a policeman look on bemusedly at the ensuing violence between Hindus and Sikhs, the latter two in army tanks with the words 'Death to Hindus!' and 'Death to Sikhs!' written on them.

The sandbags that protect Thatcher and the police officer are a figurative way of emphasizing the barriers of difference between the Caucasian British community and the British Indian community; whilst the Caucasian British community is shown as meek and pacifist in this situation, the British Indian community is shown as militant and violent (much like the Irishman under colonial rule). The battle takes place in the capital, on one of its

Figure 10 Michael Cummings, 'The good news is that our next war will be fought in outer space – the bad news is that other people's wars will be fought in the streets of Britain' (*Daily Express*, 13 June 1984). Copyright Cummings/Daily Express/1984.

most important roads: Downing Street (as can be seen by the street sign above Thatcher's head) against a backdrop of the bullet-riddled Houses of Parliament in the process of being destroyed. The image is meant to shock and raise the question: 'If the Sikh and Hindu community in Britain are so concerned with events that are taking place in a different country, are they truly British?' By showing the destruction of the very heart of British democracy by the actions of the British Indian community, the answer Cummings wants the reader to arrive at is an emphatic 'no'. Interestingly, the image of Big Ben being destroyed is echoed in image 4.6 – also by Cummings – showing a preoccupation of the political threat immigration posed in his view.

Despite the message of this cartoon, the reality was that by the 1980s, a growing number of the Sikh community were born in Britain,[51] which meant that the Sikh community had 'changed from an immigrant community to a minority group'.[52] Thus, by the time of the publication of image 4.10, the majority of Sikhs had accepted their stay in Britain as more permanent and yet, at the same time, were deeply affected by the political events taking place in India. In this context, many within the Sikh community were divided over their own heritage – were they tied primarily to India or Khalistan? Simultaneously, were they tied to Britain, despite the racial discrimination they experienced?[53]

Stanley Franklin's 'Evil of the Sky' (*Sun*, 24 June 1985) (4.11)[54] also comments on the events surrounding the campaign for an independent Khalistan. The cartoon depicts a giant vulture, standing on top of the world crushing airplanes beneath its feet. The vulture has the word 'TERRORISM' written across its left wing. Another airplane is being crushed in its beak with the words 'AIR INDIA'. The image refers to the bombing of Air India Flight 182 on 23 June 1985 which killed 329 people. It is believed that the bombing took place in retaliation against the storming of the Golden Temple by the Sikh militant group Babbar Khalsa. Contrasted against image 4.10, what is interesting is that 4.11 does not explicitly – nor implicitly for that matter – link the Sikh religion to terrorism. Rather, Franklin is indicting terrorism *per se*, where terrorism is presented as a global threat, whilst in 4.10, Cummings pits British Indians against Caucasian Britons in a way that juxtaposes peaceful Caucasians against violent Indians. Pertinently, Cummings places the Khalistan issue within the context of Britain and its effect on the British Indian community. In doing so, image 4.10 detracts from those who were victims of the violence in India and turns the event on its head by making Caucasian Britons the 'real' victims of the atrocity of the military operation on the Golden Temple and the apparent failure of multiculturalism.

Turbans and the Other

As we can see, the depiction of the turban is used as a recurring trope to highlight the Otherness of the Sikh community in Britain. As Sikh immigration grew during the 1950s, the turban was still seen as a symbol of difference, morphing into a 'cultural threat to the nation'.[55] This then changed in the 1980s, due to the rise of Sikh militancy, during which the turban was identified with fundamentalism. The turban is still a powerful symbol of Otherness and subversion, where turbaned Sikhs have been mistaken for Muslims – as witnessed by the attacks on gurdwaras in Kent and Leeds in the aftermath of the London terror attacks in 2005.[56] Gill argues that as a result, the turban has reacquired the cultural threat symbol it once had in the 1950s, the difference being that this is no longer with reference to the Sikh faith.[57]

However, though the turban is most commonly associated with Sikhism, it has (and is) also closely identified with more general Orientalist ideas of the Other. For example, JAK's 'Sold! to the gent with the large diamond in his turban!' (*Evening Standard*, 11 November 1971) (4.12)[58] and Trog's 'What I always say is, exports are exports!' (*Daily Mail*, 18 October 1968) (4.13)[59] deal with issues completely unrelated to Sikhism. Relating back to my previous point concerning the turban and gender, the two cartoons perpetuate the idea of a man who is patriarchal and chauvinist, in which the turban demonstrates that such 'regressive' ideas have been imported from foreign cultures. The very absence of any pictorial representation of 'the gent' being referred to in JAK's cartoon exemplifies this idea: the reader is left to imagine what he looks like, with only 'the large diamond in his turban' to go on.

Emmwood's 'Now that we're all European, Sahib, I suppose wogs begin at Malta!' (*Daily Mail*, 2 January 1973) (4.14)[60] illustrates the turban's potency in the debate surrounding integration and immigration, without being specifically about the Sikh community. The term 'wog' – an offensive racist slang word – is now no longer commonly used. Paul Gilroy writes about how the term was used against him when he was growing up in the 1960s and how the word's 'importance lies in the way that it identifies a liminal yet intimate position: on the inside but never welcome; present, yet firmly excluded from belonging'.[61] The caption refers to a well-known slur at the time, 'wogs begin at Calais', meaning that those not native to Britain were outsiders. The man in the turban is desperate to belong by literally pushing this geographical line back to Malta, demonstrating the turban's function of highlighting Otherness from the Caucasian Briton. The word 'sahib' hints at the turbaned man's South Asian origins. In this cartoon, the turban and the rest of the South Asian man's attire serve as a contrast against what the Caucasian man wears.

The Maltese reference is in regard to the headline on the newspaper the Caucasian man is reading: 'MINTOFF THREATENS BRITAIN'. A prominent politician in Malta, Dominic Mintoff, campaigned for the country's independence from Britain (gained in 1964) and, at the time of publication, was prime minister. It is ironic in itself that the turbaned man uses the term 'wog' to describe people from Malta who more aptly fit the 'European' description than the turbaned man himself does. Further still, Malta had been under British rule less than a decade before, retaining Queen Elizabeth II as head of state until the following year in 1974.

'Tennis fashions for Wimbledon' (*Daily Mirror*, 22 June 1925) (4.15)[62] by W. K. [William Kerridge] Haselden (1872–1953) comments on the tennis player, Suzanne Lenglen, who was renowned for her distinctive fashion sense on and off the court – especially her bandeau – of which people would often bet on the colour in Lenglen's next match.[63] Haselden mocks the public's scrutiny of Lenglen's attire by transforming the bandeau into an ostentatious turban and speculating that she may adopt 'other Eastern headgear', whilst male tennis players may opt for 'something Chinese or Ancient Egyptian'. This echoes the sentiments in image 4.2 in which the bearskin and the cowboy hat are deemed to belong as part of the Anglosphere, whilst the turban falls outside of it. Thus, the bandeau sufficiently falls inside of the Anglosphere but is dangerously close to becoming something different.

The publication of Keith Waite's 'How the heck would I know what Jim Callaghan meant?' (*Sun*, 1 March 1968) (4.16)[64] coincided with the day the 1968 Commonwealth Immigration Act received Royal Assent, having taken only three days to pass through parliament and coming into force immediately.[65] The Act restricted entry to those who had been born in the UK, or who had a grandparent born in the UK. This effectively barred the thousands of Asian Kenyans who held British passports, fleeing for Britain due to the then Kenyan President, Jomo Kenyatta's threat to expel those who did not have Kenyan citizenship. The Act was the brainchild of the then Labour Home Secretary, Jim Callaghan, who defended the Bill in parliament by stating that the 'test that is adopted is geographical, not racial'.[66]

The cartoon's caption refers to the confusing position the Act put the Asian Kenyans in who could not enter the country of which they were citizens. What is most interesting about this image is the depiction of the newly arrived Asian Kenyan family, consisting of two men in a turban and a female wearing the *niqab*. The men's beards and turbans suggest that they are most likely Sikh and so to have a female Sikh family member wearing a specifically Muslim garment would be most unlikely. Whilst 4.15 contrasts the benign bandeau with other, more 'exotic', forms of headdress, 4.16 includes the turban and the *niqab* to indicate the Asian Kenyan family's immigrant identity. Thus, both cartoons use the turban and the *niqab* to convey an Otherness that is not specific to a religion or ethnicity, but one that indicates 'the immigrant' in general. Image 4.15 goes so far as to say that such attire isn't simply un-British, but is also not befitting of Caucasians, since Lenglen was a Caucasian Frenchwoman.

A number of cartoons feature or reference Enoch Powell, alongside turbaned men, within the wider context of immigration, demonstrating the impact the politician's views had. JAK's 'Now give us your honest opinion!' (*Evening Standard*, 23 April 1968) (4.17)[67] and Stanley Franklin's 'You having another of your nightmares, Enoch?' (*Daily Mirror*, 24 April 1968) (4.18)[68] were published in response to the fears Powell expressed in his 'Rivers of Blood' speech regarding immigration. As a result of his speech, Powell was sacked from the Shadow Cabinet.[69] Franklin's image takes a tongue-in-cheek approach to Powell's views portraying a Sikh prime minister on the doorsteps of Number 10 Downing Street, guarded by an African-Caribbean policeman. Here, Franklin shows how for people like Powell, integration by ethnic communities was something to be discouraged precisely because it would lead to a scenario in which it was no longer a Caucasian fulfilling such job roles, thereby expanding what it means to be British to include other races.

Set in Powell's constituency of Wolverhampton, image 4.17 portrays a small Caucasian man surrounded by turbaned and non-turbaned South Asian men reading newspapers headlined 'POWELL'. The caption indicates that the South Asian men have taken umbrage at Powell's words and have singled out the Caucasian man for his views on the state of immigration by virtue of his race. However, the intimidated look on the man's face and the fact that he is literally dwarfed by the Asian men in the cartoon make it apparent that he cannot express his honest opinion which seems to presuppose that he does have sympathies with Powell. In this way, JAK seems to have reversed the situation by making the Caucasian man the real victim of Powell's speech, as opposed to the Asians depicted. Both images 4.17 and 4.18 employ the image of turbaned men to emphasize an immigrant background. This is problematic because it presents a duality of 'the immigrant' and 'the native', thereby giving support to Powell's views of the way mass immigration inevitably breeds social discord between different races where 'the black man will have the whip hand over the white man'.[70]

Turbans and power

The final image examined in this chapter is Peter Brookes' uncaptioned cartoon, (*The Times*, 29 July 2010) (4.19),[71] published twenty-six years after image 4.10 – the last cartoon examined here which features a turban. In the intervening years, there is almost no archival material directly relating to Sikhs in Britain, illustrating how the community was no longer in the national media spotlight. Moreover, image 4.19 is not about Sikhs in Britain *per se*. Instead, the cartoon highlights the Otherness of the then British Prime Minister, David Cameron, in India in contrast to the then Indian Prime Minister, Manmohan Singh.

There are undertones of post-colonial anxiety in the image – portraying a Britain which once ruled a vast empire now asking its former colony for financial help. Where Singh is fully dressed, Cameron is dirty, wearing a vest and patched shorts and is begging, emphasizing Britain's subservient position in contrast to India. Singh walks past Cameron, his body language demonstrating indifference. Here, the Sikh emanates power and dominance over the Anglo-Saxon, in contrast to the previous images discussed. The lack of cartoons relating to the Sikh community in Britain in the preceding years shows that the issue of the turban was no longer a nationally controversial issue owing to an acceptance of Sikhs as a part of British society. Rather, what Brookes' cartoon shows is how the negative image of the troublesome Sikh with his un-British demands has been replaced by the prominent and influential figure of Manmohan Singh – the first Sikh prime minister of India. Though the turban has lost the negative connotations once attached to it, it is perhaps true that it has also lost the positive connotations it had during the British Empire where it was connected to ideas of military bravery.

Conclusion: Turbans and 'terrorist masculinity'

Paul Gilroy discusses the idea that post-war Britain 'found it hard to adjust to the presence of semi-strangers who, disarmingly, knew British culture intimately as a result of their colonial education'.[72] The cartoons examined in this chapter demonstrate this degree of discomfort and awkwardness at the idea that a person wearing a turban could ever be accepted as being unquestionably British. Rather, as the first Sikh immigrants found, they were made to divest themselves of their visibly Sikh identity by conforming to styles of dress in order to find employment. This was in direct contrast to those Sikhs who had lived under British rule in India, where the Sikh male was encouraged to practise his faith in order to serve as part of the Armed Forces, thereby risking his life for Britain. Those who came to Britain after the collapse of the empire therefore found that the shared history between their countries – mainly as a result of British imperialism – had been forgotten.

The case of the plight of Asian Kenyans as seen in Image 4.16 and whose history lies in being taken to Kenya as labourers in the nineteenth century by the British is a key example of how the idea of the Commonwealth was being challenged. Thus, images 4.2 and 4.10 demonstrate the idea of transactionality: 'the immigrant' must be prepared to give up certain parts of their identity and take on what is deemed as belonging to the Anglosphere. This is symbolized by the bearskin in 4.2, whilst in 4.10, there is an expectation of giving up a sense of home in relation to India because to be a British citizen is to forsake such feelings.

Thus, in the context of racial tension, the turban was often used as a symbol of foreignness, as can be seen in images 4.14 and 4.6. In both these images the man in the turban represents 'the immigrant' – reminiscent of the Afghan man in image 6.4. There is an undertone to the images which belie a sense of unease at the prospect of 'the immigrant' transitioning to 'settler' status. This is because of the permanency of such a change and the fact that the ethnic make-up of Britain will be ethnically diverse, as opposed to what the men expect in 4.6. On the other hand, some of the cartoons mock this fear, such as in image 4.3. The image seems to echo the fears of the reader and yet the image is absurd: a domed bus is perhaps not what the reader had in mind when thinking about the consequences of allowing Sikh transport workers to wear the turban. With regard to the issue of the turban for Sikh motorcycle riders, the turban became less of a sign of cultural Otherness, as opposed to a symbol of resistance, as can be seen in image 4.9. In this context, the cartoons demonstrate a sense of confusion as to why the Sikh community were fighting for such a cause when the issue revolved around safety rather than religious freedom.

The lack of archival material between 1985 and 2009 is one way of understanding how ideas of nation and home have changed in relation to the Anglo-Sikh community since the publication of the first cartoon looked at above, in 1968. Whereas the reader then was led to question popular beliefs about the turban and the impact it would have on British society, now such questions are seldom raised in cartoons and, indeed, it would be considered racist to do so. For example, it is a common occurrence to see a turbaned bus driver or to see identifiably Sikh men playing in the England cricket team. Therefore, the turban is seen more as a sign of permissible difference and, in turn, the Sikh community is no longer one to be feared or questioned simply because of their appearance. Although this is positive, this is also partly to do with the Muslim community being viewed in much the same way as Sikhs were, especially in the 1980s. This has had huge repercussions for the Sikh community who are often mistaken for being Muslim and, therefore, subject to anti-Muslim attacks.

As the context has changed significantly with a shift of focus towards the British Muslim community in the wake of 9/11 and the 7/7 London bombings, this has resulted in a more explicit association between the turban and terrorism, rather than simply immigration. According to Puar:

> The turban is accruing the marks of a terrorist masculinity. The turbaned man – no longer merely the figure of a durable and misguided tradition, a community and familial patriarch ... now inhabits the space and history of monstrosity, of that which can never become civilized. The turban is not only imbued with the nationalist, religious and cultural symbolics of the Other. The turban both reveals and hides the terrorist, a constant sliding between that which can be disciplined and that which must be outlawed.[73]

Although Puar's main focus is Sikhs in an American context, the examination of British political cartoons demonstrates similar views of the turban across the Atlantic. Puar's use of the word 'monstrosity' shows how the threat the turban represents has changed from subversion of culture to a subversion of humanity. The turban acts as a barrier, where the turban bearer is dehumanized and placed in a separate sphere. Notably, one of the observations Puar makes about the attacks perpetrated against Sikhs being mistaken for Muslims in America post-9/11 is how they became 'increasingly bizarre in their execution; often the turban itself was the object of the assault, upon which the unraveling of hair signified a humiliating and intimate submission'.[74]

The very nature of such attacks demonstrates a recognition on behalf of the perpetrator of the significance of the turban through forcible removal. Puar, commenting with specific regard to the plight of American Sikhs, discusses how many decided no longer to wear the turban, in order to fit the mould of the 'masculine patriotic' for fear of being associated with 'terrorist bodies'.[75] The turban issue for Sikh employees gives context to the debates surrounding the *burqa/niqab* today, sharing commonalities with attitudes towards what is deemed compatible with British identity and what is not. I now turn to this topic in my next chapter.

4

Burqas on the beach: Muslim women in political cartoons

Introduction

Following on from the previous chapter on Sikhs, I focus on the portrayal of Muslims in British political cartoons after the 9/11 attack, looking at how the same messages of Otherness can be applied to totally different communities. This chapter focuses on the depiction of Muslim women wearing the face veil in Britain and abroad. Exotic and alluring, yet at the same time, dangerous and subversive, media representations of Muslim women are multi-faceted and complex. In the political cartoons examined below, I find that the iconography of the burqa and niqab are used interchangeably to make a wider point about the *veiling of the face*, as opposed to veiling of the hair, which is seemingly deemed acceptable.

Starting from the fall of the Taliban in 2001, I argue that this event has contributed to the idea of the *burqa/niqab* as a garment that is imposed on all Muslim women and is therefore an imposition from which they must be liberated. Examining the function of the *burqa/niqab*, I argue that such tropes convey messages of political and cultural deception, suspicion and oppression against women. The *burqa/niqab* is perceived as a visual marker of subversion against Western ideals such as democracy, free speech and the freedom of movement for women. I look at how this is translated in visual culture and the implications of these tropes in the wider context relating to perceptions of gender, national identity and violence.

Many Muslims believe that it is a religious obligation for female Muslims to veil themselves, based on several verses in the Qur'an, such as Q33:59:

> Prophet, tell your wives, your daughters, and women believers to make their outer garments hang low over them so as to be recognized and not insulted: God is most forgiving, most merciful.[1]

Following on from this, there is a multitude of different interpretations of what the Qur'an means in relation to the practise of veiling. The most common form of veiling across the globe comes in the form of wearing a headscarf, commonly known as *hijab* or *khimaar* with which the Muslim female covers her hair. In addition to the headscarf, many women also choose to wear a cloak over their clothes known as a *jilbab* or *abaya*, often worn by women in the Middle East. The *chador*, mainly worn by women in Iran, is a cloak covering the entire body which is held closed at the front. Other Muslim women opt to wear the *burqa*, a one-piece veil covering the entire face and body – mostly associated with women in Afghanistan – or the *niqab*, a veil covering the face, leaving the eyes clear.

Muslims in Britain

I have written at length about the Sikh community's history in Britain and how their struggle for rights was often met with resistance, as illustrated in the cartoons I examine. In much the same way, calls to be able to wear the face veil have proven to be major points of contention in Britain, sparking debate surrounding where – and whether – the Muslim community fits into British society.[2] One of the biggest differences between the Sikh and Muslim communities is the fact that whilst the former originates from a specific geographical area (the Punjab), the 'Muslim community' is made up of different ethnicities and races. This makes it problematic when speaking about 'the' Muslim community in Britain because, in essence, there is not one.

Demonstrating this, in their analysis of the 2011 Census, The Muslim Council of Britain (MCB) observed that the ethnic diversity of the Muslim population in Britain is on the increase as those who describe themselves as 'Black African', 'Black other' and 'Asian other' have risen in population numbers. Notwithstanding this fact, a large part of today's Muslim presence can be traced back to Commonwealth immigration from South Asia in the 1950s, of which Pakistanis make up the largest single ethnic group at just over one million in the 2011 Census.[3] Many of these South Asian immigrants came to satisfy the demand for industrial workers in Britain, with their wives and children joining them from around the 1970s onwards.[4]

Tariq Modood recounts his own experience of growing up in Britain where he was brought up to 'never deny that we are Pakistanis (later this became Asian, and then Muslim)',[5] showing the fluid and multi-dimensional character of Muslim identity in Britain. Precisely because of this, Modood's focus on discourses surrounding race and ethnicity in Britain provides a more useful insight than a historical analysis of Muslims in Britain today. One important issue in his analysis centres on the fact that whilst the Jewish and the Sikh communities are legally recognized as ethnic groups, the Muslim community do not enjoy such status. This is due to the fact that much like Christianity, Islam is theologically non-ethnic and universal. Hence, before religious discrimination was recognized in legislation in 2003 as mentioned above, the focus on race and ethnicity meant that though Muslims may have been discriminated as Muslims, they often had to reference being Pakistani or Arab, for example, to seek protection.[6]

Therefore, the experience of the Muslim immigrant is more likely to be predominantly bound with his/her race, rather than religion. Modood criticizes the approach taken in the 1970s through to the early 1980s of 'political blackness', in which Britons fell into two categories: black or white. This meant those who fell in the 'black' category included anyone 'who were potential victims of colour racism'. Such an approach was at first embraced and then later rejected by 'Asian political activists' who sought 'a more particular ethnic or religious identity rather than this all-inclusive non-whiteness.'[7] Modood highlights the controversy surrounding *The Satanic Verses* as one of the key events that demonstrated this quest for an alternative identity.

The Rushdie affair

First published in 1988, Salman Rushdie's novel *The Satanic Verses* included a re-telling of the life of the Prophet Muhammad (known as Mahound in the novel), as well as prostitutes who share the same names as the wives of the Prophet. The title of the novel itself refers to a legend involving verses recited by the Prophet purportedly from the devil permitting intercession to Meccan pagan goddesses. Amongst other elements of the novel, these were just a few that sparked outrage in the Muslim community across the world, eventually leading to a fatwa issued by Ayatollah Khomeini, calling for Rushdie's death.[8] The fatwa provoked debate surrounding freedom of expression within Muslim and non-Muslim circles. Indeed, Rushdie was attacked in New York in 2022, losing an eye and injuring his hand. Although the attacker, Hadi Matar's, motives remain unclear at the time of writing, the Foundation to Implement Imam Khomeini's Fatwas in Iran announced in February 2023 that they were awarding Matar land due to his actions.[9]

Critically, though the event was 'seen by all concerned as a Muslim versus the West battle', its primary impact was domestic in terms of group formation. The event mobilized Muslims in Britain in a way that was not seen before, engendering a strong sense of solidarity created through religious affiliation.[10] Kate Zebiri, in her essay on British Islamophobia, highlights the impact the Rushdie affair had on perceptions towards the Muslim community living in Britain in the late 1980s. This incident saw 'religion as the core element not just in British Muslim identity but also in anti-Muslim hostility', where 'images of bearded, robed, foreign-looking Muslims [...] contributed to a view of Islam and Muslims as anti-modern, repressive, intolerant',[11] because they were attacking the right to free speech.

The Rushdie affair illustrates how such ideas of the Muslim community have existed for some time, gaining prominence in the last decade following the events of 9/11 and 7/7. I argue that whilst the outcry following the publication of *The Satanic Verses* is seen as a crucial moment for the way British Muslims are still perceived to this day, the focus was more centred on the way Muslim *men* were perceived, rather than the Muslim woman in her own right. Thus, starting with the fall of the Afghanistan government, the Taliban, in 2001 as a consequence of the United States' War on Terror, I argue that this event has been fundamental in the way Muslim women are perceived today. I look at how ideas have developed in cartoons in relation to the treatment of women, portraying an image of Muslims in Britain unwilling to embrace ideas such as gender equality and democracy, which are considered fundamental British values.

According to the 2011 Census, there are over 2.7 million Muslims living in England and Wales – making up 4.8 per cent of the population. Of this, just under 1.3 million are women.[12] Interestingly, the MCB found that 73 per cent of Muslims in Britain 'consider British to be their only national identity',[13] even though over half of them were born outside of the UK. The events of 9/11 and especially 7/7 have had a huge impact on Muslims in Britain today with an increased focus on their role in wider society and measures, such as new anti-terror laws, designed to combat the radical Islamic terror threat. One important point to note is the different ways in which Muslim men and women engage and respond to the issues that they face today. As Tahir Abbas highlights:

> Young Muslim women have been shown to better engage with the theological, political and social pressures placed on their identities as British-born and Muslim people. Without doubt, it is reasonably well confirmed that Muslim women outperform their male counterparts in higher education, and are more

successful in negotiating issues of ethnicity, identity and high profile religious minority status.[14]

Despite the strong evidence in relation to Abbas' point, I look at the treatment of Muslim women by British cartoonists who are portrayed as unwilling – and even unable – to embrace ideas such as gender equality, democracy and transparency, which are considered fundamental British values.

'Terrorist femininity': veiled, unnamed and oppressed

Following the Bank of England's decision to replace the image of Elizabeth Fry on the £5 banknote with that of Winston Churchill,[15] there was a public outcry that there would no longer be any females featured other than the Queen.[16] In a separate interview a few months later, the then Business Secretary, Vince Cable, likened the Bank of England to the Taliban in relation to its fiscal policies.[17] Commenting on the subsequent decision to feature Jane Austen on £10 banknotes[18] and the Taliban comment, Peter Brookes' cartoon 'New Jane Austen £10 Note (as designed by Vince Cable)' (*The Times*, 25 July 2013) (5.1)[19] shows Jane Austen (the ringlets of hair and eyes in the likeness of the portrait by James Andrews[20]) wearing the *niqab*.

Consequently, the use of the *niqab* in the cartoon is contentious because it explicitly connects the Muslim religion with gender inequality. This demonstrates Weaver's point on how the 'incongruity' of satirical cartoons is so fundamental in the different ways they can be read, leading 'to various reactions because they do not create a literal or denotive meaning. They set up chains of connotation and create the "liquidity" of the images.'[21] The incongruity here is the veiling of a famous English (Caucasian) author, who would never have dressed as such and lived well before the Taliban came into existence. This leads the reader to conclude how gender inequality is connected to this specifically Muslim garment, which is reinforced in several ways: Austen in the foreground dressed in a black *niqab*; the well-known opening words of *Pride and Prejudice*, 'It is a truth universally acknowledged, that a single man in possession of a good fortune, must be in want of a wife', have been amended to refer to the 'Taleban' (*sic*), and the image of Austen in green in the centre, writing at her desk fully cloaked. This is all despite the fact that the Taliban or Islam has never had any influence in the Bank of England's decision on who should appear on English bank notes.

In the previous chapter, I looked at the fact that many American Sikhs no longer wear the turban for fear of being associated with 'terrorist bodies'. Extrapolating this argument, the veil is the feminine obverse to the turban; the Muslim 'feminine patriotic' who does not wear the *burqa/niqab*. In this way, the turban and the *burqa/niqab* create a subtle link between Sikhism and Islam in their function of identifying the Other, one that is unavoidably linked to gender.[22] Thus, image 5.1 illustrates the perception of the *Muslimah* (I use this term which is feminine for 'Muslim' in Arabic), wearing a face veil as equating to something that is un-British and alien. Through using the stereotype of the veiled *Muslimah*, there is a presumption that the *niqab* represses both femininity and the ability to participate fully in British society. Consequently, though the cartoon's main criticism is levelled at Vince Cable, image 5.1 attempts to highlight anti-feminist aspects of British society through focusing on the *Muslimah* by portraying Austen *as a Muslim*, insinuating that to be so is to be anti-feminist.

Thus, in order to combat the prejudice that women face in British society, one must accentuate anti-Islamic prejudice. Here, the veiled *Muslimah*'s body is presented as the locus of 'terrorist femininity' (as opposed to Puar's 'terrorist masculinity'), in political cartoons after the 9/11 and 7/7 terror attacks. By reversing the message of the cartoon, the reader understands that were the woman unveiled she would undoubtedly be unoppressed and fully exercise her rights as a British citizen. The underlying message of the cartoon perpetuates the idea of Islam as a sexist religion against women and that the Muslim 'feminine patriot' does not wear the *burqa* or *niqab*. Pertinently, she does not veil herself because there are different ways of practising one's faith with or without veiling. Rather, it is because she knows that the practice of veiling *per se* is inherently sexist and incompatible with her patriotism towards Britain, thus rendering her faith invisible, private. This ignores the reality that many women who wear the face veil choose to do so out of their own volition and further still, see no conflict between their faith and their British nationality.

Moreover, the assumption that veiling only serves to repress one's femininity disregards the different reasons and meanings behind a woman wearing it, thereby creating an illusion of the *Muslimah* who is oppressed and voiceless, in need of saving from the Muslim male.[23] Such portrayals of the *Muslimah* are instructive because they are also a comment on the Muslim male and the perception that they are 'the barbaric controlling Other'.[24] The idea of the Muslim male as the 'barbaric controlling Other' is exemplified in Dave Brown's uncaptioned image (*Independent*, 3 August 2005) (5.2).[25] In this image, the then counter-terrorism minister, Hazel Blears, is caricatured in a manner to make her seem unattractive. Against the silhouette of a mosque, two Muslim men look on at Blears in distaste, one of whom comments 'Y'know … Just occasionally … Enforcing the burka doesn't seem like a bad idea!'.

Here, Brown refers to the broad powers granted to the police to stop and search anyone without cause.[26] This led to feelings of resentment amongst Muslim communities who felt that they were being racially profiled by the police, especially following the 7/7 attacks.[27] The *burqa* acts as a way to shield the men – as well as wider society – from both the sight of Blears' ostensibly unattractive physical appearance as well as serving to disempower her from implementing her unpopular counter-terrorism measures. The image insinuates that there is power for those who can be seen, whilst those who are cloaked are left powerless. Furthermore, that both the women in images 5.1 and 5.2 are not even Muslim, demonstrates the idea of Islam as a tool to stealthily take over Britain in such a manner as to make *all* women invisible.

The caricature of Blears in such a manner indicates Brown's criticism of her, suggesting that she will be disempowered and unable to implement her unpopular counter-terrorism measures if she were to be veiled in a *burqa*. By deploying misogyny in order to criticize Blears, there is the suggestion of the Muslim male imposing the veil on the female in order to oppress her if she does not conform to his ideas of what beauty and femininity both mean. Interestingly, in Myfanwy Franks' research of Caucasian Muslim converts, one of the women interviewed, Miriam, speaks about her husband's ambivalence at her decision to wear the headscarf. Miriam cites the Bosnian War as the main reason for her decision to do so. In this example, Miriam goes against the prevailing view of the dominant Muslim male forcing her to veil. Furthermore, Miriam's identity is bound up in political events abroad, relating her decision to wearing the headscarf in terms of ethnicity and the fact that her physical appearance is not so different to those who were persecuted in Bosnia on the grounds of their faith.[28] This is just one example of the many reasons why the *Muslimah* may choose to wear the veil – be it the *hijab, burqa* or *niqab* – and how there are contesting ideas surrounding it within the Muslim community.

The fall of the Taliban

The US-led invasion of Afghanistan in 2001 resulted in the collapse of the Taliban regime after five years of brutal rule. This led to significant changes allowing Afghan women the right to vote, work and be educated.[29] Perhaps most

110   *Religious and Cultural Difference in Modern British Political Cartoons*

famously, women no longer had to wear the *burqa* as had been enforced by the Taliban regime.[30] The next image, Paul Thomas' uncaptioned cartoon (*Daily Express*, 12 November 2001) (5.3; Figure 11),[31] celebrates the end to the regime by depicting two refuse banks – a 'BURKHA BANK' and a 'BEARD BANK'. Despite being amongst the rubble caused by the war, the Afghan women and men depicted are happy as they discard their garments and shave off their beards.

The next cartoon also comments on the ability of Afghan women to dress as they please; Peter Brookes' 'Meanwhile, in downtown Kabul ... ' (*The Times*, 16 November 2001) (5.4)[32] depicts two women in heels and fishnets, wearing short dresses. An Afghan man in traditional clothing (known as a *perahan tunban*) who whistles at them receives an angry retort from one of the women to 'BURKA OFF, MATE!'. The juxtaposition of the women in western clothing against the street seller in traditional clothing suggests how their attire reflects their contrasting attitudes towards gender.

Peter Schrank's 'What am I doing here?' (*Independent on Sunday*, 11 March 2012) (5.5; Figure 12)[33] shows the impact of the ongoing war in Afghanistan on British soldiers (a swatch of the Union Jack visible on the right arm of the soldier). Next to the soldier stands an Afghan man in traditional attire, almost sneering

Figure 11 Paul Thomas, uncaptioned image (*Daily Express*, 12 November 2001). Copyright Thomas/Daily Express/2001.

at the soldier as he wonders 'What is he still doing here?'. Behind the two men stand a woman and little girl, the former in a blue *burqa* and the latter wearing a blue headscarf. The woman gives away her anxiety at the thought of foreign soldiers leaving Afghanistan, 'What will we do when he's gone?'. Images 5.3, 5.4 and 5.5 illustrate how central women's rights are seen, viewing the war in Afghanistan as a means to liberate Afghan women. Furthermore, 5.5 conveys the image of the helpless *Muslimah*, under the control of the Muslim male. Image 5.3 goes so far as to belittle and disregard the human cost of the war; although the Afghans depicted in the image are likely to be standing in the ruins of their own homes, the fact that they no longer need to wear the *burqa* or grow a beard are shown as the key outcomes of the war.

Images 5.1, 5.3 and 5.4 all conflate the Taliban with the issue of women's rights as symbolized by the *burqa*. For example, image 5.1 appropriates the imagery of a woman in a black *burqa*, comparing Britain to the collapsed Taliban state in Afghanistan, insinuating a demise of an egalitarian society where women are not allowed to participate fully in society. The cartoon's focus on the veiled woman serves to emphasize her alien status in a democratic country. In fact, this line of thinking shares common ground with the Taliban's view of women: those who did *not* veil had no place in such a political system, demonstrating how women and their right to participate in society are so often predicated on whether or not she wears the veil.

Figure 12 Peter Schrank, 'What am I doing here?' (*Independent on Sunday*, 11 March 2012). © Schrank, the Independent on Sunday.

Moreover, the rhetoric employed such as 'Taliban' and 'jihadist' in relation to the Bank of England is interesting in understanding the message conveyed by Cable and the policy official quoted in the *Independent* article.[34] In using such terminology, there is a clear intention to portray the Bank of England as the enemy, starkly presented as the aggressor because of its policies towards banks. In the way that image 4.9 brings two separate issues together, the same is also true of 5.1. Both cartoons use religious attire as a vehicle for conveying a political message and, at the same time, portray such articles of clothing unfavourably. For Gibbard, the turban in 4.9 is a safety issue whilst for Brookes, the *burqa* in 5.1 is a women's rights issue. Thus, whilst the Rushdie Affair was the catalyst for group formation of the British Muslim community, images 5.1 and 5.5 having been printed over a decade after the collapse of the Taliban regime in 2001 (the Taliban is now back in power since 2021) demonstrate the impact of 9/11 and the United States' War on Terror on more recent perceptions of the Muslim community both in Britain and abroad.

The face veil: to ban or not to ban?

Depicting a woman wearing the *niqab* being chased by a policeman on a topless beach in 'St Tropez', Matt's uncaptioned image (*Daily Telegraph*, 12 April 2011) (5.6)[35] shows the irony of the newly imposed French ban on face veils in public, whilst people are free to (not) wear anything they like – provided it is not the face veil. The cartoon shows a topless mother shielding her child's eyes from the veiled woman, further adding to the absurdity of the situation. The idea that a woman covered head to toe would be deemed too explicit for the child to witness serves to break down negative perceptions and stereotypes. Through using humour, Matt enables the reader to identify with the fugitive woman wearing a *niqab* in her plight to escape the policeman, criticizing the blanket ban on the face veil in France. Indeed, the accompanying article in the *Daily Telegraph* takes a cynical view because of the problems of enforcement without causing religious tensions as well as presenting the ban as a waste of police time.[36] Furthermore, Image 5.6 relates to a long-standing tradition of caricaturing the French, such as William Hogarth's illustrations from the eighteenth century.[37] In 5.6, Matt presents the French as debauched, holding skewed views towards the naked female body where to uncover is the norm.

Commenting on the same issue as image 5.6, Peter Brookes' uncaptioned cartoon (*The Times*, 12 April 2011) (5.7)[38] depicts the then French President,

Nicolas Sarkozy, holding a placard reading 'BAN THE BURKA' and a woman beside him wearing a *niqab* holding a placard reading 'BAN STACKED HEELS ON JUMPED UP LITTLE RUNTS ... ' against the backdrop of the French flag. The cartoon refers to the well-known fact that Sarkozy often wore stack heels to make him seem taller.[39] The focus on this is intentional; women are more often associated with wearing heels than men, and yet Sarkozy – in much the same way as the *Muslimah* wearing the *niqab* – goes against the norm.

Thus, similar to Matt's cartoon at 5.6, Brookes' cartoon at 5.7 attempts to highlight how the ban created further inequalities and restrictions, rather than dissolve them as purported.[40] This echoes the sentiments of *The Times* editorial on the issue of the face veil ban, that 'it is surely an irony to seek to defend liberal European values of tolerance and sexual freedom by restricting the freedom of women to dress as they wish.'[41] In this way, the cartoons present two Others: the *Muslimah* and the French, thus demonstrating the multi-dimensional character of political cartoons, where seemingly unrelated topics are woven into a single image.

Situating the issue of a *burqa* ban in Britain, the decision by Belgium and France to ban face veils in public sparked debate about a potential ban in this country. Resisting calls for a ban to be imposed, the then Immigration Minister, Damian Green, stated that it would be '"un-British" and run contrary to the conventions of a tolerant and mutually respectful society.'[42] As in the Matt cartoon at 5.6, we see the reiteration of the French as an Other in Green's rhetoric. Peter Schrank's uncaptioned cartoon (*Independent,* 19 July 2010) (5.8)[43] depicts an elderly Caucasian man sitting on a park bench, looking on at the passers-by dressed in summer clothing. A thought bubble above his head reads 'Sometimes I rather wish it could be made compulsory', in response to the newspaper's headline in his hands, 'No burka ban for Britain'.

The image illustrates the issue from a different perspective; the enforcement of the *burqa* on *non*-Muslims would be welcome so that those who, according to the elderly man, dress inappropriately are made to wear more modest attire. At the same time, perhaps Schrank is also conveying how such ideas are outdated and regressive – as symbolized by the juxtaposition of an elderly man looking on at a much younger generation. Therefore, Schrank exposes the irony of orthodox Muslim views on veiling being in-line with retrograde gender attitudes held by members of the elderly Caucasian population. This is in contrast to that of the more 'tolerant' younger Caucasian generation – if the man sitting on the bench was in fact young, he would be more accepting of the diversity of attire. Similar to Matt's cartoon at 5.6, Schrank depicts an absurd situation in which (non-Muslim)

Britons are shown to dress in a way that seems distasteful and yet are seemingly more accepted by society than a woman dressed in a *burqa* or *niqab*.

In July 2010, the then Environment Secretary, Caroline Spelman, shared her views on the *burqa* in an interview, stating that 'for a woman it is empowering to be able to choose each morning when you wake up what you wear'.[44] Her support for the *burqa* and the use of the word 'empowering' in relation to it made national headlines.[45] Mac's 'Doris, love. How would you like to feel empowered?' (20 July 2010, *Daily Mail*) (5.9)[46] depicts a Caucasian couple where the husband poses the question to his wife. In her survey of the perception of veiled women, Sonya Fernandez argues that the dichotomous presentation of the West vs Islam leads to a

> focus on gender issues such as veiling, honour killing and forced marriage [which act] as the perfect prop for justifying the forceful imposition of western values on the cultural Other, by pointing to the oppression of women in Other cultures while simultaneously ignoring the oppression of women within the dominant culture.[47]

The scene presented to the reader lends credence to this argument: the husband sits at the kitchen table, reading a newspaper headlined 'BURKAS EMPOWER WOMEN SAYS MINISTER', whilst his wife Doris carries a tray with two mugs over to a sink full of dirty crockery. There is an irony of the situation presented: Doris fulfils the role of a wife who is figuratively tied to the kitchen sink and yet, is unveiled. By posing the question to Doris, perhaps the husband wishes to trick her into further disempowerment by making her wear the *burqa* and ensuring her subservience to him.

Further still, despite it not being incumbent in Islam to veil in the presence of one's husband (as well as certain other male family members), the fact that Doris' husband wishes his wife to do so indicates that perhaps he does not find her physically attractive and wishes to remedy this by getting her to wear the *burqa*, thus echoing the sentiments in 5.2. By regarding the *burqa* as a way of empowering women (as the cartoon suggests she does), Spelman disregards the underlying issues of gender inequality the *burqa* represents. Image 5.9 raises further questions about the different ways gender inequality exists and the focus on particular cultures in relation to this issue. The cartoons perpetuate the idea that such inequalities are almost exclusive to Muslims in Britain, ignoring the fact that gender inequalities exist amongst non-Muslims too.

Matt's 'And don't be late tomorrow, it's the school photo ...' (*Daily Telegraph*, 17 September 2013) (5.10)[48] responds to Birmingham Metropolitan College lifting its eight-year ban on face veils following a petition instigated by a complaint from a prospective student.[49] The cartoon shows a male teacher instructing his students – all of whom wear the *niqab* – to ensure they arrive in time for the school photo tomorrow. Images 5.6 and 5.10 deride both the ban in France and the school removing the ban on face veils. The two conflicting messages in the cartoons demonstrate the complexity of the issue and its divisiveness.

Published two years after the ban in France, Image 5.10 seems to view the issue of veiling from a different angle. The reader is presented with an image of an all-female, all Muslim class who are incidentally taught by a Caucasian male. The juxtaposition of a *niqab*-wearing *Muslimah* being willingly educated in a Western educational establishment deftly illustrates the British approach of 'tolerance' towards such issues, where apparent contradictions and conflicts between different cultures are absorbed. This is reflected in the ambivalence in this cartoon that is not found in image 5.6. For example, image 5.10 demonstrates the apparent ease of the interaction between the teacher and the veiled students. Importantly, the act of veiling does not pose any barriers to the students' education, nor to the teacher being able to perform his job properly. Therefore, the fact that their faces cannot be fully seen does not mean that the girls do not wish to partake fully in society, nor do they believe the veil stops them from doing so.

Whilst images 5.1 and 5.2 focus on the way the face veil can be a tool for disempowerment and to cloak one's looks, Image 5.10 demonstrates that this is not necessarily true. By educating themselves, the schoolgirls are becoming empowered, where the issue of physical beauty is not something that they are concerned with. At the same time, the cartoon seems to echo fears that by lifting the ban on face veils, it gives way to an interpretation of Islam that does not accept diversity and seemingly encourages gender inequality. This is symbolized in the image of very young Muslim girls (the text 'CLASS 8C' on the noticeboard in the background indicates that these girls are twelve to thirteen years of age) who seemingly accept this inequality by choosing to wear the *niqab*.

According to Nasar Meer and Tehseen Noorani, this is in contrast to the legal system which takes a rigid view of Jews qua 'racial' minority and Muslims qua 'religious' minority. As a result, it is more likely that 'common beliefs and underlying value systems' are more apparent when analysing the media. As Meer and Noorani explain:

> if one was to consider the dynamics of media discourse as being more epiphenomenal with respect to wider societal concerns, analysis would still

reveal views held, even if these are not in and of themselves efficacious (and pernicious). [... There is ...] a conflation between fact and fiction when there is a reliance 'on the unchallenged reproduction of anecdotal facts usually taken from newspapers'.[50]

Therefore, both the positive and negative messages in 5.10 may be explained because of a more fluid approach to the representation of different minorities in the media. Thus, the image challenges the reader to make up her own mind as to what allowing the face veil in the classroom means in relation to British society: is it a question of religious freedom or is this a sign that Islam and British identity are incompatible?

The *burqa/niqab* as disguise

Aside from the gender equality issue, another trend emerges of presenting the face veil as a tool for deception. Peter Brookes' 'Silly Burka ... ' (*The Times*, 5 November 2013) (5.11)[51] consists of three frames of the same woman wearing a blue *burqa*. The cloaked woman has a red ministerial box, indicating her prominent position in government. In the final scene, the red box is lifted to reveal the minister's leopard skin heels. The minister depicted is Theresa May, the then Home Office minister, who is well-known for her leopard skin heels and whose remit included anti-terror legislation. May was criticized when terror suspect, Mohammed Ahmed Mohamed, managed to escape wearing a *burqa* despite strict restrictions placed on him known as a terrorism prevention and investigation measure.[52] The caption suggests May's frustration and embarrassment at the situation. The image suggests a shirking of ministerial responsibility but also a sense of naivety; May attempts to replicate the apparent ease with which Mohamed was able to escape the authorities by wearing a *burqa* to avoid having to confront the issue in her capacity as Home Office minister. However, her striking heels and red box give her away.

Commenting on the same topic, Matt's 'Wait till I catch that cat ... ' (8 November 2013, *Daily Telegraph*) (5.12)[53] shows a cat (distinguishable by its tail) in plain view, wearing a *niqab*. However, the cat's owner seems not to see it as he complains about the damage done to his armchair by his pet. Both images reflect incredulity at the way Mohamed was able to evade the authorities. Image 5.11 takes a more nuanced political view, whilst in 5.12 Matt focuses on the simplicity of Mohamed's escape. Following the fall of Tripoli into rebel hands, Matt's uncaptioned image (*Daily Telegraph*, 30 August 2011) (5.13)[54] shows a woman wearing a *niqab* and sunglasses and is decorated in military medals and epaulettes. The woman walks past a sign: 'SEARCH FOR GADDAFI', the implication being that 'she' is actually Colonel Muammar Gaddafi, the former Libyan dictator, evading capture by donning the *niqab*. Illustrating a sense of mistrust and suspicion towards the face veil, cartoons 5.11, 5.12 and 5.13 present the *burqa* and *niqab* as a form of disguise, where the cat, May and Gaddafi seek to evade culpability for their actions by (ab)using the Islamic veil.

Such sentiments are echoed in Brighty's 'Nothing to hide' (*Sun*, 16 September 2013) (5.14),[55] published in response to a court trial during which a *Muslimah* argued against having to take the face veil off when giving evidence.[56] The cartoon visualizes the defendant in *niqab* in the witness box; the angle from which the reader sees the *Muslimah* makes her tower over the reader in an almost intimidating manner. This, along with the simple statement coming from the *Muslimah* that she has 'Nothing to hide', convey to the reader the very opposite – this particular *Muslimah* does in fact have something to hide – and it is not just her face. In much the same way as images 5.11, 5.12 and 5.13, the face veil acts as a tool for deception and evasion in 5.14.

The portrayal of the veiled *Muslimah* is often an unnamed, unidentifiable individual as can be seen in images 5.5, 5.6, 5.7, 5.10 and 5.14. Within this, a process of disembodiment and dehumanization occurs when it comes to the 'typical' *Muslimah* which serves to both emphasize the *burqa/niqab* as a tool for oppression, but also disassociating the reader from the object, turning the *Muslimah* into an Other. In this way, the *burqa/niqab* function in much the same way as the mask in relation to the Irish terrorist and the Daesh fighter. This is in stark contrast to May and Gaddafi, two political figures, who are given the 'privilege' of being instantly recognizable in the cartoons, despite their attempts at going undercover. This seems to contradict the idea that the *burqa/niqab* is a tool for suppressing one's individuality; rather, this suggests that the *burqa/niqab* is unsuccessful in doing so because there are other ways of expressing one's self – be it high heels or epaulettes.

On the other hand, perhaps this signifies how the *burqa/niqab* should be seen as one of the myriad ways women choose to *clothe* themselves (as opposed to veiling themselves in a way that is disconnected to any other garments that they choose to wear with or without it). Brian Klug's theory of the 'new antisemitism' posits the idea that it is 'an *a priori* prejudice that revolves around a fiction, a figment of what Jews are like.'[57] In other words, it is a predisposed perception of Jews that *then* seeks substantiation with the wider world. Drawing from this, Modood and Meer argue that the same occurs with the Muslim community today. If views presented in political cartoons are symptomatic of a wider assumed consensus, as I assert they are, it follows on that this informs the reader of pre-existing stereotypes and views which are then built upon in these images. From the cartoons looked at here, there is an assumption that the very act of veiling is borne out of a desire to prevent the *Muslimah* from being able to participate fully in British society by causing her to be unseen or unheard in a somewhat similar way women were treated under Taliban rule in Afghanistan.

The idea of subversion is apparent in Christian Adams' 'Trojan horse in niqab' (*Daily Telegraph*, 4 May 2014) (5.15; Figure 13).[58] The cartoon shows a wooden horse, cloaked in a black and purple *niqab*, entering the 'SCHOOL' gates. Adams' cartoon refers to the alleged 'Operation Trojan Horse' plot by Muslim groups in Birmingham attempting to pursue a Muslim agenda within a number of schools through governing on school boards.[59] The cartoon follows the inspection of twenty-one schools in the city by Ofsted to investigate the claims.[60] What is remarkable is that the horse is cloaked in such a manner, denoting 'Muslim'. By visualizing the very name of the alleged plot and situating the Trojan horse outside school gates, Adams' cartoon contains strong allusions to the legend of how the Greeks managed to enter Troy. From the cartoon, the reader understands that something very similar is happening here: a battle between two sides, where the Muslims as 'the enemy within' use subterfuge as a way to achieve their goals. By depicting the horse in such attire, Adams gives the reader a sense of what these goals are, such as imposing rules on the veiling of women.

Furthermore, the veiling of the horse ironically gives itself away, rather than disguising it. Through presenting the situation as a battle, it suggests an 'us' versus 'them' mentality, where the veiled Trojan horse symbolizes something alien and an enemy to combat. This is all the more pertinent when remembering that the original story of the Trojan horse was used to win a foreign invasion by the Achaeans against the city of Troy. Commenting on the same issue, the next image is by Nicholas Newman who has been at the *Sunday Times* since 1989 and has also appeared in *Punch* and the *Spectator*. 'Oh no! A Trojan Horse School!' (*Sunday Times*, 27 July 2014) (5.16)[61] comments on the same issue, depicting goldfish cloaked in the *niqab* and donning the *topi* (round cap often worn by Muslim men) and beard, encountering non-Muslim goldfish wearing nothing. Whilst one of the dismayed non-Muslim goldfish exclaims the words in the caption, the (male) Muslim goldfish are angered at what they see. Although 5.16 takes a more humorous approach to the subject in contrast to 5.15, Image 5.16 makes reference to the *niqab* (as well as the *topi* and beard) as denoting 'Muslim'.

Figure 13 Christian Adams, 'Trojan horse in niqab' (*Daily Telegraph*, 4 May 2014). © Christian Adams Telegraph Media Group Limited 2014.

Whose values?

The *Charlie Hebdo* shooting which took place in Paris on 7 January 2015 was carried out by the Yemeni branch of Al Qaeda (Al Qaeda in the Arabian Peninsula – AQAP), in which twelve people died. AQAP claimed that the motive behind the attack was because of the publication of satirical cartoons of the Prophet by the *Charlie Hebdo* newspaper.[62] In response to the attack, the hashtag 'Je suis Charlie' was used in social media to demonstrate solidarity with the victims. Peter Brookes' 'New UK Poll … ' (*The Times*, 26 February 2015) (5.17; Figure 14)[63] depicts a *Muslimah* in a *niqab*, walking along a street carrying a handbag in one hand and a Tesco carrier bag in the other. Crucially, she wears a white vest over her *abaya* which reads 'JE SUIS 75 per cent CHARLIE'. The statement refers to the results of a survey for BBC Radio 4 Today of 1,000 Muslims in Britain, in which 27 per cent agreed with the statement: 'I have some sympathy for the motives behind the attacks on Charlie Hebdo in Paris'.[64]

Brookes picks up on the significant number of Muslims who sympathized with the attack, demonstrating how the *Muslimah* in a *burqa/niqab* is often used to symbolize the entire British Muslim community. This image also demonstrates

Figure 14 Peter Brookes, 'New UK Poll…' (*The Times*, 26 February 2015). Copyright The Times/News Licensing.

how there is an expectation of British Muslims by the wider British public to speak out against attacks that are carried out by other Muslims around the world. Despite the fact that the overwhelming majority of those polled (62 per cent) said they disagreed with the statement, Brookes' cartoon draws attention to the minority who did agree (8 per cent answered 'don't know' and 2 per cent 'refused').[65] The act of veiling serves to unmask what the person *really* thinks; by wearing the *burqa* underneath the vest it undermines the poll results. The insinuation being that one who dresses in such a manner cannot possibly be part of the 75 per cent, thereby rendering the poll results invalid. In many ways, the image conveys a sense of incredulity that there exists diversity of thought and opinion within the British Muslim community, especially in relation to this particular topic. This suggests that were the same poll to be conducted with non-Muslims, there would undoubtedly be unanimous disagreement with such a statement.

The final image I look at is Ben Jennings' 'This is what I'm talking about people! The "Burka" is an affront to our Christian values!' (*i News*, 29 April 2017) (5.18).[66] Image 5.18 is the first of three Jennings images examined here. Images 5.18, 6.27 and 6.32 are taken from *i News*, where Jennings was one of two winners of 'Cartoon Idol' – a competition run by the paper in 2011.[67] Jennings has also contributed to the *Guardian, Independent* and the *Economist*. Image 5.18 comments on Ukip's proposals to ban the face veil as part of their 2015 general election campaign.[68] In the first frame, the party leader, Paul Nuttall, points to the backs of two women cloaked in black as they walk along the street and exclaims the words in the caption. The second frame then shows the two women turn around, one of whom asks Nuttall, 'What's that, luv?'. Their garments and the large crucifixes hanging from both their necks give away the fact that they are indeed nuns and not Muslim women, illustrating the irony of Nuttall's statement. Much like the debate that was sparked in Britain by the French face veil ban, Ukip's policy proposal prompted people to ask what such a ban would mean in Britain. For example, the party was asked at a press conference whether such a ban would apply to beekeepers.[69] The cartoon shows how the act of veiling is not unique to the Muslim religion, and yet it is synonymous with Islam. Therefore, the mistake that Nuttall makes in the image is one that many members of the British public would also be likely to make.

Furthermore, image 5.18 highlights how one can be considered 'more British' by virtue of being a Christian through the depiction of two Catholic nuns – one of whom is Caucasian and the other African-Caribbean. Salam Al-Mahadin compares the different reactions necessitated by the *hijab* and the nun's habit in which the *hijab* symbolizes that which is hidden and inaccessible to the gaze, thereby causing the subject anxiety. On the other hand, the 'nun's habit does not arouse the same kind of anxiety because it has one meaning: I am the bride of Christ'.[70] Applying this to image 5.18, the implication is that by being a Christian nun, one has *chosen* to veil in such a manner for obvious reasons, thereby affording nuns a permissibility to dress as such and to be honoured for doing so. In contrast, the *Muslimah* does not choose to wear the *burqa/niqab* (and if she does, it is because she is oppressed and in need of saving such as in 5.5) and therefore, should not be allowed nor respected for wearing such attire. Consequently, in the first frame Nuttall is enraged by the image of what he thinks are two veiled Muslim women walking down the street because he does not believe that veiling is compatible with 'Christian values'. When confronted by the confused nuns, he is rendered speechless in the second frame.

Gender

The focus on Muslim women contrasts starkly to that of the portrayal of Jewish, Sikh and Irish women in cartoons, demonstrating the strength of feeling and debate surrounding the female Muslim community. Moreover, not all the eighteen cartoons examined in this chapter feature women.[71] There are four (22 per cent) cartoons which are women-only and eleven (61 per cent) women-mixed. Of the images featuring women, six of them feature non-Muslim women only, in contrast to the seven that are identifiably Muslim. Furthermore, there were two (9 per cent) cartoons where the gender was none/not clear and one (5 per cent) men-only. These include the cat in image 5.12, the wooden horse in 5.15 and Colonel Gaddafi in disguise in 5.13. The dominance of men is surprising, given the subject matter. Conversely, the fact that the dominance of men in cartoons is applicable across all the communities studied here perhaps makes the absence of women more consistent with how cartoonists tend to portray them.

It can be argued that the cartoons which do not feature women do not comment on women's inequality, but on the use of the *burqa/niqab* as a tool for deception and subversion. However, I reject this argument on the basis that the *burqa/niqab* are inextricably linked to the *Muslimah*'s body – so much so that the depiction of the *Muslimah* is not always necessary as demonstrated by such images – and is therefore a comment on gender. This shows how the female image is made so dependent on the image of the male. Commenting on the *Muslimah*, whilst precluding her from cartoons, raises questions of the cartoonists themselves. Inequality and women's rights are major themes of many of the cartoons (5.3, 5.5 and 5.7) and yet, the portrayal of the *Muslimah* is so unequal. This makes the reader dubious as to whether the cartoonists – who are all male – are qualified to raise such pressing questions.

Conclusion

My examination of the portrayal of Muslim women sheds light on the way different communities are made into an Other by using specific tropes as markers of difference in order to define what fits the definition of 'British' and what falls outside of it. Indeed, as we saw with the question of banning the face veil in Britain, the rebuttal to this was the fact that such a move fell outside the concept of what it means to be 'British', bound up in ideas of tolerance. My analysis of the cartoons above exposes the idea that through veiling herself, the *Muslimah* takes a visible stand by refusing to integrate and accept British values. Thus, the religious element of wearing the *burqa* is ignored and belittled and is only seen as 'a self-conscious public statement'.[72] As Fernandez states:

The gradual mutation of the veil from a symbol of religious identity to a contentious marker of difference paves the way for further contamination of the hijab as a sign of inequality, hostility to a democratic society, fundamentalism, as well as the blurred line between Islam and terror, breathing life into the savages-victims-saviours construct.[73]

The use of the term 'mutation' by Fernandez denotes how the veil has undergone a transformation into a symbol that imputes negative messages, where the Muslim faith is equated with ideas of danger and fear. More specifically, I argue that this is less true of the *hijab* within the context of British political cartoons post-9/11. Rather, it is the *burqa/niqab* that leads to issues of contention, indicating an acceptance of the act of veiling of women in British society, so long as the face is not covered. This serves to highlight the extent to which the British public wish to tolerate diversity. The resistance to accept the *burqa/niqab* may be partly explained by how it is frequently identified with the Taliban regime that governed Afghanistan from 1996 to 2001 (such as in images 5.1, 5.2 and 5.4), and is therefore seen as a foreign, cultural practice imposed on women. This has had a huge impact on how the *burqa* and *niqab* are used to highlight gender inequality and the oppression of women even after the collapse of the regime, such as in images 5.2 and 5.9.

In this way, Islam is conflated as a system of political ideals, with the veil serving as evidence. By framing the veil in this manner, it links Islam and Muslims to deception, subversion and resistance through portrayals of the *burqa/niqab*. This view of the veil converges with the way Puar argues the turban is viewed where '[i]t is fear then, as it materializes the turban, rather than the turban itself [...] these boundaries do not exist that then produce fear, but rather that fear produces these boundaries.'[74] This follows Klug's theory that if 'antisemitism is the process of turning Jews into "Jews" then Islamophobia is the process of turning Muslims into "Muslims."'[75] I contend that the way the turban is identified as an object of fear in America today, as Puar demonstrates, is less true in Britain, where the *burqa/niqab* is a symbol of Otherness and danger.

This is because, as Meyda Yegenoglu argues, the process of unveiling is connected to ideas of truth in which vision is 'the central instrument'.[76] Therefore, unveiling the *Muslimah* is to uncover truth because by covering one's face, it becomes an obstacle to comprehension. This can be seen most prominently in image 5.14 which creates a sense of mistrust towards the woman in the witness box wearing a *niqab*. The image implies that were the woman to take her face veil off, the reader (and the courtroom) would be able to trust her more easily precisely because her face is key in understanding and accessing the truth. This helps to explain why there is little or no resistance to the *hijab*, whilst the *burqa* and *niqab* are the cause of such contention.

In August 2018, the ex-Cabinet Minister and future Prime Minister Boris Johnson weighed into the debate by stating his opposition to a ban on the face veil. However, his comments caused controversy because he likened those who wore the face veil to bank robbers and letter boxes. Most interestingly, he stated that:

> If a constituent came to my MP's surgery with her face obscured, I should feel fully entitled [...] to ask her to remove it so that I could talk to her properly. If a female student turned up at school or at a university lecture looking like a bank robber then ditto: those in authority should be allowed to converse openly with those that they are being asked to instruct.[77]

Such sentiments indicate how important it has become for many members of the British public to be able to see someone's face in order to feel as though they are communicating with them fully. At the same time, Johnson's resistance to the idea of a ban on face veils because of the implications of 'telling a free-born adult woman what she may or may not wear, in a public place, when she is simply minding her own business'[78] demonstrates the difficulty of the situation in a liberal Western society.

Modood argues that rather than only looking to government policy and the law, a wider understanding of 'the political' is needed. In this way, cartoons are an important manifestation of contemporary understandings of ideas relating to national identity and 'the public imagining of groups *qua* groups'.[79] In the same way that the representation of Sikhs served to perpetuate negative attitudes towards the community from the 1960s to the 1980s, the cartoons looked at above are more recent examples of the same occurring today, with the difference being that they relate to Muslims. This is not only because the cartoons reflect contemporary concerns of terrorism originating from the Muslim community, but it also demonstrates the ease with which iconography of the *burqa/niqab* explicitly links Islam to such negative attitudes because it is synonymous with Muslims. Consequently, there is a binary where to be 'more Muslim' is to be more anti-Western.

Bhikhu Parekh points out that Muslims in Europe have multi-faceted identities (like anyone else), where gender and citizenship are just two examples of the many different composites. Thus, the term 'British Muslim' can mean a number of things – including denoting those who reside in the country without any patriotic sentiment – to those who do have a sense of patriotism and further still, 'Britishized Muslims', who consider Britain their home as well as being influenced by British values and culture. Parekh emphasizes the importance of the Muslim describing one's identity along with words denoting their citizenship or country of residence vis-à-vis those who simply describe themselves as Muslim. This is because of the latter's desire to homogenize Muslims and 'mould them in their image of "true" Islam'. The danger is such that '[w]hen we refer to individuals and groups as Muslims *sans phrase*, we wittingly or unwittingly strip away or marginalize their other identities and walk into the Islamist trap.'[80]

I find this marginalization occurring within the cartoons, where a particular ideology of Islam is presented as dominant and overarching, thereby muting the different discourses within the Muslim religion. Parallels can be drawn between the way orthodox Sikhism is presented as an accurate portrayal of the faith in cartoons examined in the previous chapter, and the way Saudi inspired Wahhabi Islam is presented in the cartoons looked at here. Consequently, the cartoons perpetuate the image of the *Muslimah* as veiled, hidden and disembodied as typical, ignoring (on a superficial level) the different styles of veiling observed amongst the *Muslimah* population. On a deeper level, such illustrations of the typical *Muslimah* reflect the perception of Islam as monolithic in terms of its theology and adherents. By presenting the *Muslimah* in such a manner she is shown to be blind to her own situation of being oppressed – whilst the wider British public are immediately able to perceive and understand her situation from her attire. The cartoons attempt to demonstrate the futility of the *burqa/niqab* as a way to protect the *Muslimah*'s modesty precisely because it attracts so much attention in a society which seemingly demands a woman *not* to cover in order to not be seen.

Michel Foucault, using Jeremy Bentham's idea of the Panopticon, argued that the power of seeing and being seen was a relationship of power in which a person finds themselves defined by the power of the gazer. Foucault argued that by permitting a permanent surveillance, the Panopticon trapped its inmates through their visibility to the supervisor in the central tower – who the inmates themselves cannot see – thus making power 'visible and unverifiable'.[81] Yegenoglu applies this to the fixation to unveil the *Muslimah* under colonial rule:

> In the light of this Foucauldian insight, the political rationality that shaped the logic behind the colonial feminist project's concern with the unveiling of women can best be made sense of if we can locate it within the context of principles of modern disciplinary power which is concerned with actively shaping individual minds and bodies based on the knowledge acquired by rendering them perfectly visible.[82]

This helps us to understand why the *Muslimah*'s body is fixated upon in a postcolonial world because, as Al-Mahadin puts it, 'it is the western gaze that is being repressed by the hijab, not the woman wearing it.'[83] Without making her visible to the subject's gaze, the veiled *Muslimah* 'is both an object of hostility and an object of fascination and these are expressed as a continual quest for knowledge'.[84] In this way, the feminine body that is not veiled is presented as the norm, whilst the veiled female body represents an oppressed and subjugated woman who embodies all that is wrong with Islam. Thus, Yegenoglu argues, by unveiling the *Muslimah* it signifies modernization and the transformation of the Orient.[85]

An interesting example of the power of the gaze can be found in Gili Hammer's study of blind women in which one of her study participants, Talia, experiences being both visible and invisible. Talia's (in)visibility is predicated on her identity as (i) a woman and (ii) being blind. In one scenario, Talia's cousin (who is sighted) 'attracts the gaze, an observation and appreciation of her body as human and sexual, Talia experiences staring, an assessment of her body as asexual and medically different. While the gaze sexualizes, staring dehumanizes'. However, Talia, as a woman, also experiences the gaze in which her blindness 'intensifies her visibility, placing her under the dominant male gaze'.[86]

Applying these concepts to the *Muslimah*, the *burqa* and *niqab* serve to avoid the gaze so that she is not sexualized. Thus, precisely because of her choice to avoid the gaze by choosing to veil in such a manner, the *Muslimah* attracts both staring and the gaze: she is at once invisible and asexual and yet her garments set her apart from most other members of the British public, identifying her to the gazer as a Muslim woman who must be unveiled. Consequently, this has led to the idea of the *burqa/niqab* as a garment that is imposed on all Muslim women, making them visibly invisible.

5

Beards, bombs and barbarians: Muslim men in political cartoons

Introduction

In a review of publications on Islamophobia, Brian Klug observes how the 'connection between word and image is hammered home day after day in media representations that blend fearful depictions of one-eyed hook-handed imams and bearded hate-filled terrorists'.[1] The Islam which these characters espouse is inherently in conflict with the values of its enemy – 'the West', where contemporary political cartoons present Muslim men as objects of distrust, bound up in their regressive cultural beliefs.

In this chapter, I look at the portrayal of Muslim men in which I find that often ethnicity features as a key trope in many of the cartoons. In such cases, there is a conflation of religion and ethnicity, where both Islam and different racial identities are homogenized, thus purportedly explaining the causes behind a lack of patriotism or committing acts of terrorism. Much like the Muslim 'sans phrase' which I look at in relation to Muslim women, the same can be said of how Muslim men are portrayed; the different discourses within Islam are ignored, giving the impression of an overarching Islamist ideology which begets suspicion for the non-Muslim of the Muslim.

In the immediate aftermath of the 9/11 attacks in 2001, Osama Bin Laden, dressed in traditional Afghan fashion in a white turban and a *perahan tunban*, became the archetypal image of the terrorist. Even when Bin Laden was not the primary subject, terrorists were depicted wearing similar garb and often possessing similar facial features. However, as the 'War on Terror' has evolved and changed following the '7/7' bombings in London, events in Syria and the formation of Daesh (otherwise known as Islamic State of Iraq and Syria), so too has the image of Muslim men.

A huge part of this change is due to the way the terrorists present themselves. For example, Osama Bin Laden desired to be the public face of Al Qaeda, willingly allowing video footage of himself. This has meant that in the years following the attacks of 9/11 and 7/7, the Other was easy to identify and portray as the immigrant Muslim male living in Britain or political figures such as Osama Bin Laden, as the figurehead of Al Qaeda. In contrast, Daesh videos feature graphic images of beheadings carried out by men such as 'Jihadi John' speaking in an Estuary English accent, clad in a black balaclava. Despite the change in iconography to reflect the rapid changes, I argue that the masked man in black is a sharpening and a confirmation of what the immigrant male in ethnic garb represents: the idea of what I call the 'Muslim Barbaric'.

The media-generated Muslim

The ethnic and racial makeup of the Muslim community in Britain is diverse and varied, with an overwhelming 'Asian' majority of 68 and 32 per cent 'non-Asian', as found in the 2011 Census, with 8 per cent (one in twelve Muslims) as 'White'.[2] 'Pakistani' and 'Bangladeshi' constitute the two single biggest ethnic groups of Muslims in Britain at 38 per cent and 14.9 per cent, respectively.[3] Due to the predominance of Muslims of South Asian ethnicity, the cartoons viewed below demonstrate the perception of Muslim men in Britain coming from a specific cultural background. This is evidenced through attire – most often the *salwar kameez* (loose trousers and shirt) – worn by men and women on the Asian continent, as well as the *topi* (round cap often worn by Muslim men).

These are used as visual markers of difference in much the same way as the *burqa/niqab* for women. However, the *burqa/niqab* is a *religious* trope, specifically connected to Islam in that non-Muslim women do not wear the *burqa/niqab*, whereas the *salwar kameez* is not specific to one religion (in that non-Muslims also wear it) and so is more connected to ethnicity. Consequently, the image of the Muslim male in *salwar kameez* is a useful iconographic shorthand that is not only a comment on religion, but also on a perceived monolithic and transnational Asian culture.

Whilst newspaper editorials and articles purport to tell the reader what a Muslim is *like*, cartoons illustrate to the reader what a Muslim *looks* like; both the imagery and the writing work symbiotically.[4] As Halim Rane et al. argue, there is 'an almost universal awareness of the religion and its adherents [...]. What it does mean is that a media version of Islam is widely known; what we are familiar with are media-generated Muslims.'⁵ Thus, though there is widespread acknowledgment of Islam as a religio-political force, a nuanced understanding of the religion is rare and indeed obscured by this media prevalence. The ubiquity of the *burqa/niqab* in the cartoons examined in the previous chapter demonstrates one facet of a nuanced understanding of the *Muslimah*; the *burqa/niqab* is *the* symbol of the woman's refusal to integrate into British society.

However, with regard to the depiction of the Muslim male, the iconography is much more varied, where the 'media-generated' Muslim male has developed over time as the terror threat has changed. The Muslim male is portrayed as a figure to be both reviled and feared because he is shown as an active agent of terror. An important part of the development of the way the Muslim male is depicted is due to the high profile of key figures such as Osama Bin Laden and Saddam Hussein who were seen as the embodiment of evil. In contrast, there is no single identifiable *Muslimah* who has achieved such status.[6] Bin Laden was the face of Al Qaeda, and although Abu Bakr al-Baghdadi was well known as the leader of Daesh (until his death in 2019),[7] he was not *visually* identified with the state. The apparent refusal to be filmed and the lack of authenticated photographs of al-Baghdadi indicate that he did not wish to be identified in such a way.[8] Instead, there is no single identifiable person who is attached to the state. Rather, members acting from within the state opt to cover their faces with balaclavas, becoming a visual trope synonymous with Daesh.

The 9/11 attacks

Cartoons published immediately after the 9/11 attacks in British newspapers convey a sense of solidarity with America, featuring Uncle Sam or the Statue of Liberty. Peter Schrank's uncaptioned cartoon (*Independent*, 12 September 2001) (6.1)[9] features the Statue of Liberty weeping at the sight of the devastation. Steve Bell's '1638-12-9-01_WORLDTRADEBURN' (*Guardian*, 12 September 2001) (6.2)[10] features the American flag in the guise of the Twin Towers billowing in smoke. However, Peter Brookes' uncaptioned image (*The Times*, 12 September 2001) (6.3)[11] takes a different approach to the issue. Published the day after the 9/11 attacks, Brookes depicts Saddam Hussein, Muammar Gaddafi, Yasser Arafat, Ayatollah Khomeini and Osama Bin Laden laughing above a line of skyscrapers. The image clearly places the blame of the 9/11 attacks with these men and reflects the anger the British public felt towards them in the aftermath of the tragedy.

Immediately following the attacks, there was widespread speculation that Bin Laden was behind them (he finally admitted Al Qaeda's involvement in 2004).[12]

In her research of the coverage of British Muslims in the *Guardian* and *The Times* after the 9/11 attacks, Elizabeth Poole makes the important point that the attacks brought Islam to the forefront with 'an uncomfortable familiarity. Islam is suddenly "recognizable" but it is the form in which Islam is known that is of concern'.[13] What is concerning about image 6.3 is how it portrays Islam 'recognizably' in a negative manner, pitting the West against its nemeses. This is despite the fact that Hussein, Gaddafi, Arafat and Khomeini never accepted responsibility for the attacks (indeed Khomeini died in 1989!) and that they come from very different political and sectarian backgrounds. The diversity of the figures portrayed indicates a 'clash' between Islam and the West, painting a portrait of the different countries as a homogenous group.

Following the Iran hostage crisis from 1979 to 1981, Edward Said pointed out that:

> it is always the West and not Christianity, that seems pitted against Islam. Why? Because the assumption is that whereas 'the West' is greater than and has surpassed the stage of Christianity, its principal religion, the world of Islam – its varied societies, histories, and languages notwithstanding – is still mired in religion, primitivity, and backwardness.[14]

In this way, all the countries represented – from Iran through to Palestine – are equally 'recognizable' as corrupt, evil and regressive as one another. By exposing who is considered the Other, it exposes the understanding of the Self (in this case the West) which is free of corruption, good and progressive.

However, image 6.3 places political and religious opponents alongside one another. The Shi'a Supreme Leader of Iran, Ayatollah Khamenei, is portrayed as being in league with the other figures in the image – such as Saddam Hussein – who had invaded Iran in 1988. The inclusion of Khomeini is more to do with how the Ayatollah is synonymous with Iran, demonstrating that rather than being concerned with accuracy, Brookes is making a wider point about Muslim countries based on the assumption that though they may not have had a direct hand in the attacks, neither are they unsympathetic towards whoever carried them out. It also suggests that the readership would fail to recognize the depiction of the then (and still current) Supreme Leader of Iran, Ali Khamenei, who took office after the death of Ayatollah Khomeini in 1989.

Thus, Said's point above on how 'the West' is pitted against Islam, shows the elision of the differences and complexities within Islam but also what is considered as 'the West'. Although labels such as 'the West' or 'Islam' are often used to describe things that are much more complex than these labels allow, Said argues that the sheer prevalence of such terms means that one must take them seriously.[15]

In the cartoons examined below, there is a clear context of 'us' versus 'them'. Taking Said's point into consideration, I apply the label of 'the West' to those considered to fall under 'us' and Muslims to fall under 'them'.

Mac's 'Parasite: (Chambers English Dictionary) a creature which obtains food and physical protection from a host which never benefits from its presence' (*Daily Mail*, 20 September 2001) (6.4)[16] was published a few weeks after the 9/11 attacks. Situated outside the Houses of Parliament, in the foreground a bearded, turbaned man holds a placard in one hand which reads 'DEATH TO AMERICA AND BRITAIN!' and the other hand clenched in a fist. His face is distorted in anger. There are no other visible faces, except hands holding up placards stating, 'WE SUPPORT BIN LADEN' and another with a chilling (and almost prescient) message: 'WARNING WHITEHALL AND DOWNING ST ARE LEGITIMATE TARGETS'. Much like images 4.6 and 4.10, the Palace of Westminster is used to symbolize democracy where it is literally depicted as the battleground between democracy and autocracy. The image of the angry, bearded man relates back to Zebiri's point, mentioned in the previous chapter, about the perception of the Muslim community in the wake of the Rushdie affair. The attire of the man suggests that he is possibly from Afghanistan – where they traditionally wear a *perahan tunban* often with a waistcoat.

Having been published in a context where Parliament was discussing what punitive measures should be taken against Bin Laden, as well as the Afghan Taliban because of its complicity in the 9/11 terror attacks, the image delegitimizes any opposition to war (which began on 7 October 2001). By contrasting the angry (foreign) protestors on the streets to the MPs partaking in a rational and level-headed debate within the Commons, Mac implicitly bestows legitimacy on Parliament to decide how to react to the 9/11 terror attacks. Image 6.4 conflates the idea that opposition to a war in Afghanistan must mean an (irrational) opposition to democracy and support for Bin Laden, thereby ignoring the valid fears of the cost of war on innocent civilians.

Indeed, this echoes the sentiments in image 5.3, where the outcome of the war was shown to far outweigh the impact it had on civilian life in Afghanistan. In her analysis of US media coverage of eleven terrorist events between October 2001 and January 2010, Kimberley A. Powell argues that the relationship between terrorism and the media is crucial because the '[m]aximum impact of an act of terrorism comes from widespread media coverage'.[17] It is how such acts are covered and portrayed in the media that heavily shapes and influences public opinion. In this way, both images 6.3 and 6.4 demonstrate an alignment of two national newspapers with the political will at the time, thereby legitimizing the 'War on Terror'. The War on Terror ended in August 2021, with the withdrawal of American troops from Afghanistan.[18]

However, in an effort to gain support to deal with the terror threat as he understood it, the then Prime Minister, Tony Blair, wrote an article directed at Muslims:

> The question Muslims around the world have to ask themselves is: do you want to live under the sort of regime we see today in Kabul? Because that is what Bin Laden and al-Qa'ida [sic] want for you.[19]

Nicholas Garland's uncaptioned image (*Daily Telegraph*, 16 October 2001) (6.5)[20] shows the Prime Minister in listening mode, his ear directed at the reader with the words 'British Muslims your country needs YOU'. Here, Blair is addressing *British* Muslims, depicted in the likeness of the famous 1914 Alfred Leete poster featuring Lord Kitchener during the First World War.[21]

This is important because it demonstrates how Garland seeks to both appeal to and instil a sense of patriotism in the Muslim community in Britain, in order to tackle the global terror threat. Garland's image also suggests an understanding that British Muslims were a key part of the solution in tackling terror, rather than being a part of the problem. Such messages are similar to those found in Steve Fricker's uncaptioned cartoon (*Daily Telegraph*, 17 September 2001) (6.6).[22] Published six days after the 9/11 attacks, the image focuses on American Muslims – symbolized by a young male dressed in traditional Afghan style. He stands, eyes closed with his right hand over his heart, as though listening intently to the American national anthem. The image shows how the American Muslim community's patriotism remains unwavering in the face of attacks committed by members of the same faith.

Poole talks about the process of dehumanization of tribes in Afghanistan, in stark contrast to the way victims of terror attacks are portrayed in a way to evoke feelings of sympathy and empathy from the reader in newspaper articles.[23] I argue that the same process is apparent in the images looked at here. Referring to Muslims as 'parasites', the word has strong negative connotations, chiefly connected to how a person 'lives at the expense of another, or of society in general'.[24] Such sentiments towards minority groups are not novel – the same ideas were applied to Jews by the Nazis.[25] The racial identity of the man implies that Muslims are foreign, being hosted in Britain, where they are able to live full lives to the detriment of the country in which they live. One of the troubling aspects of the caption is the perception of the Muslim community being socio-economically deprived; the implication being that Muslims in Britain take full advantage of state benefits whilst failing to contribute anything financially or otherwise to the country.

Although such a fear is not unique to Muslims and is applied to almost all immigrant groups in Britain,[26] the framing of this specific issue in such a manner vindicates Paul Gilroy's point:

> Islamophobia has increasingly shaped public debate and the figure of the traitor/terrorist has emerged to hold hands with the other well-worn iconic representations of imminent racial chaos and disorder: the street criminal, the scrounger and the illegal immigrant.[27]

Thus, by commenting on both the threat to national and economic security of the country that the Muslim community pose, we see the figure of the traitor emerge in image 6.4. In her research of the coverage of British Muslims in the *Guardian*, *The Times*, the *Observer* and *The Sunday Times* from 1994 to 2003, Poole found that prior to the 9/11 attacks, 'British Muslims were not attributed so blatantly with [terrorism]. Rather it was Muslims in Britain, exiles, who were categorised as extremists.'[28]

Mac's cartoon at 6.4 illustrates Poole's point of the perception of terrorists as immigrants who have resisted any form of integration into their host society. This relates back to the idea of transactionality which, when applied to the Muslim community, is considered to have failed. This is because the Muslim community is shown to hold onto violent and regressive ideas that are incompatible with British values. Yet, at the same time, Muslims such as those depicted in 6.4 enjoy the full benefits of living in a society that provides social welfare and free speech. This shows how the same message of Otherness, which was applied to the Sikh community, is being applied here through using different visual symbols.

The 7/7 attacks

In the immediate aftermath of the 7/7 attacks, messages of defiance and solidarity can be seen such as in David Austin's uncaptioned image (*Guardian*, 8 July 2005) (6.7)[29] and Paul Thomas' uncaptioned image (*Daily Express*, 8 July 2005) (6.8).[30] Other images placed the blame squarely with Al Qaeda, such as

Nicholas Garland's uncaptioned image (*Daily Telegraph*, 8 July 2005) (6.9)[31] and Kenneth Mahood's 'Mirror, mirror, on the wall, who is the most murderous one of all?' (*Daily Mail*, 8 July 2005) (6.10).[32] The attacks were carried out by second-generation British Muslims. The British media focused on the backgrounds of the four bombers, where all but one had been born in this country.[33] This caused widespread shock – including from the families of the bombers themselves – where affiliation to Britain was something that had been taken for granted from second-generation British Muslims.[34]

Consequently, cartoons following the 7/7 attacks take a more introspective approach to the issue of terrorism than those following the 9/11 attacks. Morten Morland's cartoon 'Mind the Gap ... ' (*The Times*, 11 July 2005) (6.11)[35] shows an Asian man in *salwar kameez* and *topi* on the Tube, being stared at and avoided by other passengers, all of whom are Caucasian. Morland seems to be criticizing the media for fear mongering and fuelling suspicion of British Muslims as demonstrated by the headlines on the newspaper exclaiming 'IT CAN HAPPEN AGAIN!' and 'BOMBERS MAY BE BRITISH BORN'. The caption is a play on words – rather than minding the gap between the train and the platform – the gap is between the Muslim man and the other passengers who are clearly shown to be very scared of him.

Whilst Morland's cartoon focuses on the knee-jerk reaction the public and the media had towards their fellow British Muslims, Nicholas Garland's 'Kicking and Screaming' (*Daily Telegraph*, 21 July 2005) (6.12)[36] shows the Government's reaction to the 7/7 attacks. The Prime Minister, Tony Blair, drags a bearded man dressed in a *thawb* (a long robe usually worn by Arab men) and *topi* who is literally kicking and screaming as the then Home Secretary, Charles Clarke, looks on. The words 'Muslim extremism' are emblazoned on the back of the Muslim man's *thawb* as Blair drags him in the direction of a signpost with the words 'Twenty-First Century'.

Following the 7/7 bombings, Blair condemned the attacks in a speech on 21 July and the overarching ideology that inspired the attackers:

> They demand the elimination of Israel; the withdrawal of all Westerners from Muslim countries [...] the establishment of effectively Taleban (sic) states and Sharia law in the Arab world en route to one caliphate of all Muslim nations. We don't have to wonder what type of country those states would be [...] Afghanistan was such a state. Girls put out of school. Women denied even rudimentary rights. People living in abject poverty and oppression. All of it justified by reference to religious faith ... Within Britain, we must join up with our Muslim community to take on the extremists.[37]

Blair's speech acknowledges that the underlying causes of terrorism are not simply a question of assimilation but also of ideology. In 6.12, Garland lends support to Blair's views of how to deal with the problem of Muslim radicalism by forcing it to come out of the (literal) fog of the past and into the present day to accept things such as democracy and equal rights for women. In this way, the image acknowledges that there are wider factors involved when looking at the causes behind terrorism; it is not simply reason enough to claim that Islam is an inherently violent religion. Rather, it is those such as the Taliban and other 'Muslim extremists' that use religion as a means to justify actions that perhaps do not correlate with Islam itself and it is these ideas that need to be tackled and dealt with.

The integration question: sufficiently British?

As examined above, the majority of the cartoons published in the immediate aftermath of the 9/11 attacks focused on the devastation caused and the sense of solidarity with the American people. However, cartoons in the days following the 7/7 attacks look more to the reasons behind why it happened. This is perhaps unsurprising since responses to an attack from the home press will be different to that from an attack that has taken place abroad. The 7/7 attacks were the first time a terrorist incident of such a nature had taken place in Britain. The cartoons following the event show how this led to questions being asked about the Muslim community in Britain and whether it was sufficiently integrated into wider British society.

Consequently, there is a belief that the Muslim male refuses to embrace his British identity and values, using his religion to hold onto outdated ideas. This is conveyed in the cartoons through facial expressions of anger and the Muslim man's choice of clothing – such as the *topi, salwar kameez* or *thawb* – thereby arousing suspicion that a Muslim man clothed as such is (more) prone to commit terrorist acts. Taking this argument further, were the Muslim male to wear more Western-style of clothing, the assumption would be that he is sufficiently integrated into British society and would not commit violent acts (we also saw how the same ideas are present in the case of the *Muslimah* in a *burqa/niqab*). What is striking about this is that despite the British background of the perpetrators of the 7/7 attacks and the fact that they were dressed in Western clothing when carrying out the bombings (as can be seen in CCTV footage of them before the attacks),[38] ethnicity is used as a conduit by which to Other them.

This may be partly because of what Powell argues that '[s]ince the 9/11 perpetrators were Arab, Muslim brown "others" became the symbol of Islam to the agenda setters in [the American] media, thus becoming representative of Islam.'[39] Applying this to the cartoons examined above following 9/11 and subsequently 7/7, the reader sees that the same is true of the British press. This demonstrates the power of the media to create and reinforce stereotypes that influence both the public *and* politicians, especially if 'the agenda is consistent among media sources [... it] has the power to create associations for people, race, culture and religion'.[40]

By robing the Muslim male in *salwar kameez* and/or *topi*, the cartoons direct criticism at both Islam and non-Western (for want of a better term) culture at having failed to keep pace with modernity. This reflects Modood's point about the Muslim immigrant having their ethnicity as their first reference point, rather than religion.[41] Thus, the identity of the Muslim male is not viewed independently to his ethnicity. Rather, the two are inextricably linked, whereby the (ethnic) Muslim male is doomed on both counts to be prone to regressive ideas. This then leads him to a segregationist way of life, set apart from his compatriots.

Post 7/7 attacks

In August 2006, arrests were made against three Britons: Abdulla Ahmed Ali, Assad Sarwar and Tanvir Hussain. The men were plotting to use liquid bombs on flights from London to the United States and Canada, disguised as soft drinks. The foiled bomb plot caused major disruptions in airports where passengers were not allowed to take on board any liquids except baby food and prescription medication. Peter Schrank's 'Back to the future' (*Independent*, 20 August 2006) (6.13; Figure 15)[42] comments on the situation, showing one door for airline passengers who are 'WHITES AND CHRISTIANS ONLY' and another door for 'MUSLIMS'. The White and Christian passengers look on at the sole Muslim passenger on the other side of the room, most of whom have an angry expression on their face. The bearded Muslim man looks annoyed, depicted wearing a *salwar kameez* and *topi*. In his hand, he carries an empty transparent bag, whilst the Whites and Christians carry fully loaded hand luggage.

Much like Morland's image at 6.11, Schrank focuses on the reaction of the wider British public in relation to another terror threat, viewing all Muslims as enemies. The caption suggests that such reactions will eventually lead to a time reminiscent of when people were discriminated against based on their race

Figure 15 Peter Schrank's 'Back to the future' (*Independent*, 20 August 2006). © Schrank, the Independent.

and religion. Such a situation, therefore, would not simply be confined to the airport, but seen in the wider world. Schrank's image challenges the assumption that it is Muslims who wish to lead a segregationist life in Britain, when in fact non-Muslims and/or Caucasians themselves desire this. Cartoons 6.11 and 6.13 pick up on the fear of the public at no longer being able to distinguish between 'them' and 'us' because of the fact that the attackers were not always foreign.[43] As Powell states:

> The evil other is no longer from the outside, but from within. Thus, the identification of the other becomes more challenged when the other is both an insider and outsider. Yet identification of Muslims with terrorism serves to keep them perpetually as the other.[44]

Nicholas Garland's 'Coming to a high street near you?' (*Daily Telegraph*, 3 July 2007) (6.14)[45] urges the Muslim community in Britain to take a public stand against terrorism. Much like the women examined in the previous chapter, the women are faceless, robed in the *niqab*, whilst the men are all dressed in *salwar kameez* with an angry expression on their bearded faces. However, in this image their anger is directed at terrorism itself as they hold placards with words such as 'SAY NO TO TERROR' and 'DROP TERROR NOT BOMBS'. The people depicted are virtual clones of one another; this is problematic in that it presents to the reader a monolithic image of the Muslim community. In one way, this could be interpreted as criticizing the unassimilated Muslim who chooses to wear the face veil or *salwar kameez*, rather than a more Western style of clothing such as jeans or a dress. However, I believe that this is more indicative of the way Garland perceives the problem of radicalism as an unresolved issue that requires dealing with by the British Muslim community itself, rather than by government.

Striking a less conciliatory tone than his uncaptioned image at 6.14, 'Coming to a high street near you?' is more direct in making the point that action is required from the Muslim community. However, in contrast to that of 'Kicking and Screaming', 'Coming to a high street near you?' implies that such a change *is* a possibility. By raising the question, the caption is asking whether Muslims in Britain are showing their solidarity with their compatriot non-Muslims and making it clear that terrorism is not aligned with the Muslim religion. Consequently, the onus is on the Muslim community to demonstrate their patriotism through loud, provocative acts such as public protests. Otherwise, there is the suggestion that those who refuse to do so are aligned with the terrorists.

There is a recognition in the Garland cartoons at 6.5, 6.12 and 6.14, that terrorism is not advocated by the religion of Islam as those such as Bin Laden and others claim (such as in 6.9), but that ordinary Muslims in Britain need to do more in order to promote this idea to the wider public. The social media trend #notinmyname being used by Muslims in condemnation to terror attacks is perhaps one such example of what Garland is encouraging in his cartoon.[46] At the same time, however, this poses problems by automatically associating Muslims with those who commit acts of terror in the name of Islam.

Thus, many of the cartoons deal with the fear the British public feel with regard to the Muslim community. Scott's uncaptioned cartoon (*Daily Star*, 24 September 2006) (6.15)[47] comments on an article published in its sister paper, the *Daily Express*, headlined 'The day an Islamic protester told the Home Secretary: How dare you come to a Muslim area?'. This was in relation to a conference in Leyton, East London, at which the then Home Secretary, John Reid, was heckled by Abu Izzadeen, a supporter of the 7/7 attacks. The cartoon features an oversized head of the '[h]ate-filled Abu Izzadeen'[48] shouting 'HOW DARE YOU COME TO A MUSLIM AREA?'. Izzadeen is surrounded by people of different ethnicities and religions laughing at him, including a Sikh man in a turban and an Irishman signified by the clover on his badge.

Scott's cartoon attempts to show a Britain in which diversity is accepted and thrives. The shop fronts read 'Kowalski' and 'Goldman & Son', further emphasizing the diversity of the neighbourhood and the absurdity of the claim. Izzadeen is depicted throwing a tantrum in a childlike manner, his face in absolute rage. He is further undermined by the implication that he is mentally unstable, symbolized by the cuckoo bird coming out of his head. In a similar vein to Garland's 'Kicking and Screaming' at 6.12, I interpret Scott's cartoon at 6.15 as highlighting the need for change in the Muslim community. However, this time, Scott and Garland are calling on Muslims to confront people from within the community – such as Izzadeen – who hold views that are deemed contrary to the values of the country in which they live.

Nicholas Garland's uncaptioned cartoon (*Daily Telegraph*, 21 September 2006) (6.16)[49] comments on the same topic. Published a few days earlier than 6.15, 6.16 cartoon presents two different scenarios. In the first frame, a Caucasian man walks on past a placard with the words 'Heckler shouts at Home Secretary'. In the second frame, the placard reads 'Muslim heckler shouts at Home Secretary'. The same person can be seen running away in fear in the opposite direction to the first frame. Here, Garland focuses on the reaction to such incidents, where simply the mention of the word 'Muslim' is enough to instil fear in the wider British public. Though both cartoons at 6.15 and 6.16 depict two different reactions to Izzadeen's outcry at Reid, there is a sense of solidarity with the public – an 'us' versus 'them' situation – where extremists like Izzadeen are social pariahs, not fitting in with the image of the common man on the streets of London. At the same time, 6.16 ignores the role the media plays in perpetuating such fears.

Another prominent Muslim figure in the media was Abu Hamza al-Masri, an imam at Finsbury Park Mosque from 1997 until its closure in 2003 (it re-opened again in 2005). Abu Hamza attracted the attention of the British authorities for his outspoken views on espousing ideas such as the killing of non-Muslims. With his glass left eye and his right-hand hook, Abu Hamza achieved notoriety for his unique look as much as his controversial views. In February 2006 he was convicted of eleven charges, including soliciting to murder and was sentenced to seven years imprisonment.[50] He was eventually extradited to the United States and sentenced to life imprisonment for charges including involvement in the hostage taking of sixteen tourists in Yemen in December 1998.[51]

Paul Thomas' uncaptioned cartoon (*Daily Express*, 27 April 2004) (6.17; Figure 16)[52] focuses on Abu Hamza's appearance, highlighting his hook and his blind left eye. The inclusion of the Union Jack on the identity card in Thomas' image draws attention to Abu Hamza's British citizenship. Here, the identity card is used as a trope to demonstrate a sense of frustration at the fact that people who seem to believe in views not compatible with British society are, in fact, members of that very society. At the same time, the use of the identity card serves to underscore the treachery of Abu Hamza against his own country. This is similar to the message in image 6.4, questioning why people who wish to see the demise of the UK are allowed to live freely here.

Dave [David Thomas] Gaskill's uncaptioned image (*Sun*, 31 January 2003) (6.18)[53] depicts a snowman with a right-hand hook and the right eye open, standing underneath a sign directing people towards 'FINSBURY PARK MOSQUE'. Again, there is a sense of frustration at Hamza being able to live in Britain freely; a billboard reads 'CALLS TO DEPORT CAPT HOOK AFTER BIGAMY REVEALED'. To the reader, the most prominent aspects of the images are the way Abu Hamza *looks*, rather than his views. This may, in part, be due to the fact that his glass eye and the right-handed hook make it easier for cartoonists to caricature Abu Hamza as a villainous figure. However, this also lends credence to the idea that one's attire and outward appearance are taken as indicators of where one stands in relation to complex issues such as democracy, freedom of religion and human rights.

Figure 16 Paul Thomas, uncaptioned cartoon (*Daily Express*, 27 April 2004). Copyright Thomas/Daily Express/2004.

The same theme is found in Brighty's 'I have decided it is time to integrate …' (*Sun*, 19 November 2012) (6.19).[54] The image demonstrates the persistence of the idea of Muslims as immigrants, despite having been published seven years after the 7/7 attacks. From the caption, the reader can assume that both are Muslim, but whilst one has decided to 'integrate' by adorning Morris dancing bells, the other is shown to be reluctant to do so. The latter has an angry and bemused expression, dressed in much the same fashion as the men in the cartoons above, where attire and attitudes towards national identity are coupled as being inextricably linked. The two men in image 6.19 portray two different extremes: one has decided to 'integrate' to the point of adopting the dress of an English folk dancer – which very few would identify as being integral or even relevant to their British identity. The other is unwilling to embrace his British identity by virtue of dressing in a *salwar kameez* and *topi* – garments which not all Muslims may identify as being relevant to their own identity.

Interestingly, Peter Brookes opens up the discussion in his cartoon, 'Absolute scandal how Muslims refuse to integrate with society, eh, chaps?' (*The Times*, 19 January 2016) (6.20).[55] The cartoon situates members of the Conservative Party, including Boris Johnson and the then British Prime Minister, David Cameron, at the 'Elite School for Boys' (a reference to the fact that they both went to Eton). The men featured wear waistcoats and matching blazers and trousers, whilst Johnson holds a bottle of 'Bolly' – a slang word for Bollinger champagne. The image suggests that the men come from wealthy backgrounds, members of an old boys' network. The caption is ironic – highlighting how different members of society have their own forms of dress, as well as the fact that people like Johnson and Cameron are perhaps not so well integrated into British society due to their upper class status.

On 22 May 2013, soldier Lee Rigby was murdered in South East London by two Muslim converts – Michael Adebolajo and Michael Adebowale. The two men first hit Rigby with a car and used knives to attack him, later attempting to decapitate the soldier using a meat cleaver. Both Christian Adams' 'Foiled' (*Daily Telegraph*, 27 May 2013) (6.21)[56] and Dave Brown's '"Thousands are at risk of radicalisation … " – Theresa May' (*Independent*, 27 May 2013) (6.22)[57] focus on the security risks the attacks exposed. Despite being known to the security services, Adebolajo and Adebowale were not kept under surveillance. Furthermore, the nature of the attack was not under a wider terrorist network which meant that MI5 were unable to detect that it was going to take place. Indeed, although MI5 were criticized for delays and errors made in relation to Adebolajo and Adebowale, the Intelligence and Security Committee of

Parliament found that it would not have been possible to have prevented the murder of Lee Rigby had these been rectified.[58]

Both images 6.21 and 6.22 simply use the meat cleaver as a trope to symbolize the attack. Image 6.21 emphasizes how more complex terror plots have been prevented by contrasting the meat cleaver against explosives and car bombs which have the word 'FOILED' stamped over them. Image 6.22 depicts a bloodied meat cleaver in the style of a RAF plane. The image hints at the motives behind the Rigby murder, where Adebolajo was filmed at the scene with his hands bloodied, stating that the 'only reason we've killed this man today is because Muslims are dying daily by British soldiers. This British soldier is one – he is an eye for an eye and a tooth for a tooth.'[59]

The absence of any imagery or explicit references to those involved in the cartoons highlight how the attack's apparent simplicity and barbaric nature made it instantly recognizable to readers. It also indicates how radical ideas are one of the underlying causes of terrorism, and not just a lack of integration. More crucially, however, both Adebolajo and Adebowale were of Nigerian descent.[60] To portray the two as an Asian male would have been grossly incorrect, and yet they both went against the Asian 'media-generated Muslim' as examined above. This demonstrates the practical difficulties political cartoonists face when actual events do not fit the stereotypes that the reader can easily identify. Therefore, in 6.21 and 6.22, the nature of the attack was the focus of the cartoons, rather than the attackers.

The Muslim Barbaric confirmed

Since 2014, the state of Daesh has been operating in parts of Iraq and Syria; at the time of writing Daesh had lost significant parts of its territory against a US-led coalition.[61] According to estimates by the Soufan Group, as many as 850 'Foreign Fighters' from the UK left for Syria or Iraq as of February 2017.[62] It is not just the numbers that have worried the British public, but the fact that young girls like Shamima Begum, Amira Abase (both fifteen at the time) and Kadiza Sultana, sixteen, travelled from London to Syria in February 2015 to join Daesh. Other high-profile cases include the Mannan family; originally from Luton, twelve members – including three young children – had gone to Syria, eventually dying there.[63] These incidents have raised questions as to what motivates Britons to leave the country and join Daesh – an organization that commits acts even Al Qaeda condemn.[64]

According to their 2015 report, the Soufan Group found that more than double the number of foreign fighters from 'Western Europe' travelled to Syria. In their 2015 findings, 'almost 3,700 of the total 5,000+ European Union foreign fighter contingent come from just four countries'[65] – France, the UK, Germany and Belgium – thereby relinquishing ties with their home nation. Under Daesh, only those who subscribe to their ideals can be considered Muslim – discounting any Muslims who live outside of the so-called caliphate and those who do not follow their interpretation of Islam, such as the Shi'a Muslim community.

Mac's 'This way, infidels!' (*Daily Mail*, 12 August 2014) (6.23)[66] illustrates the perception of 'ISIS JIHADISTS' intentionally going against 'THE ASCENT OF MAN' and directing the 'infidels' to follow in their footsteps. Bearded, with an angry expression on his face, the Muslim male is fully clothed in what seems to be a *salwar kameez* and a turban on his head, brandishing a firearm. He is cloaked in black, with the words 'ISIS JIHADISTS' emblazoned on the back. The fully evolved Caucasian Homo sapiens man is naked with nothing in his hands, no facial hair and wearing a neutral expression; the contrasts between the two men are pointed.

The image takes the idea of the regressive Muslim male and applies it in a more global context, where the reluctance is no longer about progress in terms of thinking and values, but a refusal to embrace one's humanity and to go against it. Historically, the evolutionary metaphor has been used as a way to degrade other ethnic groups, as seen in relation to the Irish, as well as Africans, to depict an innate bestial nature.[67] Thus, whilst his clothing indicates that he is not Caucasian (and therefore foreign), the words on his back are crucial in understanding that the focus is not only on the ethnicity of the ISIS Jihadist, but the particular political ideology that he symbolizes.

Chris Riddell's 'The Second Coming' (*Observer*, 28 September 2014) (6.24)[68] quotes from W. B. Yeats' poem of the same name. The words 'while the worst are full of passionate intensity' are placed directly in between the ISIS fighter and the Ukip clown, indicating that both are on a par in terms of the ideologies that they advocate: the ISIS fighter does not tolerate religious diversity, whilst the Ukip clown does not tolerate cultural diversity. This is symbolized by the Ukip clown wearing the England flag and the ISIS fighter dressed in black, brandishing a bloodied scimitar. His face is covered, leaving only the eyes visible. What is most interesting is the way the black garb of the ISIS fighter in this image has become synonymous with members of Daesh.[69] A firearm or bladed weapon are used interchangeably in cartoons to emphasize the violent acts of Daesh that have captured headlines around the world.

One such example is the case of the Daesh fighter nicknamed 'Jihadi John' who features in Michael Heath's '"Where's Jihadi John?" (with apologies to Where's Wally?)' (*Mail on Sunday*, 1 March 2015) (6.25).[70] 'Jihadi John' gained notoriety in 2014 after featuring in a video beheading the American journalist, James Foley, and subsequently appearing in later videos beheading other foreign nationals captured by Daesh. In these videos, like other members of Daesh, he wore a balaclava, leaving his identity hidden. What was remarkable was the fact that 'Jihadi John' had a British accent and in February 2015, it was revealed that the man behind the balaclava was Mohammed Emwazi. Emwazi had spent most of his childhood growing up in London and had even graduated with a degree from the University of Westminster. The only thing that makes Emwazi identifiable in the image is his beige clothing and the 'J J' on his shirt (Jihadi John). The fact that he holds a knife in his hands amongst a crowd of other Daesh fighters holding weapons highlights how nothing sets him apart from his barbaric counterparts. Emwazi was eventually killed in a drone strike in November 2015.[71]

In their examination of American political cartoons, Peter Gottschalk and Gabriel Greenberg discuss the importance of symbols and argue that:

> The symbols connoting Islam and Muslims chosen by American political cartoonists primarily derive from American and European experiences of Middle Eastern Muslims, therefore projecting onto all Muslims symbols that, by and large, do not derive their own self-understanding.[72]

Gottschalk and Greenberg refer to the use of '"Islamic" symbols',[73] one of which is the scimitar used as a 'symbol of Muslim barbarity'.[74] Applying this to the cartoons relating to Daesh above, only Riddell's 'The Second Coming' features the scimitar. However, the frequent inclusion of firearms and bladed weapons imputes the same message of such barbarity, which has been embraced and actively encouraged by Daesh.

Consequently, rather than the political cartoonists imposing their own (incorrect) personal ideas and beliefs, images 6.23–6.25 accurately portray the violence with which Daesh wish to be associated. In my previous chapter of the *Muslimah*, I examined the homogenization of women through the use of the *burqa/niqab* in cartoons. Parallels can be drawn in the way Daesh also seeks to portray a homogenous population under its control through attire, such as its members wearing black and being masked in balaclavas. Such a move disbars people under Daesh control to lay claim to any other ethnicity or nationality.

It is also difficult to ignore the intentional move by Daesh to feed into the image of the villainous masked man that is so prevalent in popular culture in the West.

I argue that the portrayal of the immigrant Muslim male in ethnic garb such as in images 6.11, 6.13 and 6.19 conveys a *suspicion* of the Muslim Barbaric. In contrast, the cartoons portraying the Muslim male in the distinctive dress of Daesh members, as well as Abu Hamza's unique appearance, serve to *confirm* that he is the Muslim Barbaric. Were he to be stripped of the black clothing and balaclava, for example, we would imagine the immigrant Muslim male, according to the logic of the cartoons. Therefore, the cartoons looked at in this chapter convey the idea of the Muslim Barbaric – namely, that every Muslim male has a proclivity towards radicalism and regressive ideas – and attire is used as the vehicle to indicate this.

Thus, the Muslim male's ethnicity and dress indicate that he has not integrated and therefore has the propensity to be violent. However, Mac's cartoon at 6.23 signifies the divergence from this idea; the words 'ISIS JIHADISTS' on his back confirm that he is indeed violent because he is attached to a specific political state. In this way, the visual trope of the villainous figure (be it the masked Daesh member or the hook-handed Abu Hamza) actually unmasks the individual in the same way as the *burqa/niqab* in relation to the *Muslimah*. Unless he fully identifies with Britain (such as in 6.19) and its values of democracy (6.4), and accepts modern values of equal rights and a multicultural society (6.12), there is a risk that the immigrant Muslim male will give into violence. Thus, in cartoon iconography, Islam is transformed into an ineluctable ethnic category that is genetic and unchangeable – to be Muslim is to be innately barbaric.

Attacks at home

Five separate terror incidents had occurred within the UK in 2017. The first such attack occurred on 22 March when fifty-two-year-old Khalid Masood drove into pedestrians on Westminster Bridge. He subsequently went on to stab a police officer on duty at Carriage Gates, one of the entrances to the Palace of Westminster. In total, Masood killed five people and injured many others. This was the first terror attack since the 7/7 bombings in 2005 on such a scale.[75] Steve Bell's '4102-230316_INCIDENT' (*Guardian*, 23 March 2017) (6.26)[76] and Ben Jennings' 'Terror Base … ' (*i News*, 25 March 2017) (6.27)[77] were both published in the wake of the attack. The images focus on its apparently rudimentary nature, as opposed to the sophisticated bomb attack of 7/7. Bell's image at 6.26 depicts a view of the Palace of Westminster from a blood-stained Westminster Bridge, with the acronym 'WTF' (i.e. 'what the fuck') printed along the barrier tape. Through situating the 'Terror Base' in the kitchen, Jennings' cartoon at 6.27 gives the impression of an ordinary person being inspired to carry out such a deadly attack in the short time it takes to brew a mug of tea, emphasizing how easy the attack was to plan and execute by Masood.

The second attack occurred on 22 May in which a bombing at the Manchester Arena during an Ariana Grande concert killed twenty-two people, including children.[78] Christian Adams' 'Who Is Smaller … ?' (*Evening Standard*, 23 May 2017) (6.28) attracted widespread acclaim.[79] The cartoon depicts the silhouette of a large suicide bomber about to detonate himself next to the silhouette of a small girl who holds a pink balloon in her hand. In another incident, on 3 June, eight people were killed and more than forty others injured in a knife attack carried out by three men on London Bridge and Borough Market. Martin Rowson's 'Enough is enough' (4 June 2017, *Guardian*) (6.29)[80] depicts the then Prime Minister, Theresa May, standing on top of the then US President Donald Trump and King Salman of Saudi Arabia as she stands at a lectern outside 10 Downing Street. The image conveys a sense of frustration aimed at world leaders for not doing enough to prevent such attacks from occurring. In contrast to 6.3, 6.29 shows how a Muslim political leader is in alignment with Western powers in dealing with extremism. Both Patrick Blower's uncaptioned cartoon (*Daily Telegraph*, 5 June 2017) (6.30)[81] and Brian Adcock's uncaptioned cartoon (*Independent*, 5 June 2017) (6.31)[82] take a different approach by depicting the Shard. The Shard in image 6.30 makes the peace sign and is lit up with the word 'democracy', whilst the Shard in 6.31 makes an obscene gesture with two fingers.

Similarly, in Ben Jennings' 'To Terror From London' (*i News*, 16 September 2017) (6.32),[83] the Tube map is in the shape of an obscene gesture in response to a bomb attack on a Tube train on 15 September, which injured more than twenty-five people.[84] A further incident occurred on 19 June with an attack by a non-Muslim on worshippers outside Finsbury Park Mosque, in which one man was killed and eleven others injured. Martin Rowson's 'Read The Sun & Daily Mail' (*Guardian*, 20 June 2017) (6.33)[85] takes a critical approach to the two tabloid papers, insinuating that the attacker was influenced by them. The *Daily Mail* criticized the publication of the cartoon, describing it as 'so deranged and offensive [… a] malicious smear'.[86]

A couple of years later, on 29 November 2019, Usman Khan stabbed Saskia Jones and Jack Merritt at Fishmongers' Hall. Khan, a convicted terrorist, was shot dead by armed police on London Bridge, resulting in the event being referred to as the 'London Bridge attack'.[87] In much the same way as the depiction of the 2017 attacks, cartoons commenting on the event do not include images of the attacker but focus on the location of the event. Ben Jennings' uncaptioned cartoon (1 December 2019, *Guardian*) (6.34) references the upcoming general election which was held on 12 December 2019; the then Prime Minister, Boris Johnson, insensitively places a campaign poster which reads 'Vote Boris', rather than laying flowers on London Bridge. Morten Morland's uncaptioned cartoon (2 December 2019, *The Times*) (6.35) also focuses on the general election, depicting Boris Johnson and the then Labour Party leader, Jeremy Corbyn racing one another to the scene of the attack. Both the cartoons are in response to criticism that Johnson was using the attack as a campaign issue,[88] whilst image 6.35 also criticizes Corbyn's stance against the Iraq War. Interestingly, image 6.29 was published a few days ahead of the June 2017 general election, in which Rowson seems to take a cynical view of the suspension of political campaigning for a day.[89]

Common themes emerge from the cartoons published in response to the different attacks. The initial shock conveyed in 6.26 and 6.27 after the Westminster attack is quickly replaced by a sense of defiance and solidarity with those affected by the subsequent attacks in images 6.28 and 6.30–6.32. For example, the use of the iconic image of the Shard as well as the Tube map instils a sense of unity and belonging, echoing the sentiments of those published immediately after the 7/7 attacks. As the shock subsided and the cartoons started to look inwards at the British Muslim community, the figure of the immigrant male in ethnic garb emerged. In contrast, the cartoons relating to the 2017 attacks focus on their *nature* and the *response* to them – as opposed to the attacker himself.

One reason could be that in the face of the constant terror threat, there is a desire to show resistance – a discourse which is often led by the public in their immediate reactions on social media. This is then emulated by the cartoonists. It can also be because the ethnicity of the attacker does not always fit the profile of the Asian male (Khalid Masood was of African-Caribbean origin for example[90]). Moreover, the immigrant man in ethnic attire would be anachronistic, with the reader unable to easily identify him as a terrorist. This is because although the black-clothed, balaclava-clad Daesh fighter has more recently become synonymous with the idea of the terrorist, it would be factually incorrect to portray the attackers as such. For example, in the case of the 2017 attacks, such as in 6.27, it is the nature of the attacks, rather than the attacker that is highlighted. Images 6.29, 6.34 and 6.35 convey a sense of frustration at the inability of political leaders to deal with terrorism effectively. However, what is different in images 6.34 and 6.35 is that the cartoonists situate political figures at the scene to highlight this sense of frustration. Importantly, 6.33 comments on a terror attack perpetrated by a Caucasian man against Muslims. In this way, the cartoons examined in this chapter expose how the reinforcement of such stereotypes can pose difficulties for the cartoonist in the case of a rapidly changing situation.

Conclusion

The focus on Muslims following the 11 September attacks, via the medium of the political cartoon, demonstrates a limited and narrowed understanding of the community. As Poole states, 'Islam's ability to be newsworthy relies on established notions of who Muslims are and what they represent to (interpretations of) British culture.'[91] What the reader finds in the cartoons immediately following the 9/11 and 7/7 attacks is a common theme of a very male-centric understanding of the British Muslim community. This may be because the perpetrators of both attacks were all men, thus presenting terrorism as an issue that primarily needs tackling amongst the Muslim male community. Furthermore, there is a notion that Muslims are immigrants and therefore one's ethnicity and attire are used as visual markers of both religion (i.e. the *topi*) and their foreignness (i.e. the *salwar kameez* and *thawb*).

Conversely, cartoons on the *Muslimah* are more static and primarily deal with the issue of women's rights in relation to the veil, where ethnicity plays little or no role and instead, the focus is on the Muslim religion itself. This exposes the different biases when depicting the different genders: the *burqa/niqab* is used as a trope to disembody and strip the *Muslimah* of all other identity other than that of her religion. It also demonstrates how the debate on the *hijab* has moved on; it is deemed to be an acceptable part of British culture and identity so that those who wear it are considered to be assimilated. In the case of the Muslim male, the debate surrounding integration is more complex because his face and clothing are visible. Therefore, the opposite occurs whereby he is embodied with a beard and wears different clothing; a foreigner who has cultural ties abroad. In much the same way as the turban in relation to Sikhs and the *burqa* for the *Muslimah*, the Muslim man's ethnicity is used as a visual marker of difference.

It is these visual markers that make the Muslim male stand out from the rest of his compatriots, lending him to suspicion of becoming the Muslim Barbaric.

Within this lies the idea that the Muslim man lacks any sort of patriotism whatsoever, where his ethnicity plays a key role in his attitudes towards integration and national identity. This can clearly be seen in the contrasting attitudes conveyed in Garland's image at 6.12 and that of 6.5. Whilst image 6.5 appeals to 'British Muslims' to take a more proactive role, image 6.12 takes a more resolute approach in to how to tackle the issue of 'Muslim extremism', by attacking the apparent inaction of the Muslim community to confront the causes behind terrorism. In contrast, although Morland's image at 6.11 and Schrank's image at 6.13 depict the archetypal ethnic Muslim male, the images are more self-reflective. In this way, 6.11 and 6.13 question the attitudes of the wider British public towards the Muslim community and whether these really are so alien to the values that the terrorists held.

Although the Jewish, Sikh and Irish chapters focus largely on men, the very fact that the Muslim community are portrayed with a strong focus on both genders, highlights how both men and women in Islam are identified differently. This is evident in the way men are given an ethnicity, whilst women are not. At the same time, it is interesting that violence and aggression are attributed to the Muslim male in much the same way as Jewish, Sikh and Irish men. This is in contrast to the *Muslimah* who is culturally and politically subversive without resorting to violence. Unsurprisingly, the largest majority are men-only – seventeen (49 per cent) images out of thirty-five.[92] However, there were eleven (31 per cent) images where the gender was none/not clear. This is a considerably large portion and is perhaps due to a more diverse catalogue of tropes that do always feature people. Of the seven images that feature women, only 6.14 includes the *Muslimah* as symbolized by the *niqab*, whereas images 6.11, 6.13 and 6.15 portray the Muslim male against a mixed gender non-Muslim group. Image 6.1 is women-only and 6.28 and 6.20 do not feature an identifiably Muslim male.

At the very crux of the images examined above is that *ethnicity* is used as a visual tool to highlight *religious* difference. Interestingly, this mirrors what Giselinde Kuipers finds in her research of Dutch jokes in relation to Muslims where there is an '"ethnification" of Muslims in the joke universe and the increasing conflation of ethnicity and religion/Islam'.[93] In the case of Daesh, the suspicion of the Muslim Barbaric is confirmed. By stripping the Muslim male of these markers of difference, such as in 6.24 and 6.25, all that is attributable is the black attire and violence which serve to highlight his true nature. Additionally, the fact that the Daesh fighters were located abroad and are depicted as such in 6.25 for example, serves to highlight their alien nature from the ordinary Briton.

As the terror threat constantly changes and becomes a part of everyday reality, the Muslim Barbaric melts into the crowd once more, where it can be anyone, going back to the scenario depicted in 6.11. The broadcaster, Katie Hopkins, called for a 'final solution'[94] following the Manchester attack in May 2017, and is one such example of how the discourse around terrorism is emotive. This is particularly relevant in image 6.33, where Rowson identifies the role of the media as contributing to the perpetrator's 'extremist hatred of Muslims'.[95] This is striking because the reactions to the 7/7 attacks focused on 'them' – Muslims – and their role in both contributing and combatting terrorism. This can be seen in the portrayal of Bin Laden in 6.9 and the Muslims protesting in 6.14.

In contrast, the reader can see how there is a shift in emphasis, so that 'us' – the West – becomes the focus of more recent cartoons. The focus is critical, looking at the wider factors in the radicalization of individuals, such as in 6.22. At the same time, it is more inclusive, so that images such as 6.28 and 6.32 use symbolism that is iconic and universal, thereby extending 'us' to include anyone who identifies with the message of the cartoon. Part of this may be because, although the binaries of 'us' and 'them' still exist, the enemy is harder to identify and therefore to portray visually. However, it perhaps also demonstrates a maturity in attitudes towards the terror threat, recognizing that not all terrorists are Muslim, and that they too are affected by terror attacks.

Conclusion

The digital era

In much the same way as technological changes in the nineteenth century impacted the way cartoons were produced and published, the advent of the digital era has made graphics software and the internet freely available. This, in turn, has had a dramatic effect on the way cartoons are produced, published and viewed. Whilst the majority of the cartoons I look at in this thesis were first experienced by people in print, research shows that online reach is now significantly higher than that of print. Figures show that over the period of July 2017–June 2018, 17.5 million viewed newsbrands on desktop or mobile, compared to 13.8 million in print.[1] Political cartoons have also evolved in how they are created. For example, Ben Jennings uses digital software to colour his images.[2] Furthermore, animation is widely accepted as being acceptable in a cartoon, such as Patrick Blower's 'Livedraw' videos for the *Guardian*[3] and the Pulitzer Prize for editorial cartooning being awarded to 'a distinguished cartoon or portfolio of cartoons [...] published as a still drawing, animation or both'.[4]

One of the possible reasons behind the survival of the political cartoon in twenty-first-century Britain could be due to the fact that, as the figures cited above show, newspapers are still read by millions of people, especially the Sunday papers which have a higher combined circulation than the daily papers.[5] Another important point to note is how social media allows cartoonists to track how many times a cartoon has been shared or viewed. For example, by looking at the number of re-tweets a cartoon gets, a cartoonist is able to get a better idea of the impact of their work, than from the print version of the newspaper. Changes in the British press have seen the *Independent* switching to an online-only format since 2016 and *The Times* and *The Sunday Times* put in place a paywall to access their online content in 2010. Such changes have forced readers to change the way they consume news content in which they may be offered a choice of subscription packages, tailored to how much content is accessible and whether it is digital, print or both. This then influences how the reader views the cartoon. For example, the *Guardian* online contains the cartoon in its 'Opinion' section which readers have to click on a weblink in order to view the image. The *Daily Telegraph*, however, displays its cartoon prominently on its homepage, allowing readers to view it without being blocked by the paywall.

Therefore, different newspapers choose to display their cartoon content in different ways, perhaps indicating how important both the website and editorial teams consider the image as part of their news reporting. This also raises questions of the sustainability of cartoons – if online readers do not click on the URL to the editorial cartoon or seek the cartoon in the printed version, is this a sign that the cartoon is irrelevant and unnecessary, or that the cartoon is not sufficiently prominent? At the same time, perhaps the diversification of the way news is published and accessed has aided the cartoon's sustainability because it is more accessible to people on a wider scale.

The internet has also led to a proliferation of cartoons and the way in which they can be viewed, commented and shared with immediacy via social media. An interesting example of how cartoons are consumed globally is the way many in Turkey felt the country was being neglected, whilst the media spotlight was on France and Belgium. All three countries had suffered terror attacks: France in November 2015 and both Turkey and Belgium within days of each other in March 2016. Despite this, Turkey did not feature in a cartoon by Plantu published in the French newspaper *Le Monde*. The cartoon depicts two people crying, their bodies in the shape of the flags of France and Belgium, with the Frenchman wrapping his arm around the Belgian.

After publication, the image was edited to include a third person symbolizing Turkey and its shared grief with the two other countries.[6] The image was shared via social media, with subsequent discussions revolving around the fact that other terrorist incidents around the world went under-reported or not at all, highlighting disparities in the way the media choose to focus on certain events around the world.[7] This demonstrates how cartoons can be edited so that they become (more) applicable to different contexts. Such practices show how the digital era has changed the idea and ease of the mutability of images. This means that even those who are not skilled artists choose to use the cartoon as a tool to convey their point.

Changing contexts

The events of 9/11 and 7/7 have opened up new discourses on integration and belonging. An interesting example of the impact of 9/11 is of the many Sikhs in America who have been mistakenly identified as Muslims, due to the profiling of the Asian-bearded male as a Muslim terrorist. The *Guardian*'s article, 'The perils of "flying while Muslim"', highlights the plight of Sikh men being embroiled in racist attacks and the discrimination they face at airports due to the turban.[8] Following 7/7, there was a public discussion on what being a multicultural society meant and to what extent Muslim communities had integrated.[9] Such discussions were further sharpened after the economic crash in 2008 which saw a rise in nationalism and, as many commentators argue, has resulted in shock events such as the election of Donald Trump as president and the vote for Brexit.[10]

My research started in a very different context, several years before the Brexit referendum. The 2016 referendum has impacted debates surrounding British identity in a profound manner. Parallels can be drawn in the way ideas of the Commonwealth challenged British identity after the end of the empire, and the debates occurring today over freedom of movement and the status of EU migrants who have settled in the UK, post-Brexit. For example, several member states opted for a transitional arrangement after the accession of Romania and Bulgaria to the EU in 2007. This meant a seven-year timeframe in which citizens of both countries had to obtain an 'accession worker card' in order to work in the UK.[11] Rules around what benefits migrants could claim were also tightened.

Within the UK, there has been growing resentment because of perceptions of the EU Parliament having more influence in legislation than that of UK MPs. Fundamental EU principles, such as the freedom of movement, have also led to the belief that this has lowered wages and migrants being offered jobs in place of native citizens. In the run up to the Brexit referendum, the debate over whether the UK should stay or leave was highly emotive, focusing on the impacts of immigration. An example of this is the outcry against the Ukip poster depicting a large queue of migrants, under the heading, 'Breaking point, the EU has failed us all' (7.1).[12] Many drew parallels between the Ukip poster and Nazi propaganda.[13] However, it was powerful rhetoric like this that helped 'Leave' campaigners win the 2016 referendum, shocking the global community.

'So long, farewell, auf wiedersehen, goodbye ... ' (*Daily Star*, 29 March 2017) (7.2)[14] by Scott (Clissold) was published the day before Article 50 was triggered by Theresa May.[15] May enthusiastically sings the words in the caption as EU leaders look on in worry. The image invokes ideas of national pride as May beats a drum with the Union Jack and 'Brexit' printed on the drumhead and 'Article 50' written across the side. The potential re-emergence of the blue passport after the UK's exit from the EU had been a point of focus in the Brexit debate and features in Scott's 'Commonwealth passport' (*Sunday Express*, 19 February 2017) (7.3)[16] and Martin Rowson's 'Blue ... ' (*Guardian*, 3 April 2017) (7.4).[17] The two cartoons convey strikingly different messages; image 7.3 depicts a hand holding the passport proudly, with a Union Jack flying on top. The image at 7.4 redesigns the coat of arms so that the then Foreign Secretary of State, Boris Johnson, and May resemble the lion and the unicorn, respectively. Scott labels it the 'Commonwealth passport', whereas Rowson attributes his to the 'Flouncy Ununited Kingdom and Ex-Dominions'.

Scott harks back to an older union that the UK is a member of, whilst Rowson mocks the very concept of a kingdom that is united, referring to the tensions between Westminster and Holyrood and the issue of Northern Ireland in the Brexit negotiations. Significantly, Rowson's image at 7.4 includes a poison pen letter which questions why Mr J. Bull Brexit (to whom the passport is attributed) would need a passport unless he is 'planning 2 visit Spain u enemy within'. Here, Rowson highlights the toxicity of the debate surrounding Brexit by showing how a British citizen (John Bull no less) is being questioned over his allegiances to his country for wanting to go abroad and visit an EU member state. The cartoon may also be hinting at the hypocrisy of many Britons who perhaps voted for Brexit but desire to live abroad in retirement in Spain.

Brian Adcock's 'Post-Brexit Immigration Policy Revealed ... ' (*Independent*, 7 September 2017) (7.5)[18] criticizes the debates surrounding immigration and the relationship with the EU after the UK's withdrawal. His use of the Union Jack above a sign reading 'Go away!' and the visualization of May's then leading Brexiteer Cabinet members overlooking a shark-infested moat convey an unwelcoming and more inward-focused Britain. Therefore, whilst the *Star* and the *Sunday Express* are pro-Brexit newspapers, other publications take a more critical stance towards the issue. Both images 7.5 and 7.4 criticize the language of patriotism surrounding the Brexit debate by showing a post-Brexit UK that is unwelcoming and dangerous against innocent members of the public – British or otherwise.

Furthermore, the Windrush scandal which broke in 2018 exposed the unfair treatment of those who had legally lived and worked in the UK for decades.

This involved detaining individuals or barring them from re-entering the UK because they were unable to prove their immigration status.[19] Peter Brookes' uncaptioned cartoon (*The Times*, 20 April 2018) (7.6)[20] comments on the situation, which came to a head at the same time as the Commonwealth Heads of Government Meeting that took place in London in April. The image depicts the late Queen making the speech at the opening of the event, with the then Home Secretary Amber Rudd using the British Prime Minister, Theresa May, as a flagpole flying the flag of surrender. The image refers to the Home Office announcing the Windrush Scheme to help those affected, signifying acceptance by the government of their wrongdoing.[21]

Christian Adams' 'Immigration Policy' (*Evening Standard*, 17 April 2018) (7.7)[22] and Martin Rowson's 'A vision of Britain, uncorrupted by the vile stain of immigration!' (*Guardian*, 16 April 2018) (7.8)[23] also comment on the Windrush scandal and the wider debates on immigration in the UK. Adams shows how the UK is literally propped up by immigration of all kinds and how such hostile policies are damaging to the country. Rowson's image depicts a lone wolf threatening the reader to 'stuff orf aht of it, ya stinkin' humans!' The newspaper headline reads, 'Tidal wave of Picts, Celts, Angles, Saxons, Jutes, Vikings, Normans, French'. The cartoon envisages a UK that is devoid of any migrants – leaving only bloodthirsty and predatory animals behind. Rowson seeks to convey how diverse the UK population is and how Caucasian Britons themselves can trace their ancestry back to migrants settling in the country. Interestingly, the wolf is shown reading the '*Daily Rabies*' newspaper whose masthead is rendered after the *Daily Mail*'s, suggesting that Rowson believes the media (particularly tabloids) play a crucial role in shaping the negative discourse around immigration. This is similar to his message in image 6.33 and how reading tabloids contributes towards a prejudiced worldview.

Despite the changing context, the images examined above show how the discourse around immigration and British identity has stayed the same, on which Brexit has had a profound impact. For example, the trope of the British passport has become symbolic of the polarization of views, harking back to the use of the national identity card used in image 6.17, which was published over a decade ago. This shows how the Brexit debate has once again raised the same questions of belonging and citizenship that were applied to people like Abu Hamza – a vocal supporter of radical Islamist ideology – and is now being applied to general members of the public in relation to where they stand on the UK's membership of the EU. The Windrush scandal exposed how those who had made a significant contribution to the UK were discriminated and mistreated.

This was symptomatic of the negative attitudes towards *anyone* considered an immigrant. This is similar to the case of the Sikh community who, despite having served in the British Army during the colonial era, had their history forgotten or ignored when they started to emigrate to the UK.

Constructions of the self and the Other

My research demonstrates how the reader is presented with the pictorial construction of 'the Jew', 'the Sikh', 'the Muslim' and 'the Irish' and how the image of the self as an Anglo-Saxon Protestant has changed over the years. This is demonstrated in the clear demarcation of the Anglo-Saxon Protestant vis-à-vis the Catholic Irish. The Anglo-Saxon Protestant becomes the Anglo-Saxon *Christian* when presented by a different Other – namely Jews, Muslims and Sikhs.

Therefore, the concept of Otherness that materializes from the cartoons examined is predicated on religious and racial difference from that of the Anglo-Saxon Protestant. This is significant because the cartoonist lampoons, satirizes and exposes hypocrisies and contradictions within society. At the same time they also cement – rather than challenge – certain perceptions and attitudes. This indicates how the cartoonist can move in two different directions at once, often creating an ambivalence in their work.

I have found how discourses surrounding belonging and integration have changed over time. For example, in Chapter 1, I find that the portrayal of the Irish is based on a perceived racial difference from that of the English. This leads to the depiction of the Irish as black, as picked up by the Irish cartoonist in image 2.5. This can also be seen in the way Jews are portrayed so that images such as 3.2 and 3.3 depict 'the Jew' as what the Anglo-Saxon Protestant man is not. Such racial differentiation serves to highlight how markedly different the English were from these groups, reflecting ideas current at the time of what Englishness meant. However, there is a gradual change in the way the Irish are perceived, so that they become 'more white' over time. This is evident in the move to a focus on sectarian divisions, in which they are either Catholic or Protestant, as a way to explain differing views towards the situation (2.32, 2.34 and 2.50). Images 3.8 and 3.9 demonstrate how a similar change occurred in relation to the Jewish community, in which they are depicted in their humanity, rather than as the fictive Jew. Such representation of these two communities shows how Otherness is based on both race and religion. Thus, although the idea of racial differentiation of the Irish and Jews is not featured in more recent cartoons, it is the extremities of religion that are then used as signifiers of Otherness. In contrast, the Sikh and Muslim communities are Othered on both their racial and religious identities in order to convey why the goal of assimilation perpetuated by the cartoonists is unattainable by these groups.

It is at times of change and upheaval for the host community – especially when minorities seek change through greater rights – that minorities are Othered. This is because it is an attempt to make sense of such disruption and to understand why it is occurring. This can be seen in the case of the Sikh community's struggle to be able to wear the turban to work. This resulted in confusion as to why the Sikh community wanted such rights when they should be grateful for having the opportunity to live and work in Britain. In return, Sikhs were expected to abide by regulations that meant they did not draw attention to the fact that they were an Other both racially *and* religiously (4.2). The issue of the *burqa/niqab* has engendered similar debates surrounding integration of the Muslim community. This is because the *burqa/niqab*, much like the turban, are seen as foreign and therefore do not belong in British society. Thus, ideas of subversion are attached to the turban and the *burqa/niqab* because they are seen as threats to the British political and cultural landscape (4.4 and 5.16). Interestingly, whilst the turban was used as a powerful reference of how the British were able to maintain their imperial power, the *burqa/niqab* carries the opposite message. Namely, the *burqa/niqab* is often associated as a symbol of the repressive Taliban regime (5.3), signifying the enemy in a war that is still ongoing. This then leads to confusion and the dismissal of the idea that the *Muslimah* may wear the *burqa/niqab* out of choice for religious reasons because of the oppression it is associated with.

Therefore, through presenting difference as something that is inherent and immutable, the minority community is deemed uncivilized and backwards vis-à-vis the progressive, civilized majority. This creates a context which furthers discrimination, marginalization and the rejection of assimilation by minorities. This idea of Otherness corresponds to Bhabha's assertion that

> the political and theoretical genealogy of modernity lies not only in the origins of the idea of civility, but in this history of the colonial moment. It is to be found in the resistance of the colonized populations to the Word of God and Man – Christianity and the English language.[24]

This is especially pertinent in the case of the Jewish community, whose Othering is based on the perception of a rejection of the Christian faith, leading to antisemitic myths such as the blood libel. In more recent times, the establishment of Israel has resulted in a conflation of the Israeli political actor and the Jewish religious believer.

It is also important to bear in mind how Othering also occurs to those within the Christian faith – as can be seen in the example of Irish Catholics. The impact of colonization by the British both perpetuated and resulted in the idea of the inherently violent Irish Catholic, who was in need of being governed by a more stabilizing influence.

Where the Jewish and Irish communities converge is in their association with political conflicts which were a direct result of British imperialism. Thus, in instances of armed struggle against the colonial power, these have been portrayed negatively by cartoonists as an attack on the British who are unfairly misconstrued by these groups. In the case of the Jewish community, this can be seen in 3.5 where an unarmed British soldier is about to be attacked by armed Jewish men. In the Irish case study, image 2.3 shows how the Fenian movement led to the simianization of the Irish in Victorian political cartoons as a tool to underscore how such violent actions were subhuman. However, in more recent times, as the Arab-Israeli conflict shows no signs of abating, there has been an increased focus on the Jewishness of Israeli politicians and how this is exacerbating the situation (3.20). In contrast, the 1998 Good Friday Agreement has led to a more stable situation in Ireland. This has resulted in cartoonists shifting their focus away from the violent nature of the Irishman. This can be seen in the way the situation is compared to other international conflicts, illustrating a sense of bemusement at why such violence occurs in such close proximity to Britain and moreover that it is between Caucasians (2.28). In this way, the trope of the masked man being applied to both unionists and loyalists successfully symbolizes violence and terror, as well as granting the Caucasian reader an aloofness from the Caucasian terrorist (2.51).

This can also be seen in the case of Daesh who are depicted in black clothing and balaclavas as a way to highlight their barbarity – something on which the group gladly capitalize. Such iconography is a useful visual tool to highlight the inhumanity of those who carry out heinous crimes by rendering them faceless and unidentifiable (6.24). The similarity to how Daesh and Irish paramilitaries are depicted is striking and indicates how the image of the masked man lends itself to the idea of the barbarian. These groups have chosen to dehumanize themselves at a superficial level through their choice of clothing and at a deeper level through their violent deeds. In a similar way, the *Muslimah*, by being depicted wearing either the *burqa/niqab,* is also disembodied and dehumanized. However, I argue that by virtue of her gender, the *Muslimah* in the *burqa/niqab* is not depicted as being violent. As Yegenoglu states,

> The veil represents for the colonial gaze the Orient's/woman's mask; it is an exterior surface which is assumed to conceal the site of interiority, the essence of the culture, i.e. femininity as the embodiment of culture's authentic core.[25]

This reflects a sense of discomfort towards the *burqa/niqab* because it is primarily seen as masking something, rather than as a garment some Muslim women choose to wear out of religious observance. It is her femininity that prevents the *Muslimah* from being violent. Instead, by representing the *Muslimah* in this way, the cartoons portray her as an unknowable silent threat, thereby engendering a sense of suspicion and hostility towards her.

This study shows how the power lies within the remit of the viewer – the communities that are depicted in the cartoons are Othered in a way that, although may make sense to the presumed reader, may not to the communities being depicted. One example is of the way Muslim men post-7/7 are depicted as being insufficiently integrated into British life. In order to convey this message, Muslim men are visualized as being from an ethnic minority, wearing ethnic garb, despite the fact that the 7/7 bombers wore Western clothing when carrying out the attack. The perceived transnational Asian culture that is conveyed in the cartoons depicting Muslim men is not applicable to the entire Muslim community in Britain and one that perhaps even those of Asian heritage do not recognize as being as integral to their identity.

On a practical level, depicting a Caucasian male in Western clothing would be unconvincing as a visually identifiable Muslim – perhaps even impossible for cartoonists – without clear signifiers such as captions and labels identifying the Caucasian male as Muslim. At the same time, it is also up to the cartoonist as to what topic s/he chooses to depict and which devices to use. For example, David Low depicted Neville Chamberlain in the likeness of his infamous umbrella to convey his policy of Appeasement towards the Nazi regime. The fact that trends do emerge, such as depicting the Muslim male as an immigrant, or the use of centuries-old antisemitic stereotypes, raises questions of an internal reception history and how cartoonists possibly refer to one another's iconography in order to ensure their cartoons are understood by the reader, as well as by other cartoonists. This suggests a conscious effort by cartoonists to perpetuate certain stereotypes which, importantly, perhaps they themselves believe. This shows how cartoons can function on multiple levels – by participating, perpetuating and creating visual stereotypes.

Therefore, the subject is reliant on the cartoonist and how s/he chooses to depict them – whether they are portrayed as an Other and if so, what tropes are used to illustrate this point. Thus, cartoons not only inform the reader of the perceived social reality, but also influence it by creating a visual context of what is deemed as rejectionist – such as the *burqa* or the *salwar kameez* – and what is assimilationist. Consequently, this disenfranchises minority groups by presenting the difficult and complicated issue of integration as a choice and one which is reduced to a question of appearance. At the same time, however, the woman who wears the *burqa/niqab* identifies herself as a *Muslimah* and similarly the male who wears the *kippah* identifies himself as a Jew. These items of clothing in some way signpost the viewer in how the subject identifies him/herself. The medium of the cartoon demands such outward indicators in order to convey the cartoonist's point, suggesting an unintended collusion between the subject and the cartoonist.

What is interesting is how racial differentiation is then taken on at an intragroup level such as that in 2.28 and 2.39 where groups are Othered by those who are also Othered. This theme is only picked up in relation to the Irish and South Asian immigrants, perhaps indicating how both communities have a unique bond in sharing a common struggle of colonization under the British Empire (as portrayed in 2.36) as well as mass immigration to Britain. In the case of the Jewish community, images 3.4 and 3.5 depict a reversal of the Othering process in which Jews seemingly intend to be Othered by the British in their struggle over Mandatory Palestine. The Othering of the Sikh community and Muslim men occurs at a religious level in which race is used as a vehicle to reinforce this Otherness such as in 4.2 and 6.11. I argue that this is also true of the *Muslimah* who, despite being stripped of any identity other than that of her religion, is Othered in a way that links back to a practice imposed from abroad (5.5).

Gender

This highlights the importance of gender in the process of Othering and how men and women are Othered. Significantly, the focus is overwhelmingly male in cartoons depicting the Irish, Jews, Sikhs and Muslims – even when the subject is the *Muslimah*. In the case of the Jewish community, there is an attempt to feminize the Jew such as in 3.2. This changes during the Second World War, where the Jewish male is contrasted against the Jewish female (3.6). Similarly, in the Irish context, Erin/Hibernia are contrasted against the violent male (2.3). Fundamentally, whether the male is feminized or hyper-masculinized, it is in order to convey something abhorrent and unnatural in his character. This is important because it shows how the cartoonists examined – who are all male – Other the Jew, Sikh, Irish and Muslim based on racial difference. This provides an insight into how issues are perceived, such as the Zionist struggle for Mandatory Palestine; the Northern Ireland conflict; the battle to wear turbans instead of helmets; and Islamic fundamentalism. Such issues are portrayed as conflicts in which men play the key roles precisely because they are seen as the prime aggressors as well as the prime benefactors.

Thus, concepts relating to defiance and violence are linked to masculinity (2.49, 3.6, 4.10 and 6.4), whilst victimhood and non-aggression are linked to femininity. In Chapters 1, 2, 3 and 5, I find key themes emerge when a generic female character is depicted (as opposed to recognizable public or fictional figures). She is part of a group of men and women (2.38, 3.15 and 6.13); passive (2.30); a victim (2.26 and 3.7); or plays a very minor role in comparison to her male counterparts (4.8). In the case of the *Muslimah*, different themes emerge: misogyny (5.2); freedom to not wear the *burqa/niqab* (5.3); oppression (5.5); non-violent protest (5.8); the *burqa/niqab* as disguise (5.12); and political and cultural subversion (5.18).

Overall, of the 153 cartoons examined in Chapters 1–5, women feature in 59 (39 per cent) of them. Breaking this data down further, 73 (48 per cent) cartoons only feature men, in contrast to the 4 (3 per cent) which only feature women. Crucially, the image of the female Other as a production of male cartoonists raises questions as to how relevant the views presented are to the female readership. Do such ideas correlate with a readership that makes up just over half of the demographic (51 per cent) and yet are so under-portrayed?[26] My research sheds light on the male optic whilst exposing how the female view has been muted and ignored in a tradition that has long been in existence in Britain.

Cartoons and diversity

This shows how the depiction of minority communities is impacted by the fact that cartoonists tend to be Caucasian men. This in turn influences the views that are conveyed in cartoons because they are undoubtedly informed by the experiences and beliefs of the cartoonist themselves. The lack of diversity in both the industry and academics of political cartooning is striking. Although female artists such as Grizelda Grizlingham, Simone Lia, Nicola Jennings and Blue Lou have featured in major publications such as the *Spectator*, *Guardian* and the *Observer*, the absence of women or ethnic minorities demonstrates the dominance of Caucasian men.

Whilst there is some research on female American cartoonists,[27] there has been very limited research on female British cartoonists. *The Inking Woman: 250 Years of British Women Cartoon and Comic Artists* edited by Nicola Streeten and Cath Tate is a seminal study on the contribution women have made to the world of cartooning and comics in Britain. The cartoonist Nicola Jennings makes an enlightening remark on the way she perceives the industry as 'a centuries-old boy's club', making it more acceptable for male cartoonists to lampoon men, as opposed to being lampooned by women, which is deemed as 'criticism', rather than humorous.[28] Streeten's doctoral thesis, 'A Cultural History of Feminist Cartoons and Comics in Britain from 1970–2010', found that feminist cartoons and comics have emerged primarily in the form of the graphic novel due to the creation of feminist publishing companies.[29] Such research is crucial in understanding the contributions British women have made – and continue to make – in this field of art and sheds light on why so few women cartoonists are employed (or choose not to be employed) by the mainstream press.

Streeten's fascinating exploration of UK feminist cartoonists in her book, *UK Feminist Cartoonists and Comics: A Critical Survey*, highlights the importance of cartoons in the campaign for the women's vote in the 1900s in Britain and that despite the historical focus on male political cartoonists such as Hogarth and Gillray, it was a woman – Mary Darly – who wrote and illustrated the first book in Britain on caricature drawing in 1762. Streeten postulates that Darly is perhaps lesser known because of her focus on everyday life, rather than politics, and examines how *Punch* played a pivotal role in how women were viewed since most of the cartoonists were men who

> satirised women and, much later, excessively ridiculed the suffragettes, reinforcing through humorous cartoons that women's natural role was in the domestic sphere with children, their legal equals.[30]

Streeten's book uncovers the enduring power cartoons have to this day, specifically in the sphere of feminism. She argues that both the 'graphic novel' and the internet have been crucial enables for female cartoonists, with the former contributing to a sense of 'respectability' and the latter providing a platform to share and publish their work.[31]

This issue has been the subject of debate where the case of the Saudi female cartoonist, Hana Hajar, has been used as an example to highlight the disparity in the UK.[32] The Political Cartoon Society's President, Tim Benson, wrote a blog piece, 'Women and British Political Cartoonists' in which he opines, 'Why in the UK have we never had a full-time female political cartoonist on one of our national newspapers? It is hard to understand why there are still none in 21st century Britain.'[33] He highlights this sad fact despite there being more women in politics to caricature, such as the former British Prime Minister Theresa May and the former DUP leader Arlene Foster. There is also the #MeToo movement in which high-profile women around the world are speaking out against sexual harassment in society – especially in the workplace. Such movements have found women to be at the forefront of the media and asserting their right to live and work without the risk of being harassed.

Another point Benson makes is how there are limited opportunities to be employed as a full-time political cartoonist. Therefore, the reason why there are so few women in political cartooning may be due to more practical reasons, such as not being able to earn a stable income, resulting in women opting for other careers. It has also been argued that the definitions of 'cartoon' and 'comic', as well as who fits the criteria of 'political cartoonist', are too narrow and male-led, leading to female artists being marginalized and categorized outside of the genre of political cartooning.[34] Parallels can be drawn with that of stand-up comedy, which is often criticized for the dominance of men. For example, the writer, Christopher Hitchens, sparked outrage when he stated that 'women, bless their tender hearts, would prefer that life be fair, and even sweet, rather than the sordid mess it actually is'.[35] This was one of the reasons why, Hitchens claimed, women are less successful at comedy because they are biologically and innately less funny than men.

The above shows how different factors have resulted in women being under-represented in the field of cartooning. Perceptions of women being less funny precisely because of their gender, as well as the few career opportunities available to cartoonists in general, result in female cartoonists looking for other avenues in which to express themselves – such as the graphic novel. In her book on American humour, Rebecca Krefting comments on the way men belittle women in comedy,

> For him [it] is ideal because it leaves him and every other swinging dick with the upper hand, the 'equipment' necessary to incite laughter and the arbiter of precisely what should elicit laughter.[36]

Krefting highlights how difference, in this case, is reduced to the genitalia of the person in question, which is then perceived to determine how funny and capable one is to succeed in the industry of comedy. Such biases are similar to those reflected in the cartoons I examine so that the image of the female cartoonist is Othered against that of the male cartoonist who is funnier and more perceptive. This also feeds into the idea that the industry is an old-boys' club, because it enables the male cartoonist to succeed against his female counterpart.

When touching on sensitive issues such as race and faith, I have found that cartoonists often demonstrate a lack of understanding and engagement with the communities they portray. An interesting example is the case of the Sikh community and how the turban is used as a key visual indicator of the person's Sikh faith. As a student of religion, I am aware that the wearing of the *kara* is more indicative and more prevalent than the turban amongst the Sikh community. Significantly, however, the *kara* is not worn by any of the Sikhs depicted in the cartoons examined. Belfast-born Kenneth Mahood and Barbara Brandon-Croft (popularly known as Barbara Brandon), who in 1991 became the first Black American female cartoonist to have a national syndication in the popular press, are interesting case studies of those who comment on issues personal to them.

For Mahood, his portrayal of the Irish is insightful because it illustrates how personal experience is so crucial to how a cartoonist portrays a certain issue. Brandon-Croft herself was '[a]ware of her unique position as a cartoonist and woman of color, [… and felt] "a larger responsibility" than mere entertainment [… using] humor to address such issues as race, gender, and class'.[37] Conversely, this also demonstrates how the political cartoonist is cognisant of the fact that s/he may address issues that are not pertinent to them personally or on which they have limited knowledge, but as visual journalists they are required to comment. Factors such as the headline news and the topic of the newspaper editorial can determine what issues the cartoonist comments on, rather than what is personally important, or more accessible, to them.

The cartoonist's dilemma

A key issue that cartoonists face is how certain events are omitted or under-reported in the mainstream press and, subsequently, in their cartoons. This is not unusual and is a common accusation that the press is used to hearing. Both David Low's 'The Hard of Lot of A Cartoonist' (*Evening Standard*, 13 October 1927) (7.9)[38] and Ben Jennings' 'A Week of Idiocy' (*i News*, 10 January 2015)

(7.10)³⁹ are enlightening because of the way they show the situation from the cartoonist's viewpoint. Low's cartoon shows how he is unable to fight against his conscience when choosing what to portray in his cartoons. This is despite being implored by his editor, Lord Beaverbrook, to take a different approach in how he depicts some of Beaverbrook's friends, such as Winston Churchill. Although it is not known whether such a conversation took place, the cartoon is important because it presents his editorial independence.⁴⁰

Jennings' image contains six frames, five of which depict different scenarios – including a Daesh member, neo-Nazis and a pro-gun supporter. In the final frame, Jennings depicts himself confused as he thinks aloud, 'Urgh … where do I start!?' The image shows how there are equally important, but competing, issues for the cartoonist to pick up on. Ultimately, the cartoonist has to settle on one issue to highlight in their drawings for practical purposes. At the same time, Jennings' response demonstrates a reluctance to pick up on such negative issues and the feeling of being overwhelmed by how many there are to choose from.

'A Week of Idiocy' at 7.10 is an important reminder that cartoonists themselves are consumers of the news and subject to the process of editorializing. Indeed, in his lengthy apology in response to the Richard Sharp cartoon, 'The Copros Touch' (28 April 2023, *Guardian*),⁴¹ Rowson takes pains to explain his thinking behind the multiple iconographic symbols within the image, pointing to his desire to emulate cartoonists such as Gillray and Hogarth. However, Rowson admits that the 'tyranny of the deadline' led to the artwork to carry an antisemitic message, rather than the message he had intended.⁴²

Therefore, the cartoonist's dilemma can be a wide range of things – including what topic to highlight, how this is done and whether the newspaper's editorial team will agree to publish it. It also involves taking into account personal emotions and how those may come through the cartoonist's work – intended or otherwise. I hope my research shows the significance of taking into account the wider context of cartoons in which the cartoonist, the viewer and the subject play vital roles in the production and reception of cartoons. Such roles are flexible and can often be merged so that the cartoonist becomes the subject and vice versa.

Glossary

AQAP Al Qaeda in the Arabian Peninsula
BCA British Cartoon Archive
DUP Democratic Unionist Party
IDF Israeli Defence Forces
IRA Irish Republican Army
MCB Muslim Council of Britain
PIRA Provisional Irish Republican Army, formed in 1969 after splitting from the IRA
PLO Palestine Liberation Organisation
RIC Royal Irish Constabulary
RIRA Real Irish Republican Army, formed in 1998 in opposition to the Good Friday Agreement
UDA Ulster Defence Association
UUP Ulster Unionist Party
Abaya cloak worn over clothes, often worn by women in the Middle East. Also known as a *jilbab*.
Burqa one-piece veil covering the entire face and body, mostly associated with women in Afghanistan.
Chador cloak covering the entire body which is held closed at the front. Mainly worn by women in Iran.
Hijab headscarf with which Muslim women cover their hair. Also known as **khimaar**.
Jilbab see *abaya*
Kachha undergarments mainly worn by baptized Sikhs.
Kangha wooden comb mainly worn under the turban by baptized Sikhs.
Kara steel bangle often worn by both baptized and non-baptized Sikhs.
Kesh unshorn hair often practised by both baptized and non-baptized Sikhs.
Khimaar see *hijab*.
Kirpan sword (of any size) mainly carried by baptized Sikhs.
Muslimah feminine for 'Muslim' in Arabic.
Niqab veil covering the face, leaving the eyes clear.
Perahan tunban traditional garments worn by Afghan men consisting of loosely fitted trousers and shirt. It resembles the *salwar kameez* worn on the Indian subcontinent.
Salwar kameez traditional garments worn by both men and women in the Indian subcontinent, consisting of loosely fitted trousers and shirt. It resembles the *perahan tunban* worn in Afghanistan.
Thawb long robe usually worn by Arab men
Topi round cap often worn by Muslim men

Notes

Introduction

1. 'Remember the Victims: Shahara Islam', *Mirror*, 20 July 2005, https://www.mirror.co.uk/news/uk-news/remember-the-victims-shahara-islam-550757.
2. 'Nigeria Cartoon Protests Kill 16', *BBC News*, 19 February 2006, http://news.bbc.co.uk/1/hi/4728616.stm.
3. Anil Dawar, 'Intruder Shot at Home of Danish Cartoonist', *Guardian*, 2 January 2010, https://www.theguardian.com/world/2010/jan/02/danish-cartoonist-intruder-shot.
4. 'Cartoons Row Hits Danish Exports', *BBC News*, 9 September 2006, http://news.bbc.co.uk/1/hi/world/europe/5329642.stm.
5. 'Iran Paper's Holocaust Cartoons', *BBC News*, 13 February 2006, http://news.bbc.co.uk/1/hi/world/middle_east/4709380.stm.
6. 'Holocaust Denial: Iran Holocaust Cartoon Exhibition', United States Holocaust Memorial Museum, https://www.ushmm.org/confront-antisemitism/holocaust-denial-and-distortion/iran/iran-cartoon-exhibition/introduction/iran-holocaust-cartoon-exhibition. In 2015, a second round of the competition was held in which similar themes of Holocaust denial featured in the entries. The competition also included a separate contest on caricaturing the Israeli Prime Minister Benjamin Netanyahu.
7. 'Prophet Mohammed Cartoons Controversy: Timeline', *Telegraph*, 4 May 2015, https://www.telegraph.co.uk/news/worldnews/europe/france/11341599/Prophet-Muhammad-cartoons-controversy-timeline.html.
8. See front cover of *Charlie Hebdo*, No. 1348, 23 May 2018.
9. Gary Younge, 'The Serena Cartoon Debate: Calling Out Racism Is Not "Censorship"', *Guardian*, 13 September 2018, https://www.theguardian.com/commentisfree/2018/sep/13/serena-williams-cartoon-racism-censorship-mark-knight-herald-sun.
10. Zeba Blay, 'The Whitewashing of Naomi Osaka', *HuffPost*, 11 September 2018, https://www.huffingtonpost.co.uk/entry/the-whitewashing-of-naomi-osaka_us_5b967eb3e4b0cf7b004209b5.
11. France Diplomacy, 'National Tribute to the Memory of Samuel Paty – Speech by Emmanuel Macron, President of the Republic, at the Sorbonne (21 October 2020)', *France Diplomacy*, 21 October 2020, https://www.diplomatie.gouv.fr/en/french-foreign-policy/human-rights/freedom-of-religion-or-belief/article/national-tribute-to-the-memory-of-samuel-paty-speech-by-emmanuel-macron.

12 Sudip Kar-Gupta and Richard Lough, 'Beheaded Teacher Was "quiet hero" Who Incarnated French Values, Macron Says', *Reuters,* 21 October 2020, https://www.reuters.com/article/france-security-idINKBN2760KR.

13 Imran Khan (@ImranKhanPTI), 'Through Encouraging the Display of Blasphemous Cartoons Targeting Islam & Our Prophet PBUH', Twitter, 25 October 2023, https://twitter.com/ImranKhanPTI/status/1320286665785704448.

14 Andrew Hussey, 'Macron and the Muslim World', *New Statesman,* 11 November 2020, https://www.newstatesman.com/long-reads/2020/11/Samuel-paty-murder-macron-muslim-terror.

15 Adam Heppinstall, 'Decision Notice: The Appointment of the Chair of the Board of the British Broadcasting Corporation (BBC) 2020/2021', *The Commissioner for Public Appointments,* 28 April 2023, https://publicappointmentscommissioner.independent.gov.uk/wp-content/uploads/2023/04/2023-04-28-OCPA-DECISION-NOTICE-IN-RELATION-TO-THE-APPOINTMENT-OF-CHAIR-OF-THE-BBC-BOARD-MR-RICHARD-SHARP.pdf. 2.

16 Dave Rich (@daverich1), 'The Depiction of Richard Sharp in Today's @guardian Cartoon Falls Squarely into an Antisemitic Tradition', Twitter, 29 April 2023, https://twitter.com/daverich1/status/1652216828247015435.

17 'Corrections and Clarifications', *Guardian,* 30 April 2023, https://www.theguardian.com/news/2023/apr/30/corrections-and-clarifications.

18 Martin Rowson, https://www.martinrowson.com/.

19 Steve Bell, (@Belltoons), 'I Tweet This in Solidarity with Martin', Twitter, 2 May 2023, https://twitter.com/BellBelltoons/status/1653353346277752833.

20 Steve Bell, '2303 NUJ242-DAVIESHARP', https://www.belltoons.co.uk/bellworks/index.php/others/LATEST/2303_NUJ242-DAVIESHARP.

21 Steve Bell was dropped by the *Guardian* in October 2023. See https://www.bbc.co.uk/news/entertainment-arts-67122609.

22 Peter Morey and Amina Yaqin, *Framing Muslims* (Cambridge: Harvard University Press, 2011), 198.

23 BCA image reference number LSE7298, https://archive.cartoons.ac.uk/Record.aspx?src=CalmView.Catalog&id=LSE7298.

24 Lorenz Langer, *Religious Offence and Human Rights: The Implications of Defamation of Religions* (Cambridge: Cambridge University Press, 2014), 1–2.

25 Colin Seymour-Ure and Jim Schoff, *David Low* (London: Secker & Warburg, 1985), 63.

26 Draper Hill, *Mr. Gillray, the Caricaturist: A Biography* (London: Phaidon Press, 1965), 3.

27 Thierry Smolderen, Bart Beaty and Nick Nguyen, *The Origins of Comics: From William Hogarth to Winsor McCay* (Jackson: University Press of Mississippi, 2014), 3. http://www.jstor.org/stable/j.ctt2tvp3g.3.

28 Mark Bryant and Simon Heneage, *Dictionary of British Cartoonists and Caricaturists 1730–1980* (Aldershot: Scolar, 1994), 90.

29 Robert L. Patten, 'Conventions of Georgian Caricature', *Art Journal* 43, no. 4 (1983): 334, https://doi.org/10.1080/00043249.1983.10792251.

30 Henry J. Miller, 'John Leech and the Shaping of the Victorian Cartoon: The Context of Respectability', *Victorian Periodicals Review* 42, no. 3 (2009): 267, http://www.jstor.org/stable/27760231.
31 Frank Palmeri, 'Cruikshank, Thackeray, and the Victorian Eclipse of Satire', *Studies in English Literature, 1500–1900* 44, no. 4 (2004): 756, http://www.jstor.org/stable/3844535.
32 Miller, 'John Leech', 268.
33 Richard Scully, *Eminent Victorian Cartoonists Volume I* (London: Political Cartoon Society, 2018), 80.
34 Graham Everitt, *English Caricaturists and Graphic Humourists of the Nineteenth Century: How They Illustrated and Interpreted Their Times* (London: S. Sonnenschein, 1893), 284.
35 Miller, 'John Leech', 270.
36 T. S. R. Boase, 'The Decoration of the New Palace of Westminster, 1841–1863', *Journal of the Warburg and Courtauld Institute* 17, no. 3/4 (1954): 324.
37 Frank Palmeri, 'The Cartoon: The Image as Critique' in *History beyond the Text: A Student's Guide to Approaching Alternative Sources*, ed. Sarah Barber and Corinna Peniston-Bird (United Kingdom: Routledge, 2009), 42. ProQuest Ebook Central.
38 Palmeri, 'The Cartoon', 40.
39 Miller, 'John Leech', 278.
40 Ibid., 277.
41 W. Cosmo Monkhouse, *The Life and Work of Sir John Tenniel, R.I.* (London: The Art Journal Office, 1901), 1.
42 Frankie Morris, 'John Tenniel, Cartoonist: A Critical & Sociocultural Study in the Art of the Victorian Political Cartoon (Britain)' (PhD dissertation, University of Missouri-Columbia, 1985), iv.
43 Monkhouse, *The Life and Work*, 2.
44 BCA image reference number mudyx4l, https://archive.cartoons.ac.uk/Record.aspx?src=CalmView.Catalog&id=mudyx4l.
45 I examine this in more detail in the chapter on Jews.
46 Patten, 'Conventions', 335.
47 Robert Justin Goldstein, 'The Persecution and Jailing of Political Caricaturists in Nineteenth-Century Europe (1815–1914)', *Media History* 9 (2003): 20, https://doi.org/10.1080/1368880032000059962.
48 Colin Seymour-Ure, 'What Future for the British Political Cartoon?', *Journalism Studies* 2, no. 3 (2001): 1, https://doi.org/10.1080/14616700120062202.
49 H. C. G. Matthew, 'Gould, Sir Francis Carruthers (1844–1925), Cartoonist and Stockbroker', *Oxford Dictionary of National Biography* (Oxford: Oxford University Press), https://www.oxforddnb.com/view/10.1093/ref:odnb/9780198614128.001.0001/odnb-9780198614128-e-33493.
50 David Morgan, *Sacred Gaze: Religious Visual Culture in Theory and Practice* (Berkeley, CA: University of California Press, 2005), 3.

51 Salam Al-Mahadin, 'The Social Semiotics of Hijab: Negotiating the Body Politics of Veiled Women', *Journal of Arab & Muslim Media Research* 6, no. 1 (2013): 4, https://doi.org/10.1386/jammr.6.1.3_1.
52 Edward W. Said, *Orientalism* (London: Penguin Classics, 2003), 5.
53 Said, *Orientalism*, 7.
54 Samir Amin, Russell Moore and James Membrez, *Eurocentrism* (New York: Monthly Review Press, 2010), 175.
55 Homi K. Bhabha, *The Location of Culture* (London: Routledge, 2004), 94.
56 Bhabha, *Location*, 100.
57 Ibid., 64.
58 Ibid., 96.
59 Ibid., 101.
60 Ibid., 95.
61 Ibid., 40.
62 Ania Loomba, *Colonialism/Postcolonialism* (London: Routledge, 2015), 117.
63 Amin, Moore, and Membrez, *Eurocentrism*, 174.
64 Loomba, *Colonialism,* 120.
65 William A. Gamson, David Croteau, William Hoynes and Theodore Sasson, 'Media Images and the Social Construction of Reality', *Annual Review of Sociology* 18 (1992): 383, http://www.jstor.org/stable/2083459.
66 Peter L. Berger and Thomas Luckmann, *The Social Construction of Reality: A Treatise in the Sociology of Knowledge* (New York: Open Road Integrated Media, 2011), 45.
67 Gamson, Croteau, Hoynes and Sasson, 'Media Images', 382.
68 Berger and Luckmann, *Social Construction,* 97.
69 Mick Temple, *British Press* (Berkshire: McGraw-Hill Education, 2008), 13.
70 Temple, *British Press*, 69.
71 Chris Curtis, 'How Britain Voted at the 2017 General Election', table entitled 'Vote by Newspaper Readership', YouGov UK, published 13 June 2017, https://yougov.co.uk/news/2017/06/13/how-britain-voted-2017-general-election/.
72 Antonio Gramsci, *Selections from the Prison Notebooks* (London: The Electric Book Company, 2005), 430.
73 L. Perry Curtis Jr., *Apes and Angels: The Irishman in Victorian Caricature* (Washington, DC and London: Smithsonian Institution Press, 1997), x.
74 Pierre Bourdieu and Randal Johnson, *The Field of Cultural Production: Essays on Art and Literature* (New York: Columbia University Press, 1993), 70–1.
75 Nicholas Davey, 'Hermeneutics and Art Theory', in *A Companion to Art Theory*, ed. Paul Smith and Carolyn Wilde (Oxford and Malden, MA: Blackwell, 2002), 443.
76 Lucy Brown, *Victorian News and Newspapers* (Oxford: Clarendon, 1985), 27.
77 Brown, *Victorian*, 31–2.

78 Richard D. Altick, *The English Common Reader: A Social History of the Mass Reading Public, 1800–1900* (Chicago and London: University of Chicago Press, 1957), 394.
79 'News Consumption in the UK: 2021', figure 6.1, *Ofcom*, published 27 July 2021, https://www.ofcom.org.uk/__data/assets/powerpoint_doc/0026/222479/news-consumption-in-the-uk-2021-report.pptx, p. 36.
80 'News Consumption in the UK: 2021', figure 6.5, 40.
81 'News Consumption in the UK: 2021', figure 2.1, 13.
82 Ibid., 13.
83 'News Consumption in the UK: 2019', figure 6.4, 37.
84 Charles D. Elder and Roger W. Cobb, *The Political Uses of Symbols* (New York: Longman, 1983), 36.
85 Paul Gilroy, 'Multiculture, Double Consciousness and the "War on Terror"', *Patterns of Prejudice* 39, no. 4 (2005): 435, http://dx.doi.org/10.1080/00313220500347899.
86 Anthony S. Wohl, '"Ben JuJu": Representations of Disraeli's Jewishness in the Victorian Political Cartoon', *Jewish History* 10, no. 2 (1996): 91, www.jstor.org/stable/20101269.

Chapter 1

1 Liz Curtis, *Nothing but the Same Old Story: The Roots of Anti-Irish Racism* (London: Information on Ireland, 1984), 56.
2 Roy Douglas, Liam Harte and Jim O'Hara, *Drawing Conclusions: A Cartoon History of Anglo-Irish Relations, 1798–1998* (Belfast: Blackstaff, 1998), 3.
3 Douglas, Harte and O'Hara, *Drawing Conclusions*, 6.
4 T. W. Moody, 'Introduction: Early Modern Ireland', in *A New History of Ireland: Early Modern Ireland 1534–1691*, ed. T. W. Moody, F. X. Martin and F. J. Byrne (Oxford: Oxford University Press, 2009), 15, 10.1093/acprof:oso/9780199562527.003.0024.
5 *The Act of Supremacy, 1534*, transcript, The National Archives, http://www.nationalarchives.gov.uk/pathways/citizenship/rise_parliament/transcripts/henry_supremacy.htm.
6 Douglas, Harte and O'Hara, *Drawing Conclusions*, 65.
7 L. Perry Curtis Jr., *Anglo-Saxons and Celts: A Study of Anti-Irish Prejudice in Victorian England* (Conference on British Studies at the University of Bridgeport; distributed by New York University Press: New York, 1968), 6–7.
8 L. Perry Curtis Jr., *Apes and Angels*, xxi. See also John Tenniel's 'A Hint to the Loyal Irish' (*Punch*, 4 January 1868) as an example of how high facial angles were applied to Irishmen supportive of British rule.
9 Curtis Jr., *Apes and Angels*, 29.

10 *Vestiges of the Natural History of Creation*, published in 1844, posited the theory of transmutation as the explanation for the origins of the universe.
11 'Ireland from One or Two Neglected Points of View. by the Author of "Hints to Country Bumpkins"', *The Spectator; London*, 2 March 1889, http://archive.spectator.co.uk/article/2nd-march-1889/25/ireland-from-one-or-two-neglected-points-of-view-b.
12 Curtis Jr., *Apes and Angels*, 37.
13 Ibid., 104.
14 John Darby, *Dressed to Kill: Cartoonists and the Northern Ireland Conflict* (Belfast: Appletree Press, 1983), 25.
15 Curtis Jr., *Anglo-Saxons and Celts*, xxxii.
16 Curtis Jr., *Apes and Angels*, 57.
17 Douglas, Harte and O'Hara, *Drawing Conclusions*, 178.
18 *Government of Ireland Act, 1920*, http://www.legislation.gov.uk/ukpga/1920/67/pdfs/ukpga_19200067_en.pdf 1–2.
19 Douglas, Harte and O'Hara, *Drawing Conclusions*, 200.
20 Michael Hopkinson, 'From Treaty to Civil War, 1921–2', in *A New History of Ireland Volume VII: Ireland 1921–84*, ed. by J. R. Hill (Oxford: Oxford University Press, 2003), 25.
21 Alvin Jackson, *Ireland 1798–1998: War, Peace and beyond* (Chichester: Wiley-Blackwell, 2010), 362.
22 Douglas, Harte and O'Hara, *Drawing Conclusions*, 224.
23 Ibid., 225.
24 BCA image reference number 12760, https://archive.cartoons.ac.uk/Record.aspx?src=CalmView.Catalog&id=12760.
25 Mark Bryant, 'Jackson, Raymond Allen [pseud. JAK] (1927–1997), Cartoonist and Illustrator', *Oxford Dictionary of National Biography* (Oxford: Oxford University Press, 2007), https://www.oxforddnb.com/view/10.1093/ref:odnb/9780198614128.001.0001/odnb-9780198614128-e-67308.
26 See BCA image reference number JAD0001, https://archive.cartoons.ac.uk/Record.aspx?src=CalmView.Catalog&id=JAD0001.
27 'Raymond Jackson [Jak]', *British Cartoon Archive*, https://www.cartoons.ac.uk/cartoonist-biographies/i-j/RaymondJackson_JAK.html.
28 BCA image reference number 14007, https://archive.cartoons.ac.uk/Record.aspx?src=CalmView.Catalog&id=14007.
29 John Killen, *The Unkindest Cut: A Cartoon History of Ulster 1900–2000* (Belfast: Blackstaff Press, 2000), 103.
30 Darby, *Dressed to Kill*, 48.
31 BCA image reference number 16112, https://archive.cartoons.ac.uk/Record.aspx?src=CalmView.Catalog&id=16112.

32 BCA image reference number 16119, https://archive.cartoons.ac.uk/Record.aspx?src=CalmView.Catalog&id=16119.
33 BCA image reference number 16133, https://archive.cartoons.ac.uk/Record.aspx?src=CalmView.Catalog&id=16133.
34 Darby, *Dressed to Kill*, 56.
35 BCA image reference number 21949, https://archive.cartoons.ac.uk/Record.aspx?src=CalmView.Catalog&id=21949.
36 BCA image reference number 21916, https://archive.cartoons.ac.uk/Record.aspx?src=CalmView.Catalog&id=21916.
37 BCA image reference number 21194, https://archive.cartoons.ac.uk/Record.aspx?src=CalmView.Catalog&id=21194.
38 BCA image reference number 21234, https://archive.cartoons.ac.uk/Record.aspx?src=CalmView.Catalog&id=21234.
39 BCA image reference number 21943, https://archive.cartoons.ac.uk/Record.aspx?src=CalmView.Catalog&id=21943.
40 Darby, *Dressed to Kill*, 50.
41 BCA image reference number 19644, https://archive.cartoons.ac.uk/Record.aspx?src=CalmView.Catalog&id=19644.
42 BCA image reference number 19649, https://archive.cartoons.ac.uk/Record.aspx?src=CalmView.Catalog&id=19649.
43 John Chartres and Tim Jones, 'Three Shot in Belfast Street Clashes', *The Times*, 8 February 1971, 1.
44 BCA image reference number NG0710, https://archive.cartoons.ac.uk/Record.aspx?src=CalmView.Catalog&id=NG0710.
45 Tim Jones, 'Another British Soldier Shot Dead by Terrorists in Belfast', *The Times*, 14 July 1971, 1.
46 C.J.M. Drake, 'The Provisional IRA: A Case Study', *Terrorism and Political Violence* 3, no. 2 (1991): 44, https://doi.org/10.1080/09546559108427103.
47 Interestingly, the PIRA feature in image 4.12, which I look at in Chapter 3. The PIRA member is the only male standing in amongst a crowd of female beauty contestants.
48 Garland uses the same imagery in 'Dog in the manger', published in 1980. See BCA image reference number 34771, https://archive.cartoons.ac.uk/Record.aspx?src=CalmView.Catalog&id=34771.
49 BCA image reference number 35528, https://archive.cartoons.ac.uk/Record.aspx?src=CalmView.Catalog&id=35528.
50 BCA image reference number NG4871, https://archive.cartoons.ac.uk/Record.aspx?src=CalmView.Catalog&id=NG4871.
51 BCA image reference number 48947, https://archive.cartoons.ac.uk/Record.aspx?src=CalmView.Catalog&id=48947.

52 'IRA Kills Four in Belfast Attacks', *Guardian*, 14 November 1991, 3.
53 'Bombs in English Town Kill Child; IRA Blamed', *Washington Post*, 21 March 1993, https://global-factiva-com.libproxy.kcl.ac.uk/redir/default.aspx?P=sa&NS=16&AID=9KIN002300&an=wp00000020011102dp3l00a38&cat=a&ep=ASI.
54 BCA image reference number NG5306, https://archive.cartoons.ac.uk/Record.aspx?src=CalmView.Catalog&id=NG5306.
55 Philip Stephens, 'Bomb Puts Ulster Peace Talks in Doubt', *Financial Times*, 25 October 1993, 1.
56 Darby, *Dressed to Kill*, p. 52.
57 BCA image reference number 18411, https://archive.cartoons.ac.uk/Record.aspx?src=CalmView.Catalog&id=18411.
58 Darby, *Dressed to Kill*, p. 55. For further details on the allegations of torture, see Tim Jones, 'Ulster MPs Seek an Independent Public Inquiry into Allegations of Torture by Army', *The Times*, 19 October 1971, 2.
59 BCA image reference number NG0497, https://archive.cartoons.ac.uk/Record.aspx?src=CalmView.Catalog&id=NG0497.
60 'Kenyatta privileged those aspirants in his group who subscribed to his ethos. They became the ruling class, a landed aristocracy which wielded enormous political power. An early project of this ruling class involved the exclusion of the other ethnic groups from this plenitude of power. The Kenyatta regime also refused to accept the legitimacy of political opposition.' E. S. Atieno Odhiambo, 'Ethnic Cleansing and Civil Society in Kenya 1969–1992', *Journal of Contemporary African Studies* 22, no. 1 (2004): 30, https://doi.org/10.1080/0258900042000179599.
61 BCA image reference number 16248, https://archive.cartoons.ac.uk/Record.aspx?src=CalmView.Catalog&id=16248.
62 BCA image reference number 16254, https://archive.cartoons.ac.uk/Record.aspx?src=CalmView.Catalog&id=16254.
63 Douglas, Harte and O'Hara, *Drawing Conclusions*, 278.
64 BCA image reference number 18473, https://archive.cartoons.ac.uk/Record.aspx?src=CalmView.Catalog&id=18473.
65 BCA image reference number 16123, https://archive.cartoons.ac.uk/Record.aspx?src=CalmView.Catalog&id=16123.
66 Douglas, Harte and O'Hara, *Drawing Conclusions*, 279.
67 BCA image reference number 16249, https://archive.cartoons.ac.uk/Record.aspx?src=CalmView.Catalog&id=16249.
68 BCA image reference number 16251, https://archive.cartoons.ac.uk/Record.aspx?src=CalmView.Catalog&id=16251.
69 John Clare and David Wilsworth, 'Army "Peace Line" to Replace Barricades across Belfast', *The Times*, 10 September 1969, 1.
70 BCA image reference number LSE6183, https://archive.cartoons.ac.uk/Record.aspx?src=CalmView.Catalog&id=LSE6183.

71 Douglas, Harte and O'Hara, *Drawing Conclusions*, 195.
72 Winston Churchill, the then Secretary of State for War described the event as 'an extraordinary event, a monstrous event, an event which stands in singular and sinister isolation', *Hansard*, 8 July 1920, vol. 131, cols. 1705–819, https://api.parliament.uk/historic-hansard/commons/1920/jul/08/army-council-and-general-dyer.
73 Pierce A. Grace, 'The Amritsar Massacre, 1919: The Irish Connection', *History Ireland* 18, no. 4 (2010): 24, http://www.jstor.org/stable/27823023.
74 See chapter on Jews.
75 Bryant and Heneage, *Dictionary*, 150.
76 'The Man with a Pocketful of Laughter: Mail Cartoonist Mahood Finally Hangs Up His Quill', *Daily Mail*, 23 December 2009, https://www.dailymail.co.uk/news/article-1238107/Mail-cartoonist-Mahood-finally-hangs-quill.html.
77 BCA image reference number 16161, https://archive.cartoons.ac.uk/Record.aspx?src=CalmView.Catalog&id=16161.
78 BCA image reference number 17462, https://archive.cartoons.ac.uk/Record.aspx?src=CalmView.Catalog&id=17462.
79 Enoch Powell, 'Rivers of Blood' speech, 20 April 1968. Reprinted *Daily Telegraph*, 12 December 2007, http://www.telegraph.co.uk/comment/3643826/Enoch-Powells-Rivers-of-Blood-speech.html.
80 BCA image reference number 23291, https://archive.cartoons.ac.uk/Record.aspx?src=CalmView.Catalog&id=23291.
81 See chapter on Muslim men.
82 BCA image reference number 35319, https://archive.cartoons.ac.uk/Record.aspx?src=CalmView.Catalog&id=35319.
83 Darby, *Dressed to Kill*, 50.
84 Douglas, Harte and O'Hara, *Drawing Conclusions*, 279.
85 BCA image reference number 21684, https://archive.cartoons.ac.uk/Record.aspx?src=CalmView.Catalog&id=21684.
86 BCA image reference number 22084, https://archive.cartoons.ac.uk/Record.aspx?src=CalmView.Catalog&id=22084.
87 *The Agreement*, full text of the Good Friday Agreement, https://assets.publishing.service.gov.uk/government/uploads/system/uploads/attachment_data/file/136652/agreement.pdf.
88 P O'Neill, *Irish Republican Army (IRA) Statement on Decommissioning: (30 April 1998)*, CAIN Web Service, http://cain.ulst.ac.uk/events/peace/docs/ira30498.htm.
89 BCA image reference number PC3629, https://archive.cartoons.ac.uk/Record.aspx?src=CalmView.Catalog&id=PC3629.
90 *The 1998 Referendums*, Northern Ireland Social and Political Archive (ARK), http://www.ark.ac.uk/elections/fref98.htm.
91 'Omagh Bomb', *BBC History,* http://www.bbc.co.uk/history/events/omagh_bomb.

92 David McKittrick, 'Omagh Bombing: Sinn Fein's Shift Shown by Its Words', *Independent,* 18 August 1998, https://www.independent.co.uk/news/omagh-bombing-sinn-feins-shift-shown-by-its-words-1172426.html.
93 BCA image reference number PC5511, https://archive.cartoons.ac.uk/Record.aspx?src=CalmView.Catalog&id=PC5511.
94 BCA image reference number 85942, https://archive.cartoons.ac.uk/Record.aspx?src=CalmView.Catalog&id=85942.
95 BCA image reference number 78815, https://archive.cartoons.ac.uk/Record.aspx?src=CalmView.Catalog&id=78815.
96 United Nations Assistance Mission in Afghanistan, *Afghanistan: Protection of Civilians in Armed Conflict Midyear Update: 1 January to 30 June 2021,* 26 July 2021, 1, https://unama.unmissions.org/sites/default/files/unama_poc_midyear_report_2021_26_july.pdf.
97 BCA image reference number 16458, https://archive.cartoons.ac.uk/Record.aspx?src=CalmView.Catalog&id=16458.
98 BCA image reference number 22839, https://archive.cartoons.ac.uk/Record.aspx?src=CalmView.Catalog&id=22839.
99 BCA image reference number PC0157, https://archive.cartoons.ac.uk/Record.aspx?src=CalmView.Catalog&id=PC0157.
100 BCA image reference number SBD0423, https://archive.cartoons.ac.uk/Record.aspx?src=CalmView.Catalog&id=SBD0423.
101 BCA image reference number PC3055, https://archive.cartoons.ac.uk/Record.aspx?src=CalmView.Catalog&id=PC3055.
102 BCA image reference number PC5555, https://archive.cartoons.ac.uk/Record.aspx?src=CalmView.Catalog&id=PC5555.
103 Donna Carton, 'Ahern's IRA Arms U-Turn Sparks Crisis', *Daily Mirror,* 15 February 1999, https://global-factiva-com.libproxy.kcl.ac.uk/redir/default.aspx?P=sa&NS=16&AID=9KIN002300&an=dmirr00020010904dv2f01090&cat=a&ep=ASI.
104 BCA image reference number 62912, https://archive.cartoons.ac.uk/Record.aspx?src=CalmView.Catalog&id=62912.
105 Warren Hoge, 'Irish Protestant Leader Issues Ultimatum on Sinn Fein Ouster', *New York Times,* 9 October 2002, 6.
106 BCA image reference number 75150, https://archive.cartoons.ac.uk/Record.aspx?src=CalmView.Catalog&id=75150.
107 Michelle O'Keeffe, 'We Support the Police', *Sun,* 29 January 2007, https://global-factiva-com.libproxy.kcl.ac.uk/redir/default.aspx?P=sa&NS=16&AID=9KIN002300&an=THESUN0020070302e31t000hr&cat=a&ep=ASI.
108 Simon Hoggart, 'Northern Ireland Shootings', *Guardian,* 10 March 2009, 7.
109 I omit image 2.2 from this list.
110 'Northern Ireland-related Terrorism Threat Level Raised', GOV.UK, published 28 March 2023, https://www.gov.uk/government/news/northern-ireland-related-terrorism-threat-level-raised.

111 Morten Morland's 'The Victory Parade' (*The Times*, 12 June 2017) shows the then Prime Minister literally being paraded into 10 Downing Street by Orangemen, much like the banners used in their parades in Northern Ireland. Morland highlights the DUP's loyalist stance and the power that they held over the PM.
112 See Martin Rowson's cartoon, 28 May 2018, *Guardian*.
113 *The Abortion (Northern Ireland) (No. 2) Regulations 2020*, https://www.legislation.gov.uk/uksi/2020/503/contents/made.
114 Interestingly, in July 2019, Christian Adams depicted the then Foreign Secretary Jeremy Hunt and Boris Johnson as leprechauns in relation to the Irish backstop issue. The cartoon caused controversy for using 'anti-Irish stereotyping'. See Felix M. Larkin, 'Why the Boris Johnson, Jeremy Hunt Leprechaun Cartoon Is No Laughing Matter', *Irish Times*, 3 July 2019.
115 See Dave Brown's cartoon, 14 April 2023, *Independent* and Christian Adams' cartoon, 11 April 2023, *Evening Standard*.
116 'Confidence and Supply Agreement between the Conservative and Unionist Party and the Democratic Unionist Party', GOV.UK, updated 23 January 2020, https://www.gov.uk/government/publications/conservative-and-dup-agreement-and-uk-government-financial-support-for-northern-ireland/agreement-between-the-conservative-and-unionist-party-and-the-democratic-unionist-party-on-support-for-the-government-in-parliament.
117 'PM Speech on the Windsor Framework: February 2023', GOV.UK, published 28 February 2023, https://www.gov.uk/government/speeches/pm-speech-on-the-windsor-framework-february-2023.

Chapter 2

1 Frank Felsenstein, 'Jews and Devils: Antisemitic Stereotypes of Late Medieval and Renaissance England', *Literature and Theology* 4, no. 1 (1990): 15, www.jstor.org/stable/23927203.
2 Anonymous, 1233, Norwich, http://www.nationalarchives.gov.uk/wp-content/uploads/2014/03/e401-15651.jpg.
3 Felsenstein, 'Jews and Devils', 16.
4 Ibid., 17.
5 Cathy S. Gelbin, 'Rootless Cosmopolitans: German-Jewish Writers Confront the Stalinist and National Socialist Atrocities', *European Review of History: Revue européenne d'histoire* 23, no. 5–6 (2016): 865, 10.1080/13507486.2016.1203082.
6 Michael Clark, 'Jewish Identity in British Politics: The Case of the First Jewish MPs, 1858–87', *Jewish Social Studies* 13, no. 2 (2007): 93, www.jstor.org/stable/4467767.

Michael Everett and Danielle Nash, 'The Parliamentary Oath', 24, http://www.legco.gov.hk/general/english/library/stay_informed_parliamentary_news/the_parliamentary_oath.pdf.
7. Everett and Nash, 'The Parliamentary Oath', 24.
8. 'Article 5 – No Title.', *Manchester Guardian (1828–1900)*, 27 July 1858, 3.
9. See 'The Jewish "Emancipation."', *Huddersfield Chronicle and West Yorkshire Advertiser*, 24 July 1858, 4, and 'The Jew Bill and the Oaths' Bill', *York Herald*, 24 July 1858, 8.
10. Clark, 'Jewish Identity', 102.
11. Todd M. Endelman, 'Disraeli's Jewishness Reconsidered', *Modern Judaism* 5, no. 2 (1985), 109, www.jstor.org/stable/1396390.
12. Dominic Janes, *Oscar Wilde Prefigured: Queer Fashioning and British Caricature, 1750–1900* (Chicago and London: The University of Chicago Press, 2016), 156.
13. Wohl, 'Ben JuJu', 102.
14. Ibid., 105.
15. 'Suez Canal (purchase of shares)'. *House of Commons Papers*, paper number 14, volume page XLIX.649, https://parlipapers.proquest.com/parlipapers/docview/t70.d75.1876-052322?accountid=11862.
16. William Gladstone, *Hansard*, House of Commons, vol. 227, col. 585, 21 February 1876, https://hansard.parliament.uk/Commons/1876-02-21/debates/90976a6d-a67a-4483-a385-ad4e6890e5c1/Supply%E2%80%94%C2%A34080000SuezCanalShares.
17. Wohl, 'Ben JuJu', 90.
18. Ibid., 105.
19. Ibid., 90.
20. BCA image reference number 59398 by Dave Brown is interesting in the way that it borrows from 'Mosé in Egitto!!!' It inverts the image so that the sphinx (i.e. George W. Bush) taps its nose knowingly at Tony Blair about the War on Terror.
21. 'Jewish Zionists: British Government Support', *Manchester Guardian (1901–1959)*, 9 November 1917, 5.
22. Arie Perliger and Ami Pedahzur, *Jewish Terrorism in Israel* (New York: Columbia University Press, 2011), 27.
23. Natan Aridan, *Britain, Israel and Anglo-Jewry 1949–57*, (Abingdon: Taylor and Francis, 2004), 195.
24. Endelman, *The Jews of Modern Britain*, 219.
25. Aridan, *Britain*, 188.
26. David Cesarani, *The Jewish Chronicle and Anglo-Jewry, 1841–1991* (Cambridge: Cambridge UP, 1994), 189.
27. Cesarani, *Jewish Chronicle*, 189.
28. BCA image reference number ILW1115, https://www.cartoons.ac.uk/record/ILW1115.

29 Perliger and Pedahzur, *Jewish Terrorism*, 41.
30 BCA image reference number LSE4809, https://www.cartoons.ac.uk/record/LSE4809.
31 'Our Special Correspondent, "Terrorists' Toll in Palestine"', *The Times*, 19 November 1946, 4.
32 Cesarani, *Jewish Chronicle*, 189.
33 BCA image reference number LSE4929, https://www.cartoons.ac.uk/record/LSE4929.
34 Aridan, *Britain*, 215.
35 BCA image reference number LSE8841, https://archive.cartoons.ac.uk/Record.aspx?src=CalmView.Catalog&id=LSE8841.
36 Ahron Bregman, *Israel's Wars: A History since 1947* (Florence: Taylor & Francis Group, 2003), 14.
37 Katharine Knox and Tony Kushner, *Refugees in an Age of Genocide: Global, National and Local Perspectives during the Twentieth Century* (London: Routledge, 1999), 75.
38 Endelman, *The Jews of Modern Britain*, 224–5.
39 Andrew Sharf, *The British Press and Jews under Nazi Rule* (London: Oxford University Press, 1964), 96–7.
40 BCA image reference number LSE4337, https://www.cartoons.ac.uk/record/LSE4337.
41 BCA image reference number LSE3216, https://archive.cartoons.ac.uk/Record.aspx?src=CalmView.Catalog&id=LSE3216.
42 David Low, *Low Visibility; a Cartoon History, 1945–1953* (London: Collins, 1953), 98.
43 Britain declared war with Germany on 3 September 1939.
44 Sharf, *British Press*, 90.
45 Ibid., 90.
46 Yitzhak Arad, Yisrael Gutman and Abraham Margaliot (eds), 'From a Discussion on the Compulsory Evacuation of the Jewish Population of the Wartheland to the Government-General, 30 January 1940' *Documents on the Holocaust: Selected Sources on the Destruction of the Jews of Germany and Austria, Poland and the Soviet Union* (Oxford: Pergamon, 1987), 183.
47 Gerald Reitlinger, *The Final Solution: The Attempt to Exterminate the Jews of Europe, 1939–1945* (New York: Beechhurst Press, 1953), 57.
48 This is all the more poignant considering the fact that a few months after the publication of the cartoon, on 'October 16th, 1940, a decree was published [...] to concentrate 360,000 Jews in an area which normally housed 160,000 people' (Reitlinger, *The Final Solution*, 58).
49 For a more detailed account of what was happening to the Jews under the Nazis during this time, see Reitlinger, *The Final Solution*, chapter 6.

50 Anthony Eden, *Hansard*, House of Commons, vol. 385, col. 2082–7, 17 December 1942, http://hansard.millbanksystems.com/commons/1942/dec/17/united-nations-declaration.

51 Lawrence H. Streicher, 'David Low and the Sociology of Caricature', *Comparative Studies in Society and History* 8, no. 1 (1965): 3, https://www.jstor.org/stable/177533.

52 BCA image reference number LSE1993, https://archive.cartoons.ac.uk/Record.aspx?src=CalmView.Catalog&id=LSE1993.

53 David Low, *Low: The Twentieth Century's Greatest Cartoonist* (London: BBC History Magazine, 2002), 10–11.

54 University of Kent, BCA, Low cuttings 1938–45, Box 1, Percy Cudlipp to David Low, 9 September 1937.

55 David Low, *Low's Autobiography* (London: Michael Joseph, 1956), 280.

56 Sharf, *British Press*, 74.

57 Aridan, *Britain*, 1.

58 Ibid., 3.

59 Ibid., 231.

60 Ibid., 6.

61 Ibid., 8.

62 BCA image reference number LSE9006, https://www.cartoons.ac.uk/record/LSE9006.

63 Colin Shindler, *A History of Modern Israel* (Cambridge: Cambridge University Press, 2008), 44.

64 Sander L. Gilman, *The Jew's Body* (New York and London: Routledge, 1991), 99.

65 Such as in BCA image reference numbers LSE8871, https://archive.cartoons.ac.uk/Record.aspx?src=CalmView.Catalog&id=LSE88.71 and DL2428, https://archive.cartoons.ac.uk/Record.aspx?src=CalmView.Catalog&id=DL2428.

66 BCA image reference number LSE9032, https://www.cartoons.ac.uk/record/LSE9032.

67 Shindler, *History*, 45.

68 Ibid., 47.

69 BCA image reference number LSE1420, https://www.cartoons.ac.uk/record/LSE1420.

70 Ilan Pappé, *Britain and the Arab-Israeli Conflict, 1948–51* (Basingstoke: Macmillan in Association with St. Antony's College, Oxford, 1988), 124.

71 Pappé, *Britain and the Arab-Israeli Conflict*, 127.

72 As Pappé notes, America led efforts to find an 'economic solution … to try to solve a political problem. The results … were catastrophic for the Palestinians and, in the long run, disastrous for the area as a whole', 125.

73 BCA image reference number LSE5581, https://archive.cartoons.ac.uk/Record.aspx?src=CalmView.Catalog&id=LSE5581.

74 Aridan, *Britain*, 218.
75 Ibid., 217.
76 Ibid., 232.
77 Endelman, *The Jews of Modern Britain*, 235.
78 Ibid., 238.
79 BCA image reference number 11330, https://www.cartoons.ac.uk/record/11330.
80 BCA image reference number 24259, https://www.cartoons.ac.uk/record/24259.
81 Moshe Brilliant, 'Israelis "Kill Two Fatah Leaders" in Lebanon Raid', *The Times*, 10 April 1973, 1.
82 Avi Shlaim, 'The Oslo Accord', *Journal of Palestine Studies* 23, no. 3 (1994): 26, http://www.jstor.org/stable/2537958.
83 BCA image reference number 49145, https://www.cartoons.ac.uk/record/49145.
84 BCA image reference number NG5275, https://www.cartoons.ac.uk/record/NG5275.
85 Shindler, *History*, 267.
86 'Too Smart for His Own Fist; Mr Netanyahu Is Risking a Reversal of the Peace Process', *Guardian*, 26 September 1996, 16.
87 BCA image reference number PC0388, https://www.cartoons.ac.uk/record/PC0388.
88 BCA image reference number PPC0392, https://www.cartoons.ac.uk/record/PC0392.
89 Isaiah 2:4. Scripture Taken from the Holy Bible, NEW INTERNATIONAL VERSION®. Copyright © 1973, 1978, 1984 Biblica. All rights reserved throughout the world. Used by permission of Biblica.
90 David Remnick, 'Bibi's Blues', *The New Yorker*, 22 January 2013, http://www.newyorker.com/news/news-desk/bibis-blues.
91 Dave Brown, 'Cartoonist Michael de Adder Lost Work after Drawing an Offensive Image of Donald Trump – but That's His Job', *Independent*, 2 July 2019, https://www.independent.co.uk/voices/michael-de-adder-sacked-cartoon-donald-trump-dead-migrants-mexican-border-a8983966.html.
92 BCA image reference number DBD0001, https://archive.cartoons.ac.uk/Record.aspx?src=CalmView.Catalog&id=DBD0001.
93 Donald Macintyre, 'Israeli Raids Driven by Election, Say Palestinians', *The Independent*, 27 January 2003, http://www.independent.co.uk/news/world/middle-east/israeli-raids-driven-by-election-say-palestinians-128067.html.
94 Ciar Byrne, 'Independent Cartoon Cleared of Anti-Semitism', *Guardian*, 22 May 2003, https://www.theguardian.com/media/2003/may/22/theindependent.pressandpublishing.
95 W. D. Rubinstein, *A History of Jews in Great Britain* (Basingstoke: St Martin's Press, 1996), 39.
96 Anthony Julius divides the development of the blood libel into six periods from the mid-twelfth century to the present in Anthony Julius, *Trials of the*

Diaspora: A History of Anti-Semitism in England (Oxford: Oxford University Press, 2010), 78–102.
97 'Report 62', *Press Complaints Commission*, http://www.pcc.org.uk/cases/adjudicated.html?article=MjA5OA==&type.
98 Gerald Scarfe, 'About Gerald', *Gerald Scarfe, the Official Website,* https://www.geraldscarfe.com/about-gerald-scarfe/.
99 Josh Halliday, '*Sunday Times* Denies Antisemitism in Israeli Election Cartoon', *Guardian*, 28 January 2013, https://www.theguardian.com/media/2013/jan/28/sunday-times-antisemitism-israeli-election-cartoon.
100 Mark Gardner and Anshel Pfeffer, 'Is the *Sunday Times* Cartoon Antisemitic?', *Guardian,* 29 January 2013, Mark Gardner's section, https://www.theguardian.com/commentisfree/2013/jan/29/is-the-sunday-times-cartoon-antisemitic.
101 Rupert Murdoch, (@rupertmurdoch), 'Gerald Scarfe Has Never Reflected the Opinions of the *Sunday Times.* Nevertheless, We Owe Major Apology for Grotesque, Offensive Cartoon', Twitter, 28 January 2013, https://twitter.com/rupertmurdoch/status/295964833394851840.
102 Mark Gardner and Anshel Pfeffer, 'Is the *Sunday Times* Cartoon Antisemitic?', Mark Gardner's section.
103 BCA image reference number SBD1085, https://www.cartoons.ac.uk/record/SBD1085.
104 Jennifer Lipman, 'Guardian Cartoonist Defends Netanyahu "Puppet-Master" Image', *Jewish Chronicle,* 16 November 2012, https://www.thejc.com/news/uk-news/guardian-cartoonist-defends-netanyahu-puppet-master-image-1.38522.
105 Joël Kotek, *Cartoons and Extremism: Israel and the Jews in Arab and Western Media*, trans. Alisa Jaffa (Edgware: Vallentine Mitchell, 2009), 119.
106 Simon Weaver, *The Rhetoric of Racist Humour* (Farnham and Burlington: Ashgate, 2011), 178.
107 I omit image 3.1 from this list.

Chapter 3

1 Arthur Wesley Helweg, *Sikhs in England: The Development of a Migrant Community* (Delhi: Oxford University Press, 1979), 21.
2 Helweg, *Sikhs in England,* 2.
3 David Beetham, *Transport and Turbans: A Comparative Study in Local Politics* (London: Oxford University Press, 1970), 10.
4 W. H. McLeod, *Sikhism* (London: Penguin, 1997), 212.
5 McLeod, *Sikhism,* 240.
6 Jasbir K. Puar, '"The Turban Is Not a Hat": Queer Diaspora and Practices of Profiling', *Sikh Formations* 4 (2008): 64–5.

7   Puar, 'The Turban', 65.
8   Santokh Singh Gill, '"So People Know I'm a Sikh": Narratives of Sikh Masculinities in Contemporary Britain', *Culture and Religion* 15 (2014): 338.
9   McLeod, *Sikhism*, 209.
10 Gill, 'So People Know', 344.
11 None of the images were omitted from this list.
12 Beetham, *Transport and Turbans*, 18.
13 Dilip Hiro, *Black British, White British* (Harmondsworth: Penguin Books, 1973), 128.
14 Sebastian M. Poulter, *English Law and Ethnic Minority Customs* (London: Butterworth, 1986), 255.
15 Poulter, *English Law*, 256.
16 Beetham, *Transport and Turbans*, 85.
17 Interestingly, BCA image reference number 26314 by Michael Cummings features a map of the 'The Dis-United Kingdom' which flags the 'Sikh republic of Southall'. This demonstrates popular perceptions of the district and fears that it was being overrun by the Sikh community, thus leading to a loss of sovereignty and a fragmented UK. https://archive.cartoons.ac.uk/Record.aspx?src=CalmView.Catalog&id=26314.
18 Brian Keith Axel, *The Nation's Tortured Body: Violence, Representation, and the Formation of a Sikh 'Diaspora'* (Durham, NC: Duke University Press, 2001), 165.
19 Axel, *Nation's Tortured Body*, 164.
20 Ian R. G. Spencer, *British Immigration Policy since 1939: The Making of Multi-Racial Britain* (New York: Routledge, 1997), 54.
21 *British Nationality Act, 1948*, http://www.legislation.gov.uk/ukpga/1948/56/pdfs/ukpga_19480056_en.pdf.
22 Helweg, *Sikhs in England*, 21.
23 Sebastian M. Poulter, *Ethnicity, Law and Human Rights: The English Experience* (Oxford: Clarendon Press, 1998), 291.
24 BCA image reference number 13685, https://archive.cartoons.ac.uk/Record.aspx?src=CalmView.Catalog&id=13685.
25 BCA image reference number 13680, https://archive.cartoons.ac.uk/Record.aspx?src=CalmView.Catalog&id=13680.
26 BCA image reference number 15238, https://archive.cartoons.ac.uk/Record.aspx?src=CalmView.Catalog&id=15238.
27 BCA image reference number 17166, https://archive.cartoons.ac.uk/Record.aspx?src=CalmView.Catalog&id=17166.
28 In a way, this was true. After the Wolverhampton case was resolved in 1969, there were calls from other minority groups to be granted rights such as Muslim female bus conductors being allowed to wear headscarves. Beetham, *Transport and Turbans*, 64.

29. BCA image reference number 15236, https://archive.cartoons.ac.uk/Record.aspx?src=CalmView.Catalog&id=15236.
30. Hiro, *Black British*, 176.
31. Gurharpal Singh, 'British Multiculturalism and Sikhs', *Sikh Formations* 1 (2005): 159.
32. Powell, 'Rivers of Blood'.
33. BCA image reference number 23439, https://archive.cartoons.ac.uk/Record.aspx?src=CalmView.Catalog&id=23439.
34. Poulter, *English Law*, 259.
35. Poulter, *English Law*, 185–6.
36. The Employment Equality (Religion or Belief) Regulations 2003, http://www.legislation.gov.uk/uksi/2003/1660/contents/made.
37. Poulter, *Ethnicity*, 292.
38. BCA image reference number 25058, https://archive.cartoons.ac.uk/Record.aspx?src=CalmView.Catalog&id=25058.
39. Poulter, *Ethnicity*, 292.
40. BCA image reference number 25059, https://archive.cartoons.ac.uk/Record.aspx?src=CalmView.Catalog&id=25059.
41. BCA image reference number 25062, https://archive.cartoons.ac.uk/Record.aspx?src=CalmView.Catalog&id=25062.
42. Lord Avebury, *Hansard,* House of Lords, vol. 374, cols. 1055–69, 4 October 1976, http://hansard.millbanksystems.com/lords/1976/oct/04/motor-cycle-crash-helmets-religious#column_1056.
43. Poulter, *Ethnicity,* 296.
44. S. Bidwell and The Sikh Missionary Society, *The Turban Victory* (Southall, Middlesex: The Sikh Missionary Society, 1987), 10.
45. Poulter, *English Law,* 283.
46. Ibid.
47. 'Recognizing the militaristic qualities of the Sikhs, the English classified them as a martial race and incorporated them into the Indian Army. Their loyalty to the crown was crucial for the British to maintain control in South Asia'. A. W. Helweg, 'Sikh Identity in England: Its Changing Nature', in *Sikh History and Religion in the Twentieth Century,* ed. J. T. O'Connell, M. Israel and W. G. Oxtoby (Toronto: Centre for South Asian Studies University of Toronto, 1988), 359.
48. Poulter*, Ethnicity,* 283.
49. Gill, 'So People Know', 340.
50. BCA image reference number 46717, https://archive.cartoons.ac.uk/Record.aspx?src=CalmView.Catalog&id=46717.
51. Helweg, 'Sikh Identity', 359.
52. Helweg, 'Sikh Identity', 370.
53. Ibid., 371.

54 BCA image reference number 47635, https://archive.cartoons.ac.uk/Record.aspx?src=CalmView.Catalog&id=47635.
55 Gill, 'So People Know', 337.
56 Several incidents involving Sikhs being attacked have occurred both in Britain as well as in other parts of the world. Emine Saner, 'Why Are Sikhs Targeted by Anti-Muslim Extremists?', *Guardian*, 8 August 2012, http://www.theguardian.com/world/2012/aug/08/sikhs-targeted-anti-muslim-extremists. Furthermore, '[t]he first of the post-9 – 11 hate-crime murders was in fact a turbaned Sikh […] who was shot five times in the back at a gas station in Mesa, Arizona, on 15 September 2001.' Puar, 'The Turban', 47.
57 Gill, 'So People Know', 342.
58 BCA image reference number 21418, https://archive.cartoons.ac.uk/Record.aspx?src=CalmView.Catalog&id=21418.
59 BCA image reference number 14072, https://archive.cartoons.ac.uk/Record.aspx?src=CalmView.Catalog&id=14072.
60 BCA image reference number 23660, https://archive.cartoons.ac.uk/Record.aspx?src=CalmView.Catalog&id=23660.
61 Paul Gilroy, 'Working with "Wogs": Aliens, Denizens and the Machinations of Denialism', *Communication, Culture and Critique* 15, no. 2 (June 2022): 122, https://doi.org/10.1093/ccc/tcac012.
62 BCA image reference number WH3686, https://archive.cartoons.ac.uk/Record.aspx?src=CalmView.Catalog&id=WH3686.
63 'Women's Fashion Hits the Courts', http://news.bbc.co.uk/1/hi/events/wimbledon_98/behind_the_scenes/114681.stm, *BBC News*, 19 June 1998.
64 BCA image reference number 13143, https://archive.cartoons.ac.uk/Record.aspx?src=CalmView.Catalog&id=13143.
65 Mark Lattimer, 'When Labour Played the Racist Card', *New Statesman*, 22 January 1999, https://www.newstatesman.com/when-labour-played-racist-card.
66 Jim Callaghan, *Hansard*, House of Commons, vol. 759, col. 1251, 27 February 1968, https://api.parliament.uk/historic-hansard/commons/1968/feb/27/commonwealth-immigrants-bill#S5CV0759P0_19680227_HOC2_305.
67 BCA image reference number 13317, https://archive.cartoons.ac.uk/Record.aspx?src=CalmView.Catalog&id=13317.
68 BCA image reference number 13319, https://archive.cartoons.ac.uk/Record.aspx?src=CalmView.Catalog&id=13319.
69 Ian Aitken, 'Enoch Powell Dismissed for "Racialist" Speech', *Guardian*, 22 April 1968, http://www.theguardian.com/news/1968/apr/22/mainsection.ianaitken.
70 Powell, 'Rivers of Blood'.
71 BCA image reference number 81542, https://archive.cartoons.ac.uk/Record.aspx?src=CalmView.Catalog&id=81542.

72 Paul Gilroy, 'Multiculture, Double Consciousness and the "War on Terror"', *Patterns of Prejudice* 39, no. 4 (2005): 434.
73 Puar, 'The Turban', 54.
74 Ibid., 48.
75 Ibid., 56.

Chapter 4

1   M.A.S. Abdel Haleem, *Qur'an: English Translation with Parallel Arabic Text* (Oxford: Oxford University Press, 2010).
2   W. F. Deedes, 'Muslims Can Never Conform to Our Ways', *Telegraph*, 20 October 2006, https://www.telegraph.co.uk/comment/personal-view/3633349/Muslims-can-never-conform-to-our-ways.html.
3   Muslim Council of Britain's Research & Documentation Committee, *British Muslims in Numbers a Demographic, Socio-Economic and Health Profile of Muslims in Britain Drawing On the 2011 Census* (London: The Muslim Council of Britain, 2015), 24, https://www.mcb.org.uk/wp-content/uploads/2015/02/MCBCensusReport_2015.pdf.
4   Tariq Modood, 'British Muslims and the Politics of Multiculturalism', in *Multiculturalism, Muslims and Citizenship: A European Approach*, ed. Tariq Modood, Anna Triandafyllidou and Ricard Zapata-Barrero (New York: Routledge, 2006), 37.
5   Modood, *Multicultural Politics: Racism, Ethnicity, and Muslims in Britain* (Minneapolis: University of Minnesota Press, 2005), 4.
6   Modood, *Multicultural Politics*, 38.
7   Modood, 'British Muslims', 41.
8   Peter Murtagh, 'Rushdie in Hiding after Ayatollah's Death Threat', *Guardian*, 15 February 1989, http://www.theguardian.com/books/1989/feb/15/salmanrushdie.
9   Michael Georgy, Raju Gopalakrishnan and Kevin Liffey (ed.), 'Iranian Foundation Offers Land to Salman Rushdie's Attacker – State TV', *Reuters*, 21 February 2023, https://www.reuters.com/world/middle-east/iranian-foundation-offers-land-salman-rushdies-attacker-state-media-2023-02-21/.
10 Modood, 'British Muslims', 41.
11 Kate Zebiri, 'Orientalist Themes in Contemporary British Islamophobia', in *Islamophobia: The Challenge of Pluralism in the 21st Century*, ed. John L. Esposito and Ibrahim Kalin (Oxford: Oxford University Press, 2011), 176–7.
12 Muslim Council of Britain's Research & Documentation Committee, *British Muslims*, 40.
13 Ibid., 34.

14. Tahir Abbas, 'Muslim Minorities in Britain: Integration, Multiculturalism and Radicalism in the Post-7/7 Period', *Journal of Intercultural Studies* 28, no. 3 (2008): 292, 10.1080/07256860701429717.
15. Kevin Peachey, 'Sir Winston Churchill to Feature on New Banknote', *BBC News,* 26 April 2013, http://www.bbc.co.uk/news/business-22306707.
16. Caroline Criado-Perez, 'We Need Women on British Banknotes', *Change.org,* https://www.change.org/p/we-need-women-on-british-banknotes.
17. Heather Saul, 'Vince Cable Accuses Bank of England Officials of "Acting Like the Taliban"', *Independent,* 24 July 2013, http://www.independent.co.uk/news/business/news/vince-cable-accuses-bank-of-england-officials-of-acting-like-the-taliban-8729262.html.
18. 'Jane Austen to be Face of the Bank of England £10 Note', *BBC News,* 24 July 2013, http://www.bbc.co.uk/news/business-23424289.
19. The new £10 note came into circulation in July 2017.
20. Portrait of Jane Austen, http://www.sothebys.com/en/auctions/ecatalogue/2013/english-literature-history-l13408/lot.283.html.
21. Weaver, *Rhetoric of Racist Humour,* 177.
22. Puar, 'The Turban', 56.
23. Sonya Fernandez, 'The Crusade Over the Bodies of Women', *Patterns of Prejudice* 43, no. 3–4 (2009): 272, 10.1080/00313220903109185.
24. Fernandez, 'Crusade', 275.
25. BCA image reference number 71997, https://www.cartoons.ac.uk/record/71997.
26. These powers were repealed under the *Protection of Freedoms Act 2012* and replaced with Article 3 of *The Terrorism Act 2000 (Remedial) Order 2011*, https://www.legislation.gov.uk/uksi/2011/631/article/3/made. For further information, see 'Section 44 Terrorism Act', *Liberty,* https://www.liberty-human-rights.org.uk/human-rights/justice-and-fair-trials/stop-and-search/section-44-terrorism-act.
27. 'Blears Seeks to Reassure Muslims', *BBC News,* 2 August 2005, http://news.bbc.co.uk/1/hi/uk_politics/4736969.stm.
28. Myfanwy Franks, 'Crossing the Borders of Whiteness? White Muslim Women Who Wear the Hijab in Britain Today', *Ethnic and Racial Studies* 23 (2000): 925.
29. *The Constitution of Afghanistan,* ratified 26 January 2004, http://www.afghanembassy.com.pl/afg/images/pliki/TheConstitution.pdf.
30. 'Some of the Restrictions Imposed by Taliban on Women in Afghanistan: 1996–2001', Revolutionary Association of the Women of Afghanistan (RAWA), http://www.rawa.org/rules.htm.
31. BCA image reference number 59694, https://www.cartoons.ac.uk/record/59694.
32. BCA image reference number 59652, https://www.cartoons.ac.uk/record/59652.
33. BCA image reference number SCD0040, https://archive.cartoons.ac.uk/Record.aspx?src=CalmView.Catalog&id=SCD0040.

34 Saul, 'Vince Cable'.
35 BCA image reference number 84444, https://www.cartoons.ac.uk/record/84444.
36 Peter Allen, 'French Burka Ban: Police Arrest Two Veiled Women', *Daily Telegraph*, 11 April 2011, http://www.telegraph.co.uk/news/worldnews/europe/france/8442622/French-burka-ban-police-arrest-two-veiled-women.html.
37 For example, 'The Invasion Plate 1: France', (8 March 1756).
38 BCA image reference number 84438, https://www.cartoons.ac.uk/record/84438.
39 'Famous Men Who Wear Stack Heels', *Guardian*, 9 April 2009, https://www.theguardian.com/lifeandstyle/gallery/2009/apr/09/famous-men-stack-heels.
40 In his state of the nation speech, Sarkozy argued that the face veil meant women were 'prisoners behind a screen, cut off from all social life, deprived of all identity. That's not our idea of freedom.' Angelique Chrisafis, 'Nicolas Sarkozy Says Islamic Veils Are Not Welcome in France', *Guardian*, 22 June 2009, https://www.theguardian.com/world/2009/jun/22/islamic-veils-sarkozy-speech-france.
41 'In Your Face', *The Times*, 11 April 2011, 2, http://find.galegroup.com/dvnw/infomark.do?&source=gale&prodId=DVNW&userGroupName=kings&tabID=T003&docPage=article&docId=IF504210106&type=multipage&contentSet=LTO&version=1.0.
42 Patrick Hennessy, 'Burka Ban Ruled Out by Immigration Minister', *Daily Telegraph*, 17 July 2010, http://www.telegraph.co.uk/news/politics/7896751/Burka-ban-ruled-out-by-immigration-minister.html.
43 BCA image reference number 81488, https://www.cartoons.ac.uk/record/81488.
44 James Slack, 'Burkas Empower Women: Female Cabinet Minister Insists Freedom to Wear Muslim Veil Is a Right', *Daily Mail*, 20 July 2010, http://www.dailymail.co.uk/news/article-1295665/Banning-burkas-UK-British-says-Green.html.
45 See Rosa Prince, 'Caroline Spelman: Wearing Burka Can Be "Empowering"', *Daily Telegraph*, 19 July 2010, http://www.telegraph.co.uk/news/religion/7897848/Caroline-Spelman-wearing-burka-can-be-empowering.html, and Yasmin Alibhai-Brown, 'The Burka Empowering Women? You Must Be Mad, Minister', *Daily Mail*, 21 July 2010, http://www.dailymail.co.uk/debate/article-1296132/The-burka-empowering-women-You-mad-minister.html.
46 BCA reference 81493, https://www.cartoons.ac.uk/record/81493.
47 Fernandez, 'Crusade', 271.
48 BCA image reference number 99612, https://www.cartoons.ac.uk/record/99612.
49 NUS Black Students' Campaign, 'Birmingham Metropolitan College: Reverse Your Decision to Ban Muslim Students from Wearing Veils', *Change.org*, https://www.change.org/p/birmingham-metropolitan-college-reverse-your-decision-to-ban-muslim-students-from-wearing-veils.
50 Nasar Meer and Tehseen Noorani, 'A Sociological Comparison of Anti-Semitism and Anti-Muslim Sentiment in Britain', *The Sociological Review* 56, no. 2 (2008): 200.

51 BCA image reference number 99998, https://www.cartoons.ac.uk/record/99998.
52 Vikram Dodd, 'Burqa Fugitive Mohammed Ahmed Mohamed "faced 20 charges"', *Guardian*, 8 November 2013, http://www.theguardian.com/uk-news/2013/nov/08/burqa-fugitive-mohammed-ahmed-mohamed-20-charges.
53 BCA image reference number 100154, https://www.cartoons.ac.uk/record/100154.
54 BCA image reference number 95089, https://www.cartoons.ac.uk/record/95089.
55 BCA image reference number 102387, https://www.cartoons.ac.uk/record/102387.
56 Karen Morrison, 'Muslim Woman Will Have to Remove Veil to Give Evidence', *Sun*, 16 September 2013, https://www.thesun.co.uk/archives/news/1016924/muslim-woman-will-have-to-remove-veil-to-give-evidence/.
57 Brian Klug, 'The Collective Jew: Israel and the New Antisemitism', *Patterns of Prejudice* 37, no. 2 (2003): 135.
58 BCA image reference number 100758, https://www.cartoons.ac.uk/record/100758.
59 Interestingly, the composition of a New York school district governing board was subject to scrutiny when it emerged that the majority of the governors were Orthodox Jews. This was despite the fact that most of their children attended private yeshivas, whilst 90 per cent of the public school population was Black and Latino. Jan Ransom, 'East Ramapo School Elections Violate Voting Rights, Suit Claims', *New York Times*, 16 November 2017, https://www.nytimes.com/2017/11/16/nyregion/aclu-files-suit-against-east-ramapo-school-board-voting-rights.html.
60 'Trojan Horse "plot" Schools Timeline', *BBC News*, 16 July 2015, http://www.bbc.co.uk/news/uk-england-birmingham-28370552.
61 BCA image reference number 101084, https://www.cartoons.ac.uk/record/101084.
62 'Al-Qaeda in Yemen Claims Charlie Hebdo Attack', *Al Jazeera*, 14 January 2015, http://www.aljazeera.com/news/middleeast/2015/01/al-qaeda-yemen-charlie-hebdo-paris-attacks-201511410323361511.html.
63 BCA image reference number 102284, https://www.cartoons.ac.uk/record/102284.
64 'BBC Radio 4 Today Muslim Poll', *ComRes*, table 14, https://savanta.com/knowledge-centre/poll/bbc-radio-4-today-muslim-poll/, 14.
65 'BBC Radio 4 Today Muslim Poll', 14.
66 BCA image reference number BJD0421, https://www.cartoons.ac.uk/record/BJD0421.
67 Stefano Hatfield, 'i Editor's Letter: Winners of i Cartoon Idol Contest', *i News*, 12 December 2011, https://www.independent.co.uk/i/editor/i-editors-letter-winners-of-i-cartoon-idol-contest-6275866.html.
68 Jessica Elgot, 'Ukip to Campaign to Ban Burqa and Sharia Courts, Says Paul Nuttall', *Guardian*, 23 April 2017, https://www.theguardian.com/politics/2017/apr/23/ukip-to-campaign-to-ban-burka-and-sharia-courts-says-paul-nuttall.
69 Helena Horton, '"What about Beekeepers?": Ukip Mocked after Being Forced to Clarify Their Veil-Banning Policy', *Daily Telegraph*, 24 April 2017, http://www.

telegraph.co.uk/news/2017/04/24/beekeepers-ukip-mocked-forced-clarify-veil-banning-policy/.
70   Salam Al-Mahadin, 'The Social Semiotics', 6.
71   No images are omitted from this list.
72   Bhikhu Parekh, 'Europe, Liberalism and the "Muslim Question"', in *Multiculturalism, Muslims and Citizenship: A European Approach*. ed. Tariq Modood, Anna Triandafyllidou and Ricard Zapata-Barrero (New York: Routledge, 2006), 181.
73   Fernandez, 'Crusade', 274.
74   Puar, 'The Turban', 62.
75   Brian Klug, 'Islamophobia: A Concept Comes of Age', *Ethnicities* 12, no. 5 (2012): 678.
76   Meyda Yegenoglu, 'Sartorial Fabric-Actions: The Enlightenment and Western Feminism', in *Colonial Fantasies: Towards a Feminist Reading of Orientalism* (Cambridge: Cambridge University Press, 1998), 110, http://dx.doi.org/10.1017/CBO9780511583445.005.
77   Boris Johnson, 'Denmark Has Got It Wrong. Yes, the Burka Is Oppressive and Ridiculous – but That's Still No Reason to Ban It', *Daily Telegraph*, 5 August 2018, https://www.telegraph.co.uk/news/2018/08/05/denmark-has-got-wrong-yes-burka-oppressive-ridiculous-still/.
78   Johnson, 'Denmark'.
79   Modood, 'British Muslims', 41.
80   Parekh, 'the "Muslim question"', 200.
81   Michel Foucault, 'Panopticism', from 'Discipline & Punish: The Birth of the Prison', *Race/Ethnicity: Multidisciplinary Global Contexts* 2, no. 1 (2008): 6, https://www.jstor.org/stable/25594995.
82   Yegenoglu, 'Sartorial Fabric-Actions', 108.
83   Al-Mahadin, 'Social Semiotics of Hijab', 16.
84   Yegenoglu, 'Sartorial Fabric-Actions', 110.
85   Ibid., 99.
86   Gili Hammer, '"If They're Going to Stare, at Least I'll Give Them a Good Reason To": Blind Women's Visibility, Invisibility, and Encounters with the Gaze', *Signs: Journal of Women in Culture and Society* 41, no. 2 (2016): 419, https://www.journals.uchicago.edu/doi/pdfplus/10.1086/682924.

Chapter 5

1   Brian Klug, 'Islamophobia: A Concept Comes of Age', *Ethnicities* 12, no. 5 (2012): 678, www.jstor.org/stable/43572627.

2   Muslim Council of Britain's Research & Documentation Committee, *British Muslims,* 16.
3   Muslim Council of Britain's Research & Documentation Committee, 24.
4   Julian Petley and Robin Richardson, *Pointing the Finger: Islam and Muslims in the British Media* (Richmond: Oneworld, 2011), xv.
5   Halim Rane, Jacqui Ewart and John Martinkus, *Media Framing of the Muslim World: Conflicts, Crises and Contexts* (Houndmills, Basingstoke, Hampshire: Palgrave Macmillan, 2014), 29.
6   To a lesser extent, Samantha Lewthwaite and Sally Jones – both often referred to as 'White Widows' – have achieved such notoriety in the British press.
7   'Who Was Abu Bakr al-Baghdadi?', *BBC News,* 28 October 2019, https://www.bbc.co.uk/news/world-middle-east-50200392.
8   'Isis Leader Calls on Muslims to "Build Islamic State"', *BBC News,* 1 July 2014, http://www.bbc.co.uk/news/world-middle-east-28116846.
9   BCA image reference number 59105, http://archives.cartoons.ac.uk/Record.aspx?src=CalmView.Catalog&id=59105.
10 BCA image reference number 59102, http://archives.cartoons.ac.uk/Record.aspx?src=CalmView.Catalog&id=59102.
11 BCA image reference number 59106, http://archives.cartoons.ac.uk/Record.aspx?src=CalmView.Catalog&id=59106.
12 'Transcript: Translation of Bin Laden's Videotaped Message', *The Washington Post,* 1 November 2004, http://www.washingtonpost.com/wp-dyn/articles/A16990-2004Nov1.html.
13 Elizabeth Poole, *Reporting Islam: Media Representations of British Muslims* (London: I.B. Tauris, 2002), 3.
14 Edward Said, *Covering Islam: How the Media and the Experts Determine How We See the Rest of the World* (London: Vintage, 1997), 10.
15 Said, *Covering Islam,* 10.
16 BCA image reference number 59049, http://archives.cartoons.ac.uk/Record.aspx?src=CalmView.Catalog&id=59049.
17 Kimberly A. Powell, 'Framing Islam: An Analysis of U.S. Media Coverage of Terrorism since 9/11', *Communication Studies* 62, no. 1 (2011): 92, 10.1080/10510974.2011.533599.
18 Council on Foreign Relations, 1999-2021 The U.S. War in Afghanistan https://www.cfr.org/timeline/us-war-afghanistan.
19 Tony Blair, 'Blair: What Will the World Look Like If We Don't Stop Bin Laden?', *Independent,* 12 October 2001, http://www.independent.co.uk/news/world/asia/blair-what-will-the-world-look-like-if-we-dont-stop-bin-laden-9172514.html. This also demonstrates the point made in the previous chapter on the impact of the Taliban regime in relation to the perception of Muslim women.

20 BCA image reference number 59365, http://archives.cartoons.ac.uk/Record.aspx?src=CalmView.Catalog&id=59365.
21 *Your country needs you, a British advertisement,* poster image, British Library, https://www.bl.uk/collection-items/your-country-needs-you.
22 BCA image reference number 59069, https://archive.cartoons.ac.uk/record.aspx?src=CalmView.Catalog&id=59069.
23 Poole, *Reporting Islam,* 4.
24 'Parasite, n.' *OED Online* (Oxford University Press, June 2017), www.oed.com/view/Entry/137636.
25 The Nazis published a pamphlet entitled *Der Jude als Weltparasit* [The Jew as World Parasite] in 1943, summarizing the party's antisemitic views.
26 For example, see James Chapman, 'Migrants with No Medical Insurance "Won't Get NHS Care": Minister's Tough Stance on New Influx from the East', *Daily Mail,* 29 January 2013, http://www.dailymail.co.uk/news/article-2269838/Migrants-medical-insurance-wont-NHS-care-Ministers-tough-stance-new-influx-East.html.
27 Gilroy, 'War on Terror', 433.
28 Elizabeth Poole, 'The Effects of September 11 and the War in Iraq on British Newspaper Coverage', in *Muslims and the News Media,* ed. Elizabeth Poole and John E. Richardson (London: I.B. Tauris & Company, Limited, 2010), 95.
29 BCA image reference number 86517, https://archive.cartoons.ac.uk/Record.aspx?src=CalmView.Catalog&id=86517.
30 BCA image reference number 71847, https://archive.cartoons.ac.uk/Record.aspx?src=CalmView.Catalog&id=71847.
31 BCA image reference number 71846, https://archive.cartoons.ac.uk/Record.aspx?src=CalmView.Catalog&id=71846.
32 BCA image reference number 86519, https://archive.cartoons.ac.uk/Record.aspx?src=CalmView.Catalog&id=86519.
33 'The Bombers', *BBC News,* http://news.bbc.co.uk/1/shared/spl/hi/uk/05/london_blasts/investigation/html/bombers.stm.
34 'Bomber's Family: He Was Proud to be British', *Daily Telegraph,* 13 July 2005, http://www.telegraph.co.uk/news/1493934/Bombers-family-he-was-proud-to-be-British.html.
35 BCA image reference number 71866, https://archive.cartoons.ac.uk/Record.aspx?src=CalmView.Catalog&id=71866.
36 BCA image reference number 71922, http://archives.cartoons.ac.uk/Record.aspx?src=CalmView.Catalog&id=71922.
37 'Full Text: Blair Speech on Terror', *BBC News,* 16 July 2005, http://news.bbc.co.uk/1/hi/uk/4689363.stm.
38 Vanessa Allen, 'How MI5 Blundered over Photo of Two 7/7 Bombers', *Daily Mail,* 7 May 2011, http://www.dailymail.co.uk/news/article-1359148/7-7-inquest-How-MI5-blundered-photo-2-bombers.html.

39 Powell, 'Framing Islam', 92.
40 Ibid., 93.
41 Tariq Modood, 'British Muslims', 41.
42 BCA image reference number 74170, http://archives.cartoons.ac.uk/Record.aspx?src=CalmView.Catalog&id=74170.
43 This is not dissimilar to the Nazi fear of the assimilated Jew who was able to deceive the non-Jew. See Anson Rabinbach, and Sander L. Gilman, *The Third Reich Sourcebook* (Berkeley: University of California Press, 2013), 311.
44 Powell, 'Framing Islam', 107.
45 BCA image reference number 75988, http://archives.cartoons.ac.uk/Record.aspx?src=CalmView.Catalog&id=75988.
46 '#Notinmyname: Hundreds of Muslims Condemn Terror Attack', *BBC News*, 25 March 2017, http://www.bbc.co.uk/news/uk-england-birmingham-39392442.
47 BCA image reference number 74432, http://archives.cartoons.ac.uk/Record.aspx?src=CalmView.Catalog&id=74432.
48 David Pilditch and Tom Whitehead, 'The Day an Islamic Protestor Told the Home Secretary: How Dare You Come to a Muslim Area?', *Daily Express*, 21 September 2006, 7.
49 BCA image reference number 74418, http://archives.cartoons.ac.uk/Record.aspx?src=CalmView.Catalog&id=74418.
50 'Abu Hamza Jailed for Seven Years', BBC News, 7 February 2006, http://news.bbc.co.uk/1/hi/uk/4690224.stm.
51 'Mustafa Kamel Mustafa, A/k/a "Abu Hamza," Convicted of 11 Terrorism Charges in Manhattan Federal Court', press release, United States Department of Justice, 19 May 2014, https://www.justice.gov/usao-sdny/pr/mustafa-kamel-mustafa-aka-abu-hamza-convicted-11-terrorism-charges-manhattan-federal.
52 BCA image reference number 69363, http://archives.cartoons.ac.uk/Record.aspx?src=CalmView.Catalog&id=69363.
53 BCA image reference number 63832, http://archives.cartoons.ac.uk/Record.aspx?src=CalmView.Catalog&id=63832.
54 BCA image reference number 97679, http://archives.cartoons.ac.uk/Record.aspx?src=CalmView.Catalog&id=97679.
55 BCA image reference number, 103642, https://archive.cartoons.ac.uk/Record.aspx?src=CalmView.Catalog&id=103642.
56 BCA image reference number 98979, https://archive.cartoons.ac.uk/Record.aspx?src=CalmView.Catalog&id=98979.
57 BCA image reference number 98947, https://archive.cartoons.ac.uk/Record.aspx?src=CalmView.Catalog&id=98947.
58 Intelligence and Security Committee of Parliament, *Report on the intelligence relating to the murder of Fusilier Lee Rigby*, 25 November 2014, https://b1cba9b3-a-5e6631fd-s-sites.googlegroups.com/a/independent.gov.uk/

isc/files/20141125_ISC_Woolwich_Report%28website%29.pdf?attachau th=ANoY7cqla86ixsy5fwWzPEEBpC-JRj00HeLkP-bj6aLcY8xiEddjigN_ kTwjQS9u05X05BPh76TY9CkkUUqZ_g1VK-qbs1xWg3jUP24-akMC1oRKa8 U01dPLn2aNmnvh4KU0TJ_1ynPBTjwx7yBF-Y_uErN30cXJIMhoicBCD1o100 WoA5YdxyL4oZv72A0k21i1qJ3Co-x5B6hnZQQGBrRcZ8x3bvwy_AT0AUI9K_ YhDtzLC3xxXMLlh70CSarWwwXmEz9K-6Vz&attredirects=0, 4.

59   'Lee Rigby Trial: Jury Shown "Eye for an Eye" Video', *Telegraph*, 25 November 2014, https://www.telegraph.co.uk/news/uknews/crime/10492778/Lee-Rigby-trial-jury-shown-eye-for-an-eye-video.html.

60   Dominic Casciani, 'Woolwich: How Did Michael Adebolajo Become a Killer?', *BBC News*, 19 December 2013, http://www.bbc.co.uk/news/magazine-25424290.

61   'Islamic State and the Crisis in Iraq and Syria in Maps.' *BBC News*, 28 March 2018, http://www.bbc.co.uk/news/world-middle-east-27838034.

62   Richard Barrett, *Beyond the Caliphate: Foreign Fighters and the Threat of Returnees*, The Soufan Center, October 2017, https://thesoufancenter.org/research/beyond-caliphate/, 13.

63   'British Family of 12 Suspected of Joining Islamic State "All Die in Syria"', *Sky News*, 28 June 2019, https://news.sky.com/story/british-family-of-12-suspected-of-joining-islamic-state-all-killed-in-syria-11750813.

64   Ruth Sherlock, 'Al-Qaeda Cuts Links with Syrian Group Too Extreme Even for Them', *Daily Telegraph*, 3 February 2014, https://www.telegraph.co.uk/news/worldnews/middleeast/syria/10614037/Al-Qaeda-cuts-links-with-Syrian-group-too-extreme-even-for-them.html.

65   *Foreign Fighters: An Updated Assessment of the Flow of Foreign Fighters into Syria and Iraq*, The Soufan Center, December 2015, https://thesoufancenter.org/research/foreign-fighters-in-syria/, 12.

66   BCA image reference number 101389, http://archives.cartoons.ac.uk/Record.aspx?src=CalmView.Catalog&id=101389.

67   See BCA image references numbers JL2461, https://archive.cartoons.ac.uk/Record.aspx?src=CalmView.Catalog&id=JL2461, WH0150, https://archive.cartoons.ac.uk/Record.aspx?src=CalmView.Catalog&id=WH0150 and NEB1183, https://archive.cartoons.ac.uk/Record.aspx?src=CalmView.Catalog&id=NEB11.83 which depict Africans in a monkey-like manner.

68   BCA image reference number 101688, http://archives.cartoons.ac.uk/Record.aspx?src=CalmView.Catalog&id=101688.

69   Other examples include BCA image reference numbers SBD1345, https://archive.cartoons.ac.uk/Record.aspx?src=CalmView.Catalog&id=SBD1345 and SCD0193, https://archive.cartoons.ac.uk/Record.aspx?src=CalmView.Catalog&id=SCD0193.

70   BCA image reference number 102107, http://archives.cartoons.ac.uk/Record.aspx?src=CalmView.Catalog&id=102107.

71 *Statement from Pentagon Press Secretary Peter Cook on Airstrike in Raqqa, Syria*, press release, U.S. Department of Defense, 12 November 2015, https://www.defense.gov/News/News-Releases/News-Release-View/Article/628777/statement-from-pentagon-press-secretary-peter-cook-on-airstrike-in-raqqa-syria/.
72 Peter Gottschalk and Gabriel Greenberg, *Islamophobia: Making Muslims the Enemy* (Lanham: Rowman & Littlefield, 2008), 45–6.
73 Gottschalk and Greenberg, *Islamophobia*, 46.
74 Ibid., 47.
75 Toby Melville and William James, 'Five Dead, Around 40 Injured in Parliament "Terrorist" Attack', *Reuters*, 22 March 2017, https://uk.reuters.com/article/uk-britain-security-photographer/five-dead-around-40-injured-in-parliament-terrorist-attack-idUKKBN16T1Y7.
76 BCA image reference number SBD1782, http://archives.cartoons.ac.uk/Record.aspx?src=CalmView.Catalog&id=SBD1782.
77 BCA image reference number BJD0418, http://archives.cartoons.ac.uk/Record.aspx?src=CalmView.Catalog&id=BJD0418.
78 'Manchester Attack: What We Know So Far', *BBC News*, 12 June 2017, https://www.bbc.co.uk/news/uk-england-manchester-40008389.
79 Jen Mills, 'Powerful Cartoon Sums up Response to Manchester Attack', *Metro*, 23 May 2017, https://metro.co.uk/2017/05/23/powerful-cartoon-sums-up-response-to-manchester-attack-6655739/.
80 BCA image reference number MRD1033, https://archive.cartoons.ac.uk/Record.aspx?src=CalmView.Catalog&id=MRD1033.
81 BCA image reference number 105700, https://archive.cartoons.ac.uk/Record.aspx?src=CalmView.Catalog&id=105700.
82 BCA image reference number BAD0461, https://archive.cartoons.ac.uk/Record.aspx?src=CalmView.Catalog&id=BAD0461.
83 BCA image reference number BJD0437, http://archives.cartoons.ac.uk/Record.aspx?src=CalmView.Catalog&id=BJD0437.
84 Jason Hanna, 'The London Train Explosion Is the Latest of 5 Terror Incidents in 2017 in the UK', *CNN*, 15 September 2017, http://edition.cnn.com/2017/09/15/world/uk-terror-events-2017/index.html.
85 BCA image reference number MRD102, http://archives.cartoons.ac.uk/Record.aspx?src=CalmView.Catalog&id=MRD1023.
86 'Fake News, the Fascist Left and the Real Purveyors of Hatred; Daily Mail Comment', *Daily Mail*, 22 June 2017, Factiva, https://global-factiva-com.libproxy.kcl.ac.uk/redir/default.aspx?P=sa&an=DAIM000020170621ed6m0000i&cat=a&ep=ASE.
87 David Mercer and Alix Culbertson, 'Five Minutes of Terror: How the London Bridge Attack Unfolded', *Sky News*, 4 June 2021, https://news.sky.com/story/how-the-london-bridge-terror-attack-unfolded-11874155.

88 Peter Walker and Frances Perraudin, 'London Bridge Attack: Boris Johnson Ignores Family's Plea Not to Exploit Victims' Deaths', *Guardian*, 2 December 2019, https://www.theguardian.com/politics/2019/dec/01/boris-johnson-election-issue-london-bridge-attack.

89 PM statement following London terror attack: 4 June 2017, GOV.UK, 4 June 2017, https://www.gov.uk/government/speeches/pm-statement-following-london-terror-attack-4 June 2017.

90 Sandra Laville and Robert Booth, 'Khalid Masood: From Kent Schoolboy to Westminster Attacker', *Guardian*, 25 March 2017, https://www.theguardian.com/uk-news/2017/mar/25/khalid-masood-profile-from-popular-teenager-to-isis-inspired-terrorist.

91 Poole, 'Effects of September 11', 92.

92 None of the images were omitted from this list.

93 Giselinde Kuipers, 'Ethnic Humour and Ethnic Politics in the Netherlands: The Rules and Attraction of Clandestine Humour', in *The Politics of Humour: Laughter, Inclusion, and Exclusion in the Twentieth Century*, ed. Martina Kessel, and Patrick Merziger (Toronto and Buffalo: University of Toronto Press, 2012), 185.

94 '7 Times Katie Hopkins Hit the Headlines', *BBC News*, 26 May 2017, http://www.bbc.co.uk/news/entertainment-arts-40061888.

95 Vikram Dodd and Jamie Grierson, 'Finsbury Park Attack Suspect Was Probably "Self-Radicalised"', *Guardian*, 21 June 2017, https://www.theguardian.com/uk-news/2017/jun/21/finsbury-park-mosque-attack-two-victims-in-critical-care.

Conclusion

1 'PAMCo 3 2018 Jul17–Jun18 Fused with comScore May 2018', table, *PamCo*, 17 September 2018, https://pamco.co.uk/pamco-data/latest-results/.

2 Tim Benson, 'Political Cartoonists Are Divided: Is It OK to Ditch Their Paper and Pens to Go Digital?', *i News*, 30 October 2018, https://inews.co.uk/news/politics/political-cartoons-satire-cartoonists-art-233845.

3 Patrick Blower, 'Livedraw Animation', *Blower Cartoons*, https://blowercartoons.com/livedraw.

4 'Editorial Cartooning', *The Pulitzer Prizes*, https://www.pulitzer.org/prize-winners-by-category/215.

5 *Circulation*, UK Newspaper Market, table, Newsworks, August 2019, https://www.newsworks.org.uk/resources/circulation.

6 Louis Dor, 'Turkish People Are Sharing This Cartoon Asking Where Our Sympathy Was for Istanbul and Ankara', *indy100*, 23 March 2016, https://www.indy100.com/article/turkish-people-are-sharing-this-cartoon-asking-where-our-sympathy-was-for-istanbul-and-ankara--ZJORO9A1eb.

7   See tweets by Francis A. Konan, (@FAK__), 24 March 2016 and Dimitrije Filipovic, (@dimitrijefill), 25 March 2016.
8   Homa Khaleeli, 'The Perils of "Flying While Muslim"', *Guardian*, 8 August 2016, https://www.theguardian.com/world/2016/aug/08/the-perils-of-flying-while-muslim.
9   Speech on Multiculturalism and integration (8 December 2006), *The National Archives*, 8 December 2006, http://webarchive.nationalarchives.gov.uk/20080909022722/http://www.number10.gov.uk/Page10563.
10 Philip Stephens, 'Populism Is the True Legacy of the Global Financial Crisis', *Financial Times*, 30 August 2018, https://www.ft.com/content/687c0184-aaa6-11e8-94bd-cba20d67390c.
11 'Romania and Bulgaria EU Migration Restrictions Lifted', *BBC News*, 1 January 2014, https://www.bbc.co.uk/news/world-europe-25565302.
12 Heather Stewart and Rowena Mason, 'Nigel Farage's Anti-Migrant Poster Reported to Police', *Guardian*, 16 June 2016, https://www.theguardian.com/politics/2016/jun/16/nigel-farage-defends-ukip-breaking-point-poster-queue-of-migrants.
13 Stewart and Mason, 'Anti-Migrant Poster'.
14 BCA image reference number CLD1054, https://archive.cartoons.ac.uk/Record.aspx?src=CalmView.Catalog&id=CLD1054.
15 'Article 50' refers to the Treaty of Lisbon in which any EU member state is allowed the right to leave and details the procedure for doing so.
16 BCA image reference number CLD0984, https://archive.cartoons.ac.uk/Record.aspx?src=CalmView.Catalog&id=CLD0984.
17 BCA image reference number MRD0992, https://archive.cartoons.ac.uk/Record.aspx?src=CalmView.Catalog&id=MRD0992.
18 BCA image reference number BAD0390, https://archive.cartoons.ac.uk/Record.aspx?src=CalmView.Catalog&id=BAD0390.
19 'Windrush Victims Detained "Unlawfully" by Home Office', *BBC News*, 29 June 2018, https://www.bbc.co.uk/news/uk-politics-44651105?intlink_from_url=https://www.bbc.co.uk/news/topics/c9vwmzw7n7lt/windrush-scandal&link_location=live-reporting-story.
20 BCA image reference number 106732, https://archive.cartoons.ac.uk/Record.aspx?src=CalmView.Catalog&id=106732.
21 Windrush scheme and information, GOV.UK, https://www.gov.uk/government/publications/undocumented-commonwealth-citizens-resident-in-the-uk.
22 Christian Adams (@adamstoon), 'My #windrush @evening.standard #cartoon #illustration #sketch #Brexit #theresamay', Instagram, 17 April 2018, https://www.instagram.com/p/BhqzeythwXj/.
23 Martin Rowson (@MartinRowson), 'And Again #Windrush', Twitter, 16 April 2018, https://twitter.com/MartinRowson/status/985791339223834624.
24 Bhabha, *Location*, 48.

25 Yegenoglu, 'Sartorial Fabric-Actions', 101.
26 Male and female populations, GOV.UK, https://www.ethnicity-facts-figures.service.gov.uk/uk-population-by-ethnicity/demographics/male-and-female-populations/latest.
27 Examples include Deborah Elizabeth Whaley's *Black Women in Sequence: Re-inking Comics, Graphic Novels, and Anime* and Monika Franzen and Nancy Ethiel's *Make Way: 200 Years of American Women in Cartoons*.
28 'Nicola Jennings', in *The Inking Woman: 250 Years of Women Cartoon and Comic Artists in Britain*, ed. Nicola Streeten and Cath Tate (Brighton: Myriad, 2018), 31.
29 Nicola Streeten, 'Academic Activity', https://nicolastreeten.wordpress.com/academic-research-activity/.
30 Nicola Streeten, *UK Feminist Cartoonists and Comics: A Critical Survey* (Cham: Palgrave Studies in Comics and Graphic Novels, 2020), 17–18.
31 Streeten, *UK Feminist Cartoonists,* 262.
32 'Female Cartoonist Hana Hajar Sheds New Light on Middle Eastern Women', *Girls Can't What?*, https://www.girlscantwhat.com/female-cartoonist-hana-hajar-sheds-new-light-on-middle-eastern-women/.
33 Tim Benson, 'Women and British Political Cartoonists', http://www.original-political-cartoon.com/cartoon-history/women-and-british-political-cartoonists/.
34 Matt Salusbury, 'Where Are the Women Cartoonists?', http://www.londonfreelance.org/fl/1804cart.html.
35 Christopher Hitchens, 'Why Women Aren't Funny', *Vanity Fair*, January 2007, https://www.vanityfair.com/culture/2007/01/hitchens200701.
36 Rebecca Krefting, *All Joking Aside: American Humor and Its Discontents* (Baltimore: Johns Hopkins University Press, 2014), 107.
37 Jaye Berman Montresor, 'Comic Women Strip-Tease: A Revealing Look at Cartoon Artists', in *Look Who's Laughing: Gender and Comedy*, ed. Gail Finney (Independence: Routledge, 1994), 339.
38 BCA image reference number LSE0278, https://archive.cartoons.ac.uk/Record.aspx?src=CalmView.Catalog&id=LSE0278.
39 BCA image reference number BJD0193, https://archive.cartoons.ac.uk/Record.aspx?src=CalmView.Catalog&id=BJD0193.
40 Seymour-Ure and Schoff, *David Low,* 42.
41 Image can be found at Felix Pope, 'Guardian Editor Personally Apologised to Richard Sharp for "Antisemitic" Cartoon', *Jewish Chronicle*, 2 May 2023, https://www.thejc.com/news/news/guardian-editor-personally-apologised-to-richard-sharp-for-antisemitic-cartoon-3qGx6KMd6Tg70DSJiucOd7.
42 Rowson, https://www.martinrowson.com/.

Bibliography

Abbas, Tahir. 'Muslim Minorities in Britain: Integration, Multiculturalism and Radicalism in the Post-7/7 Period'. *Journal of Intercultural Studies* 28, no. 3 (2008): 287–300. 10.1080/07256860701429717.

Aitken, Ian. 'Enoch Powell Dismissed for "Racialist" Speech'. *Guardian*, 22 April 1968, http://www.theguardian.com/news/1968/apr/22/mainsection.ianaitken.

Alibhai-Brown, Yasmin. 'The Burka Empowering Women? You Must Be Mad, Minister'. *Daily Mail*, 21 July 2010, http://www.dailymail.co.uk/debate/article-1296132/The-burka-empowering-women-You-mad-minister.html.

Al Jazeera. 'Al-Qaeda in Yemen claims Charlie Hebdo attack'. 14 January 2015, http://www.aljazeera.com/news/middleeast/2015/01/al-qaeda-yemen-charlie-hebdo-paris-attacks-201511410323361511.html.

Allen, Peter. 'French Burka Ban: Police Arrest Two Veiled Women'. *Daily Telegraph*, 11 April 2011, http://www.telegraph.co.uk/news/worldnews/europe/france/8442622/French-burka-ban-police-arrest-two-veiled-women.html.

Allen, Vanessa. 'How MI5 blundered over photo of two 7/7 bombers'. *Daily Mail*, 7 May 2011, http://www.dailymail.co.uk/news/article-1359148/7-7-inquest-How-MI5-blundered-photo-2-bombers.html

Al-Mahadin, Salam. 'The Social Semiotics of Hijab: Negotiating the Body Politics of Veiled Women'. *Journal of Arab & Muslim Media Research* 6, no. 1 (2013): 3–18. https://doi.org/10.1386/jammr.6.1.3_1.

Altick, Richard D. *The English Common Reader: A Social History of the Mass Reading Public, 1800–1900*. Chicago and London: University of Chicago Press, 1957.

Amin, Samir, Russell Moore and James Membrez. *Eurocentrism*. New York: Monthly Review Press, 2010.

Arad, Yitzhak, Yisrael Gutman and Abraham Margaliot, eds. 'From a discussion on the compulsory evacuation of the Jewish population of the Wartheland to the Government-General, January 30, 1940'. In *Documents on the Holocaust: Selected Sources on the Destruction of the Jews of Germany and Austria, Poland and the Soviet Union*. Oxford: Pergamon, 1987.

Aridan, Natan. *Britain, Israel and Anglo-Jewry 1949–57*. Abingdon: Taylor and Francis, 2004.

Article 3 of The Terrorism Act 2000 (Remedial) Order 2011. https://www.legislation.gov.uk/uksi/2011/631/article/3/made.

Avebury, Lord. *Hansard*, House of Lords, vol. 374, cols. 1055–69. 4 October 1976, http://hansard.millbanksystems.com/lords/1976/oct/04/motor-cycle-crash-helmets-religious#column_1056

Axel, Brian Keith. *The Nation's Tortured Body: Violence, Representation, and the Formation of a Sikh "Diaspora"*. Durham, NC: Duke University Press, 2001.

Barrett, Richard. *BEYOND THE CALIPHATE: Foreign Fighters and the Threat of Returnees*. The Soufan Center. October 2017. https://thesoufancenter.org/research/beyond-caliphate/.

BBC History. 'Omagh bomb'. Accessed 19 August 2018, http://www.bbc.co.uk/history/events/omagh_bomb.

BBC News. '7 times Katie Hopkins hit the headlines'. 26 May 2017, http://www.bbc.co.uk/news/entertainment-arts-40061888.

BBC News. 'Abu Hamza jailed for seven years'. 7 February 2006, http://news.bbc.co.uk/1/hi/uk/4690224.stm.

BBC News. 'Blears seeks to reassure Muslims'. 2 August 2005, http://news.bbc.co.uk/1/hi/uk_politics/4736969.stm.

BBC News. 'The bombers'. Accessed 6 September 2023, http://news.bbc.co.uk/1/shared/spl/hi/uk/05/london_blasts/investigation/html/bombers.stm.

BBC News. 'Cartoons row hits Danish exports'. 9 September 2006, http://news.bbc.co.uk/1/hi/world/europe/5329642.stm.

BBC News. 'Full text: Blair speech on terror'. 16 July 2005, http://news.bbc.co.uk/1/hi/uk/4689363.stm

BBC News. 'Iran paper's Holocaust cartoons'. 13 February 2006, http://news.bbc.co.uk/1/hi/world/middle_east/4709380.stm.

BBC News. 'Isis leader calls on Muslims to "build Islamic state"'. 1 July 2014, http://www.bbc.co.uk/news/world-middle-east-28116846.

BBC News. 'Islamic State and the crisis in Iraq and Syria in maps'. 28 March 2018, http://www.bbc.co.uk/news/world-middle-east-27838034.

BBC News. 'Jane Austen to be face of the Bank of England £10 note'. 24 July 2013, http://www.bbc.co.uk/news/business-23424289.

BBC News. 'Manchester attack: What we know so far'. 12 June 2017, https://www.bbc.co.uk/news/uk-england-manchester-40008389.

BBC News. 'Nigeria cartoon protests kill 16'. 19 February 2006, http://news.bbc.co.uk/1/hi/4728616.stm.

BBC News. '#Notinmyname: Hundreds of Muslims condemn terror attack'. 25 March 2017, http://www.bbc.co.uk/news/uk-england-birmingham-39392442.

BBC News. 'Romania and Bulgaria EU migration restrictions lifted'. 1 January 2014, https://www.bbc.co.uk/news/world-europe-25565302.

BBC News. 'Steve Bell sacked by Guardian in antisemitism row over Netanyahu cartoon'. 16 October 2023, https://www.bbc.co.uk/news/entertainment-arts-67122609.

BBC News. 'Trojan Horse "plot" Schools Timeline'. 16 July 2015, http://www.bbc.co.uk/news/uk-england-birmingham-28370552.

BBC News. 'Who was Abu Bakr al-Baghdadi?'. 28 October 2019, https://www.bbc.co.uk/news/world-middle-east-50200392.

BBC News. 'Windrush victims detained "unlawfully" by home office'. 29 June 2018, https://www.bbc.co.uk/news/uk-politics-44651105?intlink_from_url=https://www.

bbc.co.uk/news/topics/c9vwmzw7n7lt/windrush-scandal&link_location=live-reporting-story.

BBC News. 'Women's fashion hits the courts'. 19 June 1998. Accessed 10 August 2018, http://news.bbc.co.uk/1/hi/events/wimbledon_98/behind_the_scenes/114681.stm.

Beetham, David. *Transport and Turbans: A Comparative Study in Local Politics*. London: Oxford University Press, 1970.

Bell, Steve. '2303 NUJ242-DAVIESHARP'. Accessed 14 May 2023, https://www.belltoons.co.uk/bellworks/index.php/others/LATEST/2303_NUJ242-DAVIESHARP.

Bell, Steve (@Belltoons). 'I tweet this in solidarity with Martin: https://belltoons.co.uk/bellworks/index.php/others/LATEST/2303_NUJ242-DAVIESHARP'. Twitter, 2 May 2023, https://twitter.com/BellBelltoons/status/1653353346277752833.

Bell, Steve. 'Steve Bell – Biography'. Belltoons.co.uk, http://www.belltoons.co.uk/biography.

Benson, Tim. 'Political cartoonists are divided: Is it ok to ditch their paper and pens to go digital?'. *i News*, 30 October 2018, https://inews.co.uk/news/politics/political-cartoons-satire-cartoonists-art–233845.

Benson, Tim. 'Women and British political cartoonists'. Accessed 27 October 2018, http://www.original-political-cartoon.com/cartoon-history/women-and-british-political-cartoonists/.

Berger, Peter L. and Thomas Luckmann. *The Social Construction of Reality: A Treatise in the Sociology of Knowledge*. New York: Open Road Integrated Media, 2011.

Bhabha, Homi K. *The Location of Culture*. London: Routledge, 2004.

Bidwell, S., and The Sikh Missionary Society. *The Turban Victory*. Southall, Middlesex: The Sikh Missionary Society, 1987.

Blair, Tony. 'Blair: What will the world look like if we don't stop Bin Laden?'. *Independent*, 12 October 2001, http://www.independent.co.uk/news/world/asia/blair-what-will-the-world-look-like-if-we-dont-stop-bin-laden-9172514.html.

Blay, Zeba. 'The Whitewashing of Naomi Osaka'. *HuffPost*, 11 September 2018, https://www.huffingtonpost.co.uk/entry/the-whitewashing-of-naomi-osaka_us_5b967eb3e4b0cf7b004209b5.

Blower, Patrick. 'Livedraw Animation'. Blower Cartoons. https://blowercartoons.com/livedraw.

Boase, T. S. R. 'The Decoration of the New Palace of Westminster, 1841–1863'. *Journal of the Warburg and Courtauld Institute* 17, no. 3/4 (1954): 319–58, https://doi.org/10.2307/750325.

'Bomber's family: He was proud to be British'. *Daily Telegraph*, 13 July 2005, http://www.telegraph.co.uk/news/1493934/Bombers-family-he-was-proud-to-be-British.html.

Bourdieu, Pierre, and Randal Johnson. *The Field of Cultural Production: Essays on Art and Literature*. New York: Columbia University Press, 1993.

Bregman, Ahron. *Israel's Wars: A History since 1947*. Florence: Taylor & Francis Group, 2003.

Brilliant, Moshe. 'Israelis "kill two Fatah leaders" in Lebanon raid.' *The Times*, 10 April 1973.

British Cartoon Archive. 'Raymond Jackson [Jak]'. Accessed 22 November 2019, https://www.cartoons.ac.uk/cartoonist-biographies/i-j/RaymondJackson_JAK.html.

Brown, Dave. 'Cartoonist Michael de Adder lost work after drawing an offensive image of Donald Trump – but that's his job'. *Independent*, 2 July 2019, https://www.independent.co.uk/voices/michael-de-adder-sacked-cartoon-donald-trump-dead-migrants-mexican-border-a8983966.html.

Brown, Lucy. *Victorian News and Newspapers*. Oxford: Clarendon, 1985.

Bryant, Mark. 'Jackson, Raymond Allen [pseud. JAK] (1927–1997), cartoonist and illustrator'. In *Oxford Dictionary of National Biography*. Oxford: Oxford University Press, 2007, https://www.oxforddnb.com/view/10.1093/ref:odnb/9780198614128.001.0001/odnb-9780198614128-e-67308.

Bryant, Mark, and Simon Heneage. *Dictionary of British Cartoonists and Caricaturists 1730–1980*. Aldershot: Scolar, 1994.

Byrne, Ciar. 'Independent cartoon cleared of anti-Semitism'. *Guardian*, 22 May 2003, https://www.theguardian.com/media/2003/may/22/theindependent.pressandpublishing.

Callaghan, Jim. 'Commonwealth Immigrants Bill'. *Hansard*, House of Commons, vol. 759, col. 1251. 27 February 1968, https://api.parliament.uk/historic-hansard/commons/1968/feb/27/commonwealth-immigrants-bill#S5CV0759P0_19680227_HOC2_305.

Carton, Donna. 'Ahern's IRA arms U-turn sparks crisis'. *Daily Mirror*, 15 February 1999, https://global-factiva-com.libproxy.kcl.ac.uk/redir/default.aspx?P=sa&NS=16&AID=9KIN002300&an=dmirr00020010904dv2f01090&cat=a&ep=ASI.

Casciani, Dominic. 'Woolwich: How did Michael Adebolajo become a killer?'. *BBC News*. 19 December 2013, http://www.bbc.co.uk/news/magazine-25424290

Cesarani, David. *The Jewish Chronicle and Anglo-Jewry, 1841–1991*. Cambridge: Cambridge UP, 1994.

Chapman, James. 'Migrants with no medical insurance "won't get NHS care": Minister's tough stance on new influx from the East.' *Daily Mail*, 29 January 2013, http://www.dailymail.co.uk/news/article-2269838/Migrants-medical-insurance-wont-NHS-care-Ministers-tough-stance-new-influx-East.html.

Chartres, John and Tim Jones. 'Three shot in Belfast street clashes'. *The Times*, 8 February 1971.

Chrisafis, Angelique. 'Nicolas Sarkozy says Islamic veils are not welcome in France'. *Guardian*, 22 June 2009, https://www.theguardian.com/world/2009/jun/22/islamic-veils-sarkozy-speech-france.

Churchill, Winston. 'Army Council and General Dyer'. *Hansard*, 8 July 1920, vol. 131, cols. 1705–819. Accessed 19 August 2018, https://api.parliament.uk/historic-hansard/commons/1920/jul/08/army-council-and-general-dyer.

Clare, John and David Wilsworth. 'Army "peace line" to replace barricades across Belfast'. *The Times*, 10 September 1969.

Clark, Michael. 'Jewish Identity in British Politics: The Case of the First Jewish MPs, 1858–87'. *Jewish Social Studies* 13, no. 2 (2007): 93–126. www.jstor.org/stable/4467767.

ComRes. 'BBC Radio 4 Today Muslim poll'. http://www.comresglobal.com/wp-content/uploads/2015/02/BBC-Today-Programme_British-Muslims-Poll_FINAL-Tables_Feb2015.pdf

The Constitution of Afghanistan. Ratified 26 January 2004. http://www.afghanembassy.com.pl/afg/images/pliki/TheConstitution.pdf.

Council on Foreign Relations. '1999–2021, The U.S. War in Afghanistan'. https://www.cfr.org/timeline/us-war-afghanistan.

Criado-Perez, Caroline. 'We need women on British banknotes'. *Change.org*, https://www.change.org/p/we-need-women-on-british-banknotes.

Curtis, Chris. 'How Britain voted at the 2017 general election'. table entitled 'Vote by newspaper readership'. YouGov UK. Published 13 June 2017. Accessed 25 October 2018, https://yougov.co.uk/news/2017/06/13/how-britain-voted-2017-general-election/.

Curtis, Liz. *Nothing but the Same Old Story: The Roots of Anti-Irish Racism*. London: Information on Ireland, 1984.

Curtis Jr., L. Perry. *Anglo-Saxons and Celts: A Study of Anti-Irish Prejudice in Victorian England*. Conference on British Studies at the University of Bridgeport; distributed by New York University Press: New York, 1968.

Curtis Jr., L. Perry. *Apes and Angels: The Irishman in Victorian Caricature*. Washington, DC and London: Smithsonian Institution Press, 1997.

Darby, John. *Dressed to Kill: Cartoonists and the Northern Ireland Conflict*. Belfast: Appletree Press, 1983.

Davey, Nicholas. 'Hermeneutics and art theory. In *A Companion to Art Theory*, edited by Paul Smith and Carolyn Wilde, 436–47. Oxford and Malden, MA: Blackwell, 2002.

Dawar, Anil. 'Intruder shot at home of Danish cartoonist'. *Guardian*, 2 January 2010, https://www.theguardian.com/world/2010/jan/02/danish-cartoonist-intruder-shot.

Deedes, W. F. 'Muslims can never conform to our ways'. *Telegraph*, 20 October 2006, https://www.telegraph.co.uk/comment/personal-view/3633349/Muslims-can-never-conform-to-our-ways.html.

Dodd, Vikram. 'Burqa Fugitive Mohammed Ahmed Mohamed "faced 20 charges"'. *Guardian*, 8 November 2013, http://www.theguardian.com/uk-news/2013/nov/08/burqa-fugitive-mohammed-ahmed-mohamed-20-charges.

Dodd, Vikram, and Jamie Grierson. 'Finsbury Park attack suspect was probably "self-radicalised"'. *Guardian*, 21 June 2017, https://www.theguardian.com/uk-news/2017/jun/21/finsbury-park-mosque-attack-two-victims-in-critical-care.

Dor, Louis. 'Turkish people are sharing this cartoon asking where our sympathy was for Istanbul and Ankara'. *indy100*, 23 March 2016, https://www.indy100.com/article/turkish-people-are-sharing-this-cartoon-asking-where-our-sympathy-was-for-istanbul-and-ankara–ZJORO9A1eb.

Douglas, Roy, Liam Harte, and Jim O'Hara. *Drawing Conclusions: A Cartoon History of Anglo-Irish Relations, 1798–1998*. Belfast: Blackstaff, 1998.

Drake, C.J.M. 'The provisional IRA: A Case Study'. *Terrorism and Political Violence* 3, no. 2 (1991): 43–60. https://doi.org/10.1080/09546559108427103.

Eden, Anthony. *Hansard*, House of Commons, vol. 385, col. 2082–7. 17 December 1942, http://hansard.millbanksystems.com/commons/1942/dec/17/united-nations-declaration.

Elder, Charles D., and Roger W. Cobb. *The Political Uses of Symbols*. New York: Longman, 1983.

Elgot, Jessica. 'Ukip to campaign to ban burqa and sharia courts, says Paul Nuttall'. *Guardian*, 23 April 2017, https://www.theguardian.com/politics/2017/apr/23/ukip-to-campaign-to-ban-burka-and-sharia-courts-says-paul-nuttall.

The Employment Equality (Religion or Belief) Regulations 2003, http://www.legislation.gov.uk/uksi/2003/1660/contents/made.

Endelman, Todd M. 'Disraeli's Jewishness Reconsidered'. *Modern Judaism* 5, no. 2 (1985): 109–23. www.jstor.org/stable/1396390.

Everett, Michael and Danielle Nash. 'The Parliamentary Oath'. Accessed 30 October 2017, http://www.legco.gov.hk/general/english/library/stay_informed_parliamentary_news/the_parliamentary_oath.pdf.

Everitt, Graham. *English Caricaturists and Graphic Humourists of the Nineteenth Century: How They Illustrated and Interpreted Their Times*. London: S. Sonnenschein, 1893.

'Fake news, the fascist left and the real purveyors of hatred; daily mail comment'. *Daily Mail*. 22 June 2017, Factiva https://global-factiva-com.libproxy.kcl.ac.uk/redir/default.aspx?P=sa&an=DAIM000020170621ed6m0000i&cat=a&ep=ASE.

Felsenstein, Frank. 'Jews And Devils: Antisemitic Stereotypes of Late Medieval and Renaissance England'. *Literature and Theology* 4, no. 1 (1990): 15–28. www.jstor.org/stable/23927203.

Foucault, Michel. 'Panopticism', from 'Discipline & Punish: The Birth of the Prison'. *Race/Ethnicity: Multidisciplinary Global Contexts* 2, no. 1 (2008): 1–12. https://www.jstor.org/stable/25594995.

France Diplomacy. 'National tribute to the memory of Samuel Paty – Speech by Franks, Myfanwy. 'Crossing the Borders of Whiteness? White Muslim Women Who Wear the Hijab in Britain Today'. *Ethnic and Racial Studies* 23 (2000): 917–29.

Franzen, Monika, and Nancy Ethiel. *Make Way: 200 Years of American Women in Cartoons*. Chicago: Chicago Review Press, 1988.

Gamson, William A., David Croteau, William Hoynes and Theodore Sasson. 'Media Images and the Social Construction of Reality'. *Annual Review of Sociology* 18 (1992): 373–93. http://www.jstor.org/stable/2083459.

Gardner, Mark and Anshel Pfeffer. 'Is the Sunday Times cartoon antisemitic?'. *Guardian*, 29 January 2013, https://www.theguardian.com/commentisfree/2013/jan/29/is-the-sunday-times-cartoon-antisemitic.

Gelbin, Cathy S. 'Rootless cosmopolitans: German-Jewish writers confront the Stalinist and National Socialist atrocities'. *European Review of History: Revue européenne d'histoire* 23, no. 5–6 (2016): 863–79. 10.1080/13507486.2016.1203882.

Gill, Santokh Singh. '"So People Know I'm a Sikh": Narratives of Sikh Masculinities in Contemporary Britain'. *Culture and Religion* 15 (2014): 334–53.

Gilman, Sander L. *The Jew's Body*. New York and London: Routledge, 1991.

Gilroy, Paul. 'Multiculture, Double Consciousness and the "War on Terror"'. *Patterns of Prejudice* 39, no. 4 (2005): 431–43. http://dx.doi.org/10.1080/00313220500347899.

Gilroy, Paul. 'Working with "Wogs": Aliens, Denizens and the Machinations of Denialism'. *Communication, Culture and Critique* 15, no. 2 (June 2022): 122–38. https://doi.org/10.1093/ccc/tcac012.

Girls Can't What?. 'Female Cartoonist Hana Hajar Sheds New Light on Middle Eastern Women'. Accessed 6 September 2023. https://www.girlscantwhat.com/female-cartoonist-hana-hajar-sheds-new-light-on-middle-eastern-women.

Gladstone, William. *Hansard*, House of Commons, vol. 227, col. 585. 21 February 1876, https://hansard.parliament.uk/Commons/1876-02-21/debates/90976a6d-a67a-4483-a385-ad4e6890e5c1/Supply%E2%80%94%C2%A34080000SuezCanalShares.

Goldstein, Robert Justin. 'The Persecution and Jailing of Political Caricaturists in Nineteenth-Century Europe (1815–1914)'. *Media History* 9 (2003): 19–45. https://doi.org/10.1080/1368880032000059962.

Gottschalk, Peter, and Gabriel Greenberg. *Islamophobia: Making Muslims the Enemy*. Lanham: Rowman & Littlefield, 2008.

GOV.UK. *The Agreement*. Full text of the Good Friday Agreement. Accessed 19 August 2018, https://assets.publishing.service.gov.uk/government/uploads/system/uploads/attachment_data/file/136652/agreement.pdf.

GOV.UK. 'Confidence and Supply Agreement between the Conservative and Unionist Party and the Democratic Unionist Party'. Updated, 23 January 2020, https://www.gov.uk/government/publications/conservative-and-dup-agreement-and-uk-government-financial-support-for-northern-ireland/agreement-between-the-conservative-and-unionist-party-and-the-democratic-unionist-party-on-support-for-the-government-in-parliament.

GOV.UK. 'Male and female populations'. Last updated 2 August 2023, https://www.ethnicity-facts-figures.service.gov.uk/uk-population-by-ethnicity/demographics/male-and-female-populations/latest.

GOV.UK. 'Northern Ireland-related terrorism threat level raised'. Published 28 March 2023, https://www.gov.uk/government/news/northern-ireland-related-terrorism-threat-level-raised.

GOV.UK. 'PM speech on the windsor framework: February 2023'. Published 27 February 2023, https://www.gov.uk/government/speeches/pm-speech-on-the-windsor-framework-february-2023.

GOV.UK. 'PM statement following London terror attack: 4 June 2017'. Published 4 June 2017, https://www.gov.uk/government/speeches/pm-statement-following-london-terror-attack-4-june-2017.

GOV.UK. 'Windrush scheme and information'. https://www.gov.uk/government/publications/undocumented-commonwealth-citizens-resident-in-the-uk.

Grace, Pierce A. 'The Amritsar Massacre, 1919: The Irish Connection'. *History Ireland* 18, no. 4 (2010): 24–5. http://www.jstor.org/stable/27823023.

Gramsci, Antonio. *Selections from the Prison Notebooks*. London: The Electric Book Company, 2005.

Guardian. 'IRA kills four in Belfast attacks'. 14 November 1991, https://global-factiva-com.libproxy.kcl.ac.uk/redir/default.aspx?P=sa&NS=16&AID=9KIN002300&an=grdn000020011124dnbe00ysi&cat=a&ep=ASI.

Guardian. 'Too smart for his own fist; Mr Netanyahu is risking a reversal of the peace process'. 26 September 1996.

Guardian. 'Famous men who wear stack heels'. 9 April 2009, https://www.theguardian.com/lifeandstyle/gallery/2009/apr/09/famous-men-stack-heels.

Guardian. 'Corrections and clarifications'. 30 April 2023, https://www.theguardian.com/news/2023/apr/30/corrections-and-clarifications.

Haleem, M.A.S. Abdel. *Qur'an: English Translation with Parallel Arabic Text*. Oxford: Oxford University Press, 2010.

Halliday, Josh. 'Sunday Times denies antisemitism in Israeli election cartoon'. *Guardian*, 28 January 2013, https://www.theguardian.com/media/2013/jan/28/sunday-times-antisemitism-israeli-election-cartoon.

Hammer, Gili. '"If They're Going to Stare, at Least I'll Give Them a Good Reason To": Blind Women's Visibility, Invisibility, and Encounters with the Gaze'. *Signs: Journal of Women in Culture and Society* 41, no. 2 (2016): 409–32. https://www.journals.uchicago.edu/doi/pdfplus/10.1086/682924.

Hanna, Jason. 'The London train explosion is the latest of 5 terror incidents in 2017 in the UK'. *CNN*, 15 September 2017, http://edition.cnn.com/2017/09/15/world/uk-terror-events-2017/index.html.

Hatfield, Stefano. 'i editor's letter: Winners of i Cartoon Idol contest'. *i News*, 12 December 2011, https://www.independent.co.uk/i/editor/i-editors-letter-winners-of-i-cartoon-idol-contest-6275866.html.

Helweg, Arthur Wesley. 'Sikh identity in England: Its changing nature'. In *Sikh History and Religion in the Twentieth Century*, edited by J. T. O'Connell, M. Israel and W. G. Oxtoby. Toronto: Centre for South Asian Studies University of Toronto, 1988.

Helweg, Arthur Wesley. *Sikhs in England: The Development of a Migrant Community*. Delhi: Oxford University Press, 1979.

Hennessy, Patrick. 'Burka ban ruled out by immigration minister'. *Daily Telegraph*, 17 July 2010, http://www.telegraph.co.uk/news/politics/7896751/Burka-ban-ruled-out-by-immigration-minister.html.

Heppinstall, Adam. 'Decision Notice: The appointment of the chair of the board of the British Broadcasting Corporation (BBC) 2020/2021'. The Commissioner for Public Appointments, 28 April 2023. Accessed 5 September 2023, https://publicappointmentscommissioner.independent.gov.uk/wp-content/uploads/2023/04/2023-04-28-OCPA-DECISION-NOTICE-IN-RELATION-TO-THE-APPOINTMENT-OF-CHAIR-OF-THE-BBC-BOARD-MR-RICHARD-SHARP.pdf.

Hill, Draper. *Mr. Gillray, the Caricaturist: A Biography*. London: Phaidon Press, 1965.

Hiro, Dilip. *Black British, White British*. Harmondsworth: Penguin Books, 1973.

Hitchens, Christopher. 'Why women aren't funny'. *Vanity Fair*, 1 January 2007, https://www.vanityfair.com/culture/2007/01/hitchens200701.

Hoge, Warren. 'Irish protestant leader issues ultimatum on Sinn Fein Ouster'. *New York Times*, 9 October 2002.

Hoggart, Simon. 'Northern Ireland shootings'. *Guardian*, 10 March 2009.

Hopkinson, Michael. "From treaty to civil war, 1921–2". In *A New History of Ireland Volume VII: Ireland 1921–84*, edited by J. R. Hill. Oxford: Oxford University Press, 2003.

Horton, Helena. '"What about beekeepers?": Ukip mocked after being forced to clarify their veil-banning policy', *Daily Telegraph*, 24 April 2017, http://www.telegraph.co.uk/news/2017/04/24/beekeepers-ukip-mocked-forced-clarify-veil-banning-policy/.

House of Commons Papers. 'Suez Canal (purchase of shares).' Paper number 14, volume page XLIX.649. https://parlipapers.proquest.com/parlipapers/docview/t70.d75.1876-052322?accountid=11862.

Huddersfield Chronicle and West Yorkshire Advertiser. 'The Jewish "Emancipation"'. 24 July 1858.

Hussey, Andrew. 'Macron and the Muslim world'. *New Statesman*, 11 November 2020, https://www.newstatesman.com/long-reads/2020/11/Samuel-paty-murder-macron-muslim-terror.

Intelligence and Security Committee of Parliament. 'Report on the intelligence relating to the murder of Fusilier Lee Rigby'. Printed 25 November 2014, https://isc.independent.gov.uk/wp-content/uploads/2021/01/20141125_ISC_Woolwich_Reportwebsite.pdf.

Isaiah 2. Scripture taken from the Holy Bible, NEW INTERNATIONAL VERSION®. Copyright © 1973, 1978, 1984 Biblica. All rights reserved throughout the world. Used by permission of Biblica.

Jackson, Alvin. *Ireland 1798–1998: War, Peace and beyond*. Chichester: Wiley-Blackwell, 2010.

Janes, Dominic. *Oscar Wilde Prefigured: Queer Fashioning and British Caricature, 1750–1900*. Chicago and London: The University of Chicago Press, 2016.

Johnson, Boris. 'Denmark has got it wrong. Yes, the burka is oppressive and ridiculous – but that's still no reason to ban it'. *Daily Telegraph*, 5 August 2018, https://www.telegraph.co.uk/news/2018/08/05/denmark-has-got-wrong-yes-burka-oppressive-ridiculous-still/.

Jones, Tim. 'Another British soldier shot dead by terrorists in Belfast'. *The Times*, 14 July 1971.

Jones, Tim. 'Ulster MPs seek an independent public inquiry into allegations of torture by Army'. *The Times*, 19 October 1971.

Julius, Anthony. *Trials of the Diaspora: A History of Anti-Semitism in England*. Oxford: Oxford University Press, 2010.

Kar-Gupta, Sudip, and Richard Lough. 'Beheaded teacher was "quiet hero" who incarnated French values, Macron says'. *Reuters*, 21 October 2020. https://www.reuters.com/article/france-security-idINKBN2760KR.

Khaleeli, Homa. 'The perils of "flying while Muslim"'. *Guardian*, 8 August 2016, https://www.theguardian.com/world/2016/aug/08/the-perils-of-flying-while-muslim.

Khan, Imran (@ImranKhanPTI). 'through encouraging the display of blasphemous cartoons targeting Islam & our Prophet PBUH'. Twitter, 25 October 2023, https://twitter.com/ImranKhanPTI/status/1320286665785704448.

Killen, John. *The Unkindest Cut: A Cartoon History of Ulster 1900–2000*. Belfast: Blackstaff Press, 2000.

Klug, Brian. 'The Collective Jew: Israel and the New Antisemitism'. *Patterns of Prejudice* 37, no. 2 (2003): 117–138.

Klug, Brian. 'Islamophobia: A Concept Comes of Age'. *Ethnicities* 12, no. 5 (2012): 665–81. www.jstor.org/stable/43572627.

Knox, Katharine, and Tony Kushner. *Refugees in an Age of Genocide: Global, National and Local Perspectives during the Twentieth Century*. London: Routledge, 1999.

Kotek, Joël. *Cartoons and Extremism: Israel and the Jews in Arab and Western Media*. Translated by Alisa Jaffa. Edgware: Vallentine Mitchell, 2009.

Krefting, Rebecca. *All Joking Aside: American Humor and Its Discontents*. Baltimore: Johns Hopkins University Press, 2014.

Kuipers, Giselinde. 'Ethnic humour and ethnic politics in the Netherlands: The rules and attraction of clandestine humour'. In *The Politics of Humour: Laughter, Inclusion, and Exclusion in the Twentieth Century*, edited by Martina Kessel and Patrick Merziger, 175–201. Toronto and Buffalo: University of Toronto Press, 2012.

'Lee Rigby Trial: Jury shown "eye for an eye" video'. *Daily Telegraph*, 25 November 2014, https://www.telegraph.co.uk/news/uknews/crime/10492778/Lee-Rigby-trial-jury-shown-eye-for-an-eye-video.html.

legislation.gov.uk. *The Abortion (Northern Ireland) (No. 2) Regulations 2020*. Accessed 14 May 2023, https://www.legislation.gov.uk/uksi/2020/503/contents/made.

legislation.gov.uk. *British Nationality Act, 1948*. Accessed 20 October 2014. http://www.legislation.gov.uk/ukpga/1948/56/pdfs/ukpga_19480056_en.pdf.

legislation.gov.uk. *Government of Ireland Act, 1920*. Accessed 22 November 2019, http://www.legislation.gov.uk/ukpga/1920/67/pdfs/ukpga_19200067_en.pdf.

Langer, Lorenz. *Religious Offence and Human Rights: The Implications of Defamation of Religions*. Cambridge: Cambridge University Press, 2014.

Larkin, Felix M. 'Why the Boris Johnson, Jeremy Hunt leprechaun cartoon is no laughing matter', *Irish Times*, 3 July 2019.

Lattimer, Mark. 'When Labour played the racist card'. *New Statesman*, 22 January 1999. Accessed 10 August 2018, https://www.newstatesman.com/when-labour-played-racist-card.

Laville, Sandra and Robert Booth. 'Khalid Masood: From Kent schoolboy to Westminster attacker'. *Guardian*, 25 March 2017, https://www.theguardian.com/uk-news/2017/mar/25/khalid-masood-profile-from-popular-teenager-to-isis-inspired-terrorist.

Lipman, Jennifer. 'Guardian cartoonist defends Netanyahu "puppet-master" image'. *Jewish Chronicle*, 16 November 2012, https://www.thejc.com/news/uk-news/guardian-cartoonist-defends-netanyahu-puppet-master-image-1.38522.

Loomba, Ania. *Colonialism/Postcolonialism*. London: Routledge, 2015.

Low, David. *Low: The Twentieth Century's Greatest Cartoonist*. London: BBC History Magazine, 2002.

Low, David. *Low Visibility; a Cartoon History, 1945–1953*. London: Collins, 1953.

Low, David. *Low's Autobiography*. London: Michael Joseph, 1956.

Macintyre, Donald. 'Israeli raids driven by election, say Palestinians'. *Independent*, 27 January 2003, http://www.independent.co.uk/news/world/middle-east/israeli-raids-driven-by-election-say-palestinians-128067.html.

Macron, Emmanuel. President of the Republic, at the Sorbonne (21 October 2020)', 21 October 2020. Accessed 14 May 2023, https://www.diplomatie.gouv.fr/en/french-foreign-policy/human-rights/freedom-of-religion-or-belief/article/national-tribute-to-the-memory-of-samuel-paty-speech-by-emmanuel-macron.

'The man with a pocketful of laughter: Mail cartoonist Mahood finally hangs up his quill'. *Daily Mail*, 23 December 2009, https://www.dailymail.co.uk/news/article-1238107/Mail-cartoonist-Mahood-finally-hangs-quill.html.

Manchester Guardian (1828–1900). 'Article 5 –no title'. 27 July 1858.

Manchester Guardian (1901–1959). 'Jewish Zionists: British Government Support', 9 November 1917.

Matthew, H. C. G. 'Gould, Sir Francis Carruthers (1844–1925), cartoonist and stockbroker'. In *Oxford Dictionary of National Biography*. Oxford: Oxford University Press, 2004. https://www.oxforddnb.com/view/10.1093/ref:odnb/9780198614128.001.0001/odnb-9780198614128-e-33493.

McKittrick, David. 'Omagh Bombing: Sinn Fein's shift shown by its words'. *Independent*, 18 August 1998, https://www.independent.co.uk/news/omagh-bombing-sinn-feins-shift-shown-by-its-words-1172426.html.

McLeod. W. H. *Sikhism*. London: Penguin, 1997.

Meer, Nasar and Tehseen Noorani. 'A Sociological Comparison of Anti-Semitism and Anti-Muslim Sentiment in Britain'. *The Sociological Review* 56, no. 2 (2008): 195–219.

Melville, Toby, and William James. 'Five dead, around 40 injured in parliament "terrorist" attack'. *Reuters*, 22 March 2017, https://uk.reuters.com/article/uk-britain-security-photographer/five-dead-around-40-injured-in-parliament-terrorist-attack-idUKKBN16T1Y7.

Mercer, David, and Alix Culbertson. 'Five minutes of terror: How the London Bridge attack unfolded'. *Sky News*, 4 June 2021, https://news.sky.com/story/how-the-london-bridge-terror-attack-unfolded–11874155.

Miller, Henry J. 'John Leech and the Shaping of the Victorian Cartoon: The Context of Respectability'. *Victorian Periodicals Review* 42, no. 3 (2009): 267–91. http://www.jstor.org/stable/27760231.

Mills, Jen. 'Powerful cartoon sums up response to Manchester attack'. *Metro*, 23 May 2017, https://metro.co.uk/2017/05/23/powerful-cartoon-sums-up-response-to-manchester-attack-6655739/.

Mirror. 'Remember the victims: Shahara Islam'. 20 July 2005, https://www.mirror.co.uk/news/uk-news/remember-the-victims-shahara-islam-550757.

Modood, Tariq. 'British muslims and the politics of multiculturalism'. In *Multiculturalism, Muslims and Citizenship: A European Approach*, edited by Modood, Tariq, Anna Triandafyllidou and Ricard Zapata-Barrero, 37–56. New York: Routledge, 2006.

Modood, Tariq. *Multicultural Politics: Racism, Ethnicity, and Muslims in Britain*. Minneapolis: University of Minnesota Press, 2005.

Monkhouse, W. Cosmo. *The Life and Work of Sir John Tenniel, R.I.* London: The Art Journal Office, 1901.

Montresor, Jaye Berman. 'Comic women strip-tease: A revealing look at cartoon artists'. In *Look Who's Laughing: Gender and Comedy*, edited by Gail Finney, 335–48. Independence: Routledge, 1994.

Moody, T. W. 'Introduction: Early modern Ireland'. In *A New History of Ireland: Early Modern Ireland 1534–1691*, edited by T. W. Moody, F. X. Martin and F. J. Byrne. Oxford: Oxford University Press, 2009. https://doi.org/10.1093/acprof:oso/9780199562527.003.0024.

Morey, Peter, and Amina Yaqin. *Framing Muslims*. Cambridge: Harvard University Press, 2011.

Morgan, David. *Sacred Gaze: Religious Visual Culture in Theory and Practice*. Berkeley, CA: University of California Press, 2005.

Morris, Frankie. 'John Tenniel, Cartoonist: A Critical & Sociocultural Study in the Art of the Victorian Political Cartoon (Britain)'. PhD diss., University of Missouri-Columbia, 1985.

Morrison, Karen. 'Muslim woman will have to remove veil to give evidence'. *Sun*, 16 September 2013, https://www.thesun.co.uk/archives/news/1016924/muslim-woman-will-have-to-remove-veil-to-give-evidence/.

Murdoch, Rupert (@rupertmurdoch). 'Gerald Scarfe has never reflected the opinions of the Sunday Times. Nevertheless, we owe major apology for grotesque, offensive cartoon'. Twitter, 28 January 2013, https://twitter.com/rupertmurdoch/status/295964833394851840.

Murtagh, Peter. 'Rushdie in hiding after Ayatollah's death threat'. *Guardian*, 15 February 1989, http://www.theguardian.com/books/1989/feb/15/salmanrushdie.

Muslim Council of Britain's Research & Documentation Committee. *British Muslims in Numbers a Demographic, Socio-Economic and Health Profile of Muslims in*

Britain Drawing on the 2011 Census. London: The Muslim Council of Britain, 2015. https://www.mcb.org.uk/wp-content/uploads/2015/02/MCBCensusReport_2015.pdf.

The National Archives. 'The Act of Supremacy, 1534'. *The Act of Supremacy, 1534*, transcript. Accessed 19 August 2018, http://www.nationalarchives.gov.uk/pathways/citizenship/rise_parliament/transcripts/henry_supremacy.htm.

The National Archives. 'Speech on Multiculturalism and integration (8 Dec 06)'. 8 December 2006, http://webarchive.nationalarchives.gov.uk/20080909022722/http://www.number10.gov.uk/Page10563.

Newsworks. 'Circulation, UK newspaper market'. Published August 2019. https://www.newsworks.org.uk/resources/circulation.

Northern Ireland Social and Political Archive (ARK). 'The 1998 Referendums'. Accessed 19 August 2018, http://www.ark.ac.uk/elections/fref98.htm.

NUS Black Students' Campaign. 'Birmingham Metropolitan College: Reverse Your Decision to Ban Muslim Students from Wearing Veils'. *Change.org*. https://www.change.org/p/birmingham-metropolitan-college-reverse-your-decision-to-ban-muslim-students-from-wearing-veils.

Odhiambo, E.S. Atieno. 'Ethnic Cleansing and Civil Society in Kenya 1969–1992'. *Journal of Contemporary African Studies* 22, no. 1 (2004): 29–42. https://doi.org/10.1080/0258900042000179599.

Ofcom. 'News Consumption in the UK: 2021'. Published 27 July 2021. Accessed 14 May 2023, https://www.ofcom.org.uk/__data/assets/powerpoint_doc/0026/222479/news-consumption-in-the-uk-2021-report.pptx.

O'Keeffe, Michelle. 'We support the police'. *Sun*, 29 January 2007, https://global-factiva-com.libproxy.kcl.ac.uk/redir/default.aspx?P=sa&NS=16&AID=9KIN002300&an=THESUN0020070302e31t000hr&cat=a&ep=ASI.

O'Neill, P. 'Text of Irish Republican Army (IRA) Statement on Decommissioning 30 April 1998'. CAIN Web Service, Accessed 5 September 2023, http://cain.ulst.ac.uk/events/peace/docs/ira30498.htm.

Palmeri, Frank. 'The cartoon: The image as critique'. In *History beyond the Text: A Student's Guide to Approaching Alternative Sources*, edited by Sarah Barber and Corinna Peniston-Bird, 32–48. ProQuest Ebook Central: Routledge, 2009.

Palmeri, Frank. 'Cruikshank, Thackeray, and the Victorian Eclipse of Satire'. *Studies in English Literature, 1500–1900* 44, no. 4 (2004): 753–77. http://www.jstor.org/stable/3844535.

PamCo. 'PAMCo 3 2018 Jul17–Jun18 fused with comScore May 2018'. Published 17 September 2018. https://pamco.co.uk/pamco-data/latest-results/.

Pappé, Ilan. *Britain and the Arab-Israeli Conflict, 1948–51*. Basingstoke: Macmillan in Association with St. Antony's College, Oxford, 1988.

'parasite, n'. *OED Online*, Oxford University Press, June 2017. www.oed.com/view/Entry/137636.

Parekh, Bhikhu. 'Europe, liberalism and the "Muslim question"'. In *Multiculturalism, Muslims and Citizenship: A European Approach*, edited by Tariq Modood, Anna Triandafyllidou and Ricard Zapata-Barrero, 179–203. New York: Routledge, 2006.

Patten, Robert L., 'Conventions of Georgian Caricature'. *Art Journal* 43, no. 4 (1983): 331–38. https://doi.org/10.1080/00043249.1983.10792251.

Peachey, Kevin. 'Sir Winston Churchill to Feature on New Banknote'. *BBC News*, 26 April 2013. http://www.bbc.co.uk/news/business-22306707.

Perliger, Arie, and Ami Pedahzur. *Jewish Terrorism in Israel*. New York: Columbia University Press, 2011.

Petley, Julian, and Robin Richardson. *Pointing the Finger: Islam and Muslims in the British Media*. Richmond: Oneworld, 2011.

Pilditch, David and Tom Whitehead. 'The day an Islamic protestor told the Home Secretary: How dare you come to a Muslim area?' *Daily Express*, 21 September 2006.

Poole, Elizabeth. 'The effects of September 11 and the war in Iraq on British newspaper coverage'. In *Muslims and the News Media*, edited by Elizabeth Poole and John E. Richardson, 89–102. London: I.B. Tauris & Company, Limited, 2010.

Poole, Elizabeth. *Reporting Islam: Media Representations of British Muslims*. London: I.B. Tauris, 2002.

Poulter, Sebastian M. *English Law and Ethnic Minority Customs*. London: Butterworth, 1986.

Poulter, Sebastian M. *Ethnicity, Law and Human Rights: The English Experience*. Oxford: Clarendon Press, 1998.

Powell, Enoch. '"Rivers of Blood" speech'. 20 April 1968. Reprinted, *Daily Telegraph*, 12 December 2007, http://www.telegraph.co.uk/comment/3643826/Enoch-Powells-Rivers-of-Blood-speech.html.

Powell, Kimberly A. 'Framing Islam: An Analysis of U.S. Media Coverage of Terrorism since 9/11'. *Communication Studies* 62, no. 1 (2011): 90–112. 10.1080/10510974.2011.533599.

Press Complaints Commission. 'Report 62'. Accessed 30 October 2017, http://www.pcc.org.uk/cases/adjudicated.html?article=MjA5OA==&type=.

Prince, Rosa. 'Caroline Spelman: Wearing burka can be "Empowering"'. *Daily Telegraph*, 19 July 2010, http://www.telegraph.co.uk/news/religion/7897848/Caroline-Spelman-wearing-burka-can-be-empowering.html.

'Prophet Mohammed cartoons controversy: Timeline'. *Daily Telegraph*, 4 May 2015, https://www.telegraph.co.uk/news/worldnews/europe/france/11341599/Prophet-Muhammad-cartoons-controversy-timeline.html.

Puar, Jasbir K. '"The Turban Is Not a Hat": Queer Diaspora and Practices of Profiling'. *Sikh Formations* 4 (2008): 47–91.

The Pulitzer Prizes. 'Editorial Cartooning'. https://www.pulitzer.org/prize-winners-by-category/215.

Rabinbach, Anson, and Sander L. Gilman. *The Third Reich Sourcebook*. Berkeley: University of California Press, 2013.

Rane, Halim, Jacqui Ewart and John Martinkus. *Media Framing of the Muslim World: Conflicts, Crises and Contexts*. Houndmills, Basingstoke, Hampshire: Palgrave Macmillan, 2014.

Ransom, Jan. 'East ramapo school elections violate voting rights, suit claims'. *New York Times*, 16 November 2017, https://www.nytimes.com/2017/11/16/nyregion/aclu-files-suit-against-east-ramapo-school-board-votng-rights.html.

Reitlinger, Gerald. *The Final Solution: The Attempt to Exterminate the Jews of Europe, 1939–1945*. New York: Beechhurst Press, 1953.

Remnick, David. 'Bibi's blues'. *The New Yorker*, 22 January 2013, http://www.newyorker.com/news/news-desk/bibis-blues.

Reuters. 'Iranian foundation offers land to Salman Rushdie's attacker - state TV'. 21 February 2023, https://www.reuters.com/world/middle-east/iranian-foundation-offers-land-salman-rushdies-attacker-state-media-2023-02-21/.

Revolutionary Association of the Women of Afghanistan (RAWA). 'Some of the restrictions imposed by Taliban on women in Afghanistan: 1996–2001'. http://www.rawa.org/rules.htm.

Rich, Dave (@daverich1). 'The depiction of Richard Sharp in today's @guardian cartoon falls squarely into an antisemitic tradition'. Twitter, 29 April 2023, https://twitter.com/daverich1/status/1652216828247015435.

Rowson, Martin. Accessed 14 May 2023. https://www.martinrowson.com.

Said, Edward. *Covering Islam: How the Media and the Experts Determine How We See the Rest of the World*. London: Vintage, 1997.

Said, Edward W. *Orientalism*. London: Penguin Classics, 2003.

Salusbury, Matt. 'Where are the women cartoonists?'. Accessed 27 October 2018, http://www.londonfreelance.org/fl/1804cart.html.

Saner, Emine. 'Why are sikhs targeted by anti-muslim extremists?'. *Guardian*, 8 August 2012, http://www.theguardian.com/world/2012/aug/08/sikhs-targeted-anti-muslim-extremists.

Saul, Heather. 'Vince cable accuses Bank of England officials of "acting like the Taliban"'. *Independent*, 24 July 2013, http://www.independent.co.uk/news/business/news/vince-cable-accuses-bank-of-england-officials-of-acting-like-the-taliban-8729262.html.

Scarfe, Gerald. 'About Gerald'. Gerald Scarfe, the Official Website. https://www.geraldscarfe.com/about-gerald-scarfe.

Scully, Richard. *Eminent Victorian Cartoonists Volume I*. London: Political Cartoon Society, 2018.

Seymour-Ure, Colin. 'What Future for the British Political Cartoon?'. *Journalism Studies* 2, no. 3 (2001): 333–55. https://doi.org/10.1080/14616700120062202.

Seymour-Ure, Colin, and Jim Schoff. *David Low*. London: Secker & Warburg, 1985.

Sharf, Andrew. *The British Press and Jews under Nazi Rule*. London: Oxford University Press, 1964.

Sherlock, Ruth. 'Al-Qaeda cuts links with Syrian group too extreme even for them'. *Daily Telegraph*, 3 February 2014, https://www.telegraph.co.uk/news/worldnews/

middleeast/syria/10614037/Al-Qaeda-cuts-links-with-Syrian-group-too-extreme-even-for-them.html.

Shindler, Colin. *A History of Modern Israel*. Cambridge: Cambridge University Press, 2008.

Shlaim, Avi. 'The Oslo Accord'. *Journal of Palestine Studies* 23, no. 3 (1994): 24–40. http://www.jstor.org/stable/2537958.

Singh, Gurharpal. 'British Multiculturalism and Sikhs.' *Sikh Formations* 1 (2005): 157–73.

Sky News. 'British family of 12 suspected of joining Islamic State "all die in Syria"'. 28 June 2019, https://news.sky.com/story/british-family-of-12-suspected-of-joining-islamic-state-all-killed-in-syria–11750813.

Slack, James. 'Burkas empower women: Female cabinet minister insists freedom to wear muslim veil is a right'. *Daily Mail*, 20 July 2010, http://www.dailymail.co.uk/news/article-1295665/Banning-burkas-UK-British-says-Green.html.

Smolderen, Thierry, Bart Beaty and Nick Nguyen. *The Origins of Comics: From William Hogarth to Winsor McCay*. Jackson: University Press of Mississippi, 2014. http://www.jstor.org/stable/j.ctt2tvp3g.3.

Sotheby's. 'Portrait of Jane Austen, watercolour on paper'. Accessed 15 February 2015. http://www.sothebys.com/en/auctions/ecatalogue/2013/english-literature-history-l13408/lot.283.html.

The Soufan Center. 'FOREIGN FIGHTERS: An Updated Assessment of the Flow of Foreign Fighters into Syria and Iraq'. December 2015. https://thesoufancenter.org/wp-content/uploads/2017/05/TSG_ForeignFightersUpdate_format-for-print-120915-REBRAND-031317.pdf.

The Spectator; London. 'Ireland from one or two neglected points of view. By the author of "Hints to Country Bumpkins."' Published 2 March, 1889. Accessed 22 November 2019. https://search.proquest.com/docview/1295364091?accountid=11862.

Spencer, Ian R. G. *British Immigration Policy since 1939: The Making of Multi-Racial Britain*. New York: Routledge, 1997.

Stephens, Philip. 'Bomb Puts Ulster Peace Talks in Doubt'. *Financial Times*, 25 October 1993. The Financial Times Historical Archive, 1888–2010.

Stephens, Philip. 'Populism is the true legacy of the global financial crisis'. *Financial Times*, 30 August 2018, https://www.ft.com/content/687c0184-aaa6-11e8-94bd-cba20d67390c.

Stewart, Heather, and Rowena Mason. 'Nigel Farage's anti-migrant poster reported to police'. *Guardian*, 16 June 2016, https://www.theguardian.com/politics/2016/jun/16/nigel-farage-defends-ukip-breaking-point-poster-queue-of-migrants.

Streeten, Nicola. 'Academic Activity'. https://nicolastreeten.wordpress.com/academic-research-activity/.

Streeten, Nicola. *UK Feminist Cartoonists and Comics: A Critical Survey*. Cham: Palgrave Studies in Comics and Graphic Novels, 2020.

Streeten, Nicola, and Cath Tate Jennings, ed. *The Inking Woman: 250 Years of Women Cartoon and Comic Artists in Britain*. Brighton: Myriad, 2018.

Streicher, Lawrence H. 'David Low and the Sociology of Caricature'. *Comparative Studies in Society and History*, 8, no. 1 (1965): 1–23. https://www.jstor.org/stable/177533.

Temple, Mick. *British Press*. Berkshire: McGraw-Hill Education, 2008.

The Times. 'In Your Face'. 11 April 2011, http://find.galegroup.com/dvnw/infomark.do?&source=gale&prodId=DVNW&userGroupName=kings&tabID=T003&docPage=article&docId=IF504210106&type=multipage&contentSet=LTO&version=1.0.

The Times. 'Our special correspondent, "Terrorists' Toll In Palestine."' 19 November 1946.

United Nations Assistance Mission in Afghanistan. *Afghanistan: Protection of Civilians in Armed Conflict Midyear Update: 1 January to 30 June 2021*, Published 26 July 2021. Accessed 4 April 2023, https://unama.unmissions.org/sites/default/files/unama_poc_midyear_report_2021_26_july.pdf.

U.S. Department of Defense. 'Statement from pentagon press secretary Peter Cook on airstrike in Raqqa, Syria'. Published 12 November 2015, https://www.defense.gov/News/News-Releases/News-Release-View/Article/628777/statement-from-pentagon-press-secretary-peter-cook-on-airstrike-in-raqqa-syria/.

United States Department of Justice. 'Mustafa Kamel Mustafa, A/k/a "Abu Hamza," convicted of 11 terrorism charges in manhattan federal court'. Published 19 May 2014, https://www.justice.gov/usao-sdny/pr/mustafa-kamel-mustafa-aka-abu-hamza-convicted-11-terrorism-charges-manhattan-federal.

United States Holocaust Memorial Museum. 'Holocaust Denial: Iran Holocaust Cartoon Exhibition'. Accessed 14 October 2018, https://www.ushmm.org/confront-antisemitism/holocaust-denial-and-distortion/iran/iran-cartoon-exhibition/introduction/iran-holocaust-cartoon-exhibition.

University of Kent, British Cartoon Archive. Low cuttings 1938–45, Box 1, Percy Cudlipp to David Low. 9 September 1937.

Walker, Peter, and Frances Perraudin. 'London Bridge attack: Boris Johnson ignores family's plea not to exploit victims' deaths'. *Guardian*, 2 December 2019, https://www.theguardian.com/politics/2019/dec/01/boris-johnson-election-issue-london-bridge-attack.

'Bombs in English Town kill child; IRA blamed'. *Washington Post*, 21 March 1993, https://global-factiva-com.libproxy.kcl.ac.uk/redir/default.aspx?P=sa&NS=16&AID=9KIN002300&an=wp00000020011102dp3l00a38&cat=a&ep=ASI.

'Transcript: Translation of Bin Laden's videotaped message'. *Washington Post*, 1 November 2004, http://www.washingtonpost.com/wp-dyn/articles/A16990-2004Nov1.html.

Whaley, Deborah Elizabeth. *Black Women in Sequence: Re-inking Comics, Graphic Novels, and Anima*. Seattle: University of Washington Press, 2016.

Wohl, Anthony S. "'Ben JuJu": Representations of Disraeli's Jewishness in the Victorian Political Cartoon'. *Jewish History* 10, no. 2 (1996): 89–134. www.jstor.org/stable/20101269.

Yegenoglu, Meyda. 'Sartorial Fabric-Actions: The Enlightenment and Western Feminism'. In *Colonial Fantasies: Towards a Feminist Reading of Orientalism*, 95–120. Cambridge: Cambridge University Press, 1998. http://dx.doi.org/10.1017/CBO9780511583445.005.

York Herald. 'The Jew Bill and the Oaths' Bill'. 24 July 1858.

Younge, Gary. 'The Serena cartoon debate: Calling out racism is not "censorship"'. *Guardian*, 13 September 2018, https://www.theguardian.com/commentisfree/2018/sep/13/serena-williams-cartoon-racism-censorship-mark-knight-herald-sun.

Zebiri, Kate. 'Orientalist themes in contemporary British islamophobia'. In *Islamophobia: The Challenge of Pluralism in the 21st Century*, edited by John L. Esposito and Ibrahim Kalin, 173–190. Oxford: Oxford University Press, 2011.

List of images cited

Introduction

1.1 David Low, 'IT', *The Star*, 18 August 1925, https://archive.cartoons.ac.uk/Record.aspx?src=CalmView.Catalog&id=LSE7298.
1.2 William Hogarth, 'A Harlot's progress', plate 1, April 1733. https://en.wikipedia.org/wiki/A_Harlot's_Progress.
1.3 William Hogarth, 'The four stages of cruelty: First stage of cruelty', 1 February 1751. https://en.wikipedia.org/wiki/The_Four_Stages_of_Cruelty#:~:text=Each%20print%20depicts%20a%20different,of%20the%20fictional%20Tom%20Nero.&text=Beginning%20with%20the%20torture%20of,murder%20in%20Cruelty%20in%20perfection.
1.4 James Gillray, 'The plumb-pudding in danger: - or - state epicures taking un petit souper', 26 February 1805.
1.5 John Leech, 'Cartoon, no. 1. substance and shadow', *Punch*, 15 July 1843
1.6 John Doyle, 'A scene from Shakspere (compressed!)', 8 August 1844, https://archive.cartoons.ac.uk/Record.aspx?src=CalmView.Catalog&id=mudyx4l.

Chapter 2 – Nuns, guns and balaclavas: The Irish in political cartoons

2.1 John Leech, 'The repeal farce', *Punch*, 21 January 1843.
2.2 H. Strickland Constable, no caption, *Harper's Weekly*, 1899. https://upload.wikimedia.org/wikipedia/commons/f/fa/Scientific_racism_irish.jpg.
2.3 John Tenniel, 'Two forces', *Punch*, 29 October 1881. https://www.metmuseum.org/art/collection/search/685295.
2.4 Matt Morgan, 'The Irish frankenstein', *Tomahawk*, 1869.
2.5 Anonymous, no caption, *Pat*, 1881.
2.6 Anonymous, 'The kindest cut of all', *Punch*, 10 March 1920.

2.7 Bernard Partridge, 'A forgotten patriotism', *Punch*, 24 August 1921.

2.8 Leonard Raven-Hill, 'Ireland's evil genius', *Punch*, 6 June 1923.

2.9 Jak, 'Owing to a spot of bother in Ireland, we're recruiting again for the Black and Tan', *Evening Standard*, 8 October 1968. BCA image reference number 12760, https://archive.cartoons.ac.uk/Record.aspx?src=CalmView.Catalog&id=12760.

2.10 Keith Waite, 'I don't understand the police violence – all we did was throw a few petrol bombs at them', *Sun*, 9 October 1968. BCA image reference number 14007, https://archive.cartoons.ac.uk/Record.aspx?src=CalmView.Catalog&id=14007.

2.11 Jak, 'In Christ's name', *Evening Standard*, 16 August 1969. BCA image reference number 16112, https://archive.cartoons.ac.uk/Record.aspx?src=CalmView.Catalog&id=16112.

2.12 Bernard Cookson, no caption, *Evening News*, 18 August 1969. BCA image reference number 16119, https://archive.cartoons.ac.uk/Record.aspx?src=CalmView.Catalog&id=16119.

2.13 Jon, 'It's all this wanton destruction, sir', *Daily Mail*, 18 August 1969. BCA reference 16133, https://archive.cartoons.ac.uk/Record.aspx?src=CalmView.Catalog&id=16133.

2.14 Leslie Gibbard, 'Under orders', *Guardian*, 5 February 1972. BCA image reference number 21949, https://archive.cartoons.ac.uk/Record.aspx?src=CalmView.Catalog&id=21949.

2.15 Jak, 'He fired first!', *Evening Standard*, 31 January 1972. BCA image reference number 21916, https://archive.cartoons.ac.uk/Record.aspx?src=CalmView.Catalog&id=21916.

2.16 Jak, 'I wonder how the British Press will distort this', *Evening Standard*, 26 October 1971. BCA image reference number 21194, https://archive.cartoons.ac.uk/Record.aspx?src=CalmView.Catalog&id=21194.

2.17 Paul Rigby, 'Look at this - how could anyone stoop to such brutality?', *Sun*, 20 October 1971. BCA image reference number 21234, https://archive.cartoons.ac.uk/Record.aspx?src=CalmView.Catalog&id=21234.

2.18 Nicholas Garland, no caption, *Daily Telegraph*, 4 February 1972. BCA image reference number 21943, https://archive.cartoons.ac.uk/Record.aspx?src=CalmView.Catalog&id=21943.

2.19 Bernard Patridge, 'Out of the ashes', *Punch*, 12 July 1922.

List of Images Cited 219

2.20 Mac, 'I've killed a soldier, Dad - now can I go and play football?', *Daily Sketch*, 9 February 1971. BCA image reference number 19644, https://archive.cartoons.ac.uk/Record.aspx?src=CalmView.Catalog&id=19644.

2.21 Bernard Cookson, 'He said his first word today, Paddy … "Kill!"', *Evening News*, 9 February 1971. BCA image reference number 19649, https://archive.cartoons.ac.uk/Record.aspx?src=CalmView.Catalog&id=19649.

2.22 Nicholas Garland, 'Mad dogs and Englishmen …', *Daily Telegraph*, 15 July 1971. BCA image reference number NG0710, https://archive.cartoons.ac.uk/Record.aspx?src=CalmView.Catalog&id=NG0710.

2.23 Stanley Franklin, no caption, *Sun*, 16 November 1981. BCA image reference number 35528, https://archive.cartoons.ac.uk/Record.aspx?src=CalmView.Catalog&id=35528.

2.24 Nicholas Garland, 'Remember - squeeze don't pull'. *Daily Telegraph*, 15 November 1991. BCA image reference number NG4871, https://archive.cartoons.ac.uk/Record.aspx?src=CalmView.Catalog&id=NG4871.

2.25 Mac, 'Hero of Auld Ireland', *Daily Mail*, 22 March 1993. BCA image reference number 48947, https://archive.cartoons.ac.uk/Record.aspx?src=CalmView.Catalog&id=48947.

2.26 Nicholas Garland, 'No! No! No!', *Daily Telegraph*, 26 October 1993. BCA image reference number NG5306, https://archive.cartoons.ac.uk/Record.aspx?src=CalmView.Catalog&id=NG5306.

2.27 Keith Waite, 'Look here, we ordered guns, not nuns', *Daily Mirror*, 25 August 1970. BCA image reference number 18411, https://archive.cartoons.ac.uk/Record.aspx?src=CalmView.Catalog&id=18411.

2.28 Nicholas Garland, 'I find it difficult not to feel sympathy for both sides in these tribal conflicts', *Daily Telegraph*, 16 August 1969. BCA image reference number NG0497, https://archive.cartoons.ac.uk/Record.aspx?src=CalmView.Catalog&id=NG0497.

2.29 Trog, 'Heathen Bloody Savages!', *Punch*, 27 September 1972.

2.30 Jon, 'Glory be, Mrs Murphy, isn't it terrible what the Arabs and Israelis are up to?', *Daily Mail*, 11 September 1969. BCA image reference number 16248, https://archive.cartoons.ac.uk/Record.aspx?src=CalmView.Catalog&id=16248.

2.31 Michael Cummings, 'We're pagan missionaries come to try to make peace among the bloodthirsty Christians', *Daily Express*,

12 September 1969. BCA image reference number 16254, https://archive.cartoons.ac.uk/Record.aspx?src=CalmView.Catalog&id=16254.

2.32 Michael Cummings, 'How marvellous it would be if they DID knock each other insensible!', *Daily Express*, 12 August 1970. BCA image reference number 18473, https://archive.cartoons.ac.uk/Record.aspx?src=CalmView.Catalog&id=18473.

2.33 Ronald Carl Giles, 'I don't think it's a stupid question. I simply asked how throwing a little brick through someone's window and knocking a policeman's hat off helped the Irish cause', *Daily Express*, 19 August 1969. BCA image reference number 16123, https://archive.cartoons.ac.uk/Record.aspx?src=CalmView.Catalog&id=16123.

2.34 Mac, 'Ye lying ol' devil, Paddy. Ye know mother's the same faith as us!', *Daily Sketch*, 11 September 1969. BCA image reference number 16249, https://archive.cartoons.ac.uk/Record.aspx?src=CalmView.Catalog&id=16249.

2.35 Stanley Franklin, '"Tis a strange thing that among us people can't agree the whole week because they go different ways on Sundays" Irish dramatist Farquhar 1700', *Daily Mirror*, 11 September 1969. BCA image reference number 16251, https://archive.cartoons.ac.uk/Record.aspx?src=CalmView.Catalog&id=16251.

2.36 David Low, 'Progress to Liberty - Amritsar style', *The Star*, 16 December 1919. BCA image reference number LSE6183, https://archive.cartoons.ac.uk/Record.aspx?src=CalmView.Catalog&id=LSE6183.

2.37 Kenneth Mahood, 'I hope you're not Irish or coloured?' *Punch*, 29 October 1969.

2.38 Kenneth Mahood, 'I think this chap's call should have priority – he has an Irish accent!', *Punch*, 29 May 1974.

2.39 Jak, 'Bloody foreigners!', *Evening Standard*, 29 August 1969. BCA image reference number 16161, https://archive.cartoons.ac.uk/Record.aspx?src=CalmView.Catalog&id=16161.

2.40 Jak, 'As far as I can make out, we Irish are two-and-a-half per cent more sexy than the rest of you!', *Evening Standard*, 12 March 1970. BCA image reference number 17462, https://archive.cartoons.ac.uk/Record.aspx?src=CalmView.Catalog&id=17462.

2.41 Michael Cummings, 'Please, Mr. Whitelaw! When the Irish have fought to the very last man, can we go and live in the unoccupied space?', *Daily Express*, 21 October 1972. BCA image reference number 23291, https://archive.cartoons.ac.uk/Record.aspx?src=CalmView.Catalog&id=23291.

2.42 Kenneth Mahood, 'There is no need for a Nationality Bill, says MAHOOD – all that is required is a few simple tests', *Punch*, 18 February 1981.

2.43 Michael Cummings, 'Can't you British see straight - you've imprisoned another innocent!', *Sunday Express*, 21 June 1981. BCA image reference number 35319, https://archive.cartoons.ac.uk/Record.aspx?src=CalmView.Catalog&id=35319.

2.44 Michael Cummings, 'We musn't keep him out of the Club on grounds of his species! After all, it's not his fault that the human race is descended from him!', *Daily Express*, 22 December 1971. BCA image reference number 21684, https://archive.cartoons.ac.uk/Record.aspx?src=CalmView.Catalog&id=21684.

2.45 Sidney William Martin, no caption, *Sunday Express*, 27 February 1972. BCA image reference number 22084, https://archive.cartoons.ac.uk/Record.aspx?src=CalmView.Catalog&id=22084.

2.46 Chris Priestley, no caption, *Independent*, 1 May 1998. BCA image reference number PC3629, https://archive.cartoons.ac.uk/Record.aspx?src=CalmView.Catalog&id=PC3629.

2.47 Chris Riddell, 'Hero of Omagh', *Observer*, 7 February 1999. BCA image reference number PC5511, https://archive.cartoons.ac.uk/Record.aspx?src=CalmView.Catalog&id=PC5511.

2.48 David Haldane, 'Where did you get the cash to buy that fancy balaclava?', *The Times*, 19 February 2005. BCA image reference number 85942, https://archive.cartoons.ac.uk/Record.aspx?src=CalmView.Catalog&id=85942.

2.49 Mac, 'Spot the difference', *Daily Mail*, 10 March 2009. BCA image reference number 78815, https://archive.cartoons.ac.uk/Record.aspx?src=CalmView.Catalog&id=78815.

2.50 Stanley Franklin, 'Patriotism is the last refuge of a scoundrel - Samuel Johnson', *Daily Mirror*, 14 October 1969. BCA image reference number 16458, https://archive.cartoons.ac.uk/Record.aspx?src=CalmView.Catalog&id=16458.

2.51 Emmwood, 'Faceless, senseless – brainless', *Daily Mail*, 12 July 1972. BCA image reference number 22839, https://archive.cartoons.ac.uk/Record.aspx?src=CalmView.Catalog&id=22839.

2.52 Andrzej Krauze, no caption, *Observer*, 14 July 1996. BCA image reference number PC0157, https://archive.cartoons.ac.uk/Record.aspx?src=CalmView.Catalog&id=PC0157.

2.53 Steve Bell, '1049-9-1-98_MORETEAMADDOG', *Guardian*, 9 January 1998, BCA image reference number SBD0423, https://archive.cartoons.ac.uk/Record.aspx?src=CalmView.Catalog&id=SBD0423.

2.54 Chris Priestley, no caption, *Independent*, 9 January 1998. BCA image reference number PC3055, https://archive.cartoons.ac.uk/Record.aspx?src=CalmView.Catalog&id=PC3055.

2.55 Dave Gaskill, no caption, *Sun*, 15 February 1999. BCA image reference number PC5555, https://archive.cartoons.ac.uk/Record.aspx?src=CalmView.Catalog&id=PC5555.

2.56 Dave Brown, no caption, *Independent*, 9 October 2002, BCA image reference number 62912, https://archive.cartoons.ac.uk/Record.aspx?src=CalmView.Catalog&id=62912.

2.57 JAS, no caption, *Daily Telegraph*, 29 January 2007. BCA image reference number 75150, https://archive.cartoons.ac.uk/Record.aspx?src=CalmView.Catalog&id=75150.

2.58 Jonathan Pugh, 'Oh no, not another repeat', *The Times*, 11 March 2009.

Chapter 3 – Noses, Moses and war: Jews in political cartoons

3.1 Anonymous, 1233, Norwich. http://www.nationalarchives.gov.uk/wp-content/uploads/2014/03/e401-15651.jpg.

3.2 John Tenniel, 'New crowns for old ones!', *Punch*, 15 April 1876.

3.3 Joseph Swain, 'Mose in Egitto!!!', *Punch*, 11 December 1875.

3.4 Leslie Gilbert Illingworth, no caption, *Daily Mail*, 23 July 1946. BCA image reference number ILW1115, https://www.cartoons.ac.uk/record/ILW1115.

3.5 David Low, 'What, he's not anti-semitic? We'll soon alter that', *Evening Standard*, 22 November 1946. BCA image reference number LSE4809, https://www.cartoons.ac.uk/record/LSE4809.

3.6 David Low, 'Unhappy partners in Palestine', *Evening Standard*, 7 August 1947. BCA image reference number LSE4929, https://www.cartoons.ac.uk/record/LSE4929.

List of Images Cited

3.7 David Low, 'New chapter of tribulation', *Evening Standard*, 2 January 1948. BCA image reference number LSE8841, https://archive.cartoons.ac.uk/Record.aspx?src=CalmView.Catalog&id=LSE8841.

3.8 David Low, 'Lebensraum for the conquered', *Evening Standard*, 20 January 1940. BCA image reference number LSE4337, https://www.cartoons.ac.uk/record/LSE4337.

3.9 David Low, 'I've settled the fate of Jews – and of Germans', *Evening Standard*, 14 December 1942. BCA image reference number LSE3216, https://archive.cartoons.ac.uk/Record.aspx?src=CalmView.Catalog&id=LSE3216.

3.10 David Low, 'It worked at the Reichstag - Why not here?', *Evening Standard*, 18 October 1933. BCA image reference number LSE1993, https://archive.cartoons.ac.uk/Record.aspx?src=CalmView.Catalog&id=LSE1993.

3.11 David Low, 'And now to snatch the triumph from HIM', *Evening Standard*, 4 February 1949. BCA image reference number LSE9006, https://www.cartoons.ac.uk/record/LSE9006.

3.12 David Low, 'There, yesterday, were we', *Evening Standard*, 23 March 1949. BCA image reference number LSE9032, https://www.cartoons.ac.uk/record/LSE9032.

3.13 David Low, 'Verdict', *Evening Standard*, 1 October 1946. BCA image reference number LSE1420, https://www.cartoons.ac.uk/record/LSE1420.

3.14 David Low, 'Repairs at Mount Sinai', *Manchester Guardian*, 16 November 1956. BCA image reference number LSE5581, https://archive.cartoons.ac.uk/Record.aspx?src=CalmView.Catalog&id=LSE5581.

3.15 Jak, 'So, who's minding the shop?', *Evening Standard*, 31 May 1967. BCA image reference number 11330, https://www.cartoons.ac.uk/record/11330.

3.16 Jak, 'You were in Beirut, and you couldn't find time to send a card to your mother?', *Evening Standard*, 11 April 1973. BCA image reference number 24259, https://www.cartoons.ac.uk/record/24259.

3.17 Nicholas Garland, no caption, *Daily Telegraph*, 10 September 1993. BCA image reference number 49145, https://www.cartoons.ac.uk/record/49145.

3.18 Nicholas Garland, 'David and Goliath', *Daily Telegraph*, 2 September 1993. BCA image reference number NG5275, https://www.cartoons.ac.uk/record/NG5275.

3.19 Steve Bell, '0831-27-9-96_PEACEPROCESSOR', *Guardian*, 27 September 1996. BCA image reference number PC0388, https://www.cartoons.ac.uk/record/PC0388.

3.20 Peter Brookes, 'They shall beat their swords into ploughshares … (Isaiah Ch. 2, v.4)', *The Times*, 27 September 1996. BCA image reference number PPC0392, https://www.cartoons.ac.uk/record/PC0392.

3.21 Dave Brown, no caption, *Independent*, 27 January 2003. BCA image reference number DBD0001, https://archive.cartoons.ac.uk/Record.aspx?src=CalmView.Catalog&id=DBD0001.

3.22 Gerald Scarfe, 'Will cementing the peace continue?', *Sunday Times*, 27 January 2013.

3.23 Steve Bell, '3421-161112_VOTELIKUD', *Guardian*, 16 November 2012. BCA image reference number SBD1085, https://www.cartoons.ac.uk/record/SBD1085.

Chapter 4 – Turbans, terrorism and transport: Sikhs in political cartoons

4.1 David Myers, no caption, *Evening Standard*, 4 July 1968. BCA image reference number 13685, https://archive.cartoons.ac.uk/Record.aspx?src=CalmView.Catalog&id=13685.

4.2 Keith Waite, 'Actually I'm wearing my turban underneath it', *Sun*, 4 July 1968. BCA image reference number 13680, https://archive.cartoons.ac.uk/Record.aspx?src=CalmView.Catalog&id=13680.

4.3 Stanley Franklin, 'I told you one thing would lead to another', *Daily Mirror*, 11 April 1969. BCA image reference number 15238, https://archive.cartoons.ac.uk/Record.aspx?src=CalmView.Catalog&id=15238.

4.4 Stanley Franklin, 'It makes a change from Z-cars', *Daily Mirror*, 29 January 1970. BCA image reference number 17166, https://archive.cartoons.ac.uk/Record.aspx?src=CalmView.Catalog&id=17166.

4.5 Keith Waite, 'It's all right, big boy – we're allowed to wear turbans now', *Sun*, 11 April 1969. BCA image reference number 15236, https://archive.cartoons.ac.uk/Record.aspx?src=CalmView.Catalog&id=15236.

4.6 Michael Cummings, 'If this is the "Mother" Country, cobber, I think I'd rather take the next flight back to Australia …', *Daily Express*,

List of Images Cited 225

20 November 1972. BCA image reference number 23439, https://archive.cartoons.ac.uk/Record.aspx?src=CalmView.Catalog&id=23439.

4.7 Keith Waite, 'No, I'm not a Sikh – it's just that I wasn't wearing a crash helmet', *Daily Mirror*, 11 September 1973. BCA image reference number 25058, https://archive.cartoons.ac.uk/Record.aspx?src=CalmView.Catalog&id=25058.

4.8 Mac, 'And we can't do a damned thing – the driver's wearing a crash helmet!', *Daily Mail*, 11 September 1973. BCA image reference number 25059, https://archive.cartoons.ac.uk/Record.aspx?src=CalmView.Catalog&id=25059.

4.9 Leslie Gibbard, 'No thanks - it's against my religion ...', *Guardian*, 11 September 1973. BCA image reference number 25062, https://archive.cartoons.ac.uk/Record.aspx?src=CalmView.Catalog&id=25062.

4.10 Michael Cummings, 'The good news is that our next war will be fought in outer space - the bad news is that other people's wars will be fought in the streets of Britain', *Daily Express*, 13 June 1984. BCA image reference number 46717, https://archive.cartoons.ac.uk/Record.aspx?src=CalmView.Catalog&id=46717.

4.11 Stanley Franklin, 'Evil of the sky', *Sun*, 24 June 1985. BCA image reference number 47635, https://archive.cartoons.ac.uk/Record.aspx?src=CalmView.Catalog&id=47635.

4.12 Jak, 'Sold! to the gent with the large diamond in his turban!', *Evening Standard*, 11 November 1971. BCA image reference number 21418, https://archive.cartoons.ac.uk/Record.aspx?src=CalmView.Catalog&id=21418.

4.13 Trog, 'What I always say is, exports are exports!', *Daily Mail*, 18 October 1968. BCA image reference number 14072, https://archive.cartoons.ac.uk/Record.aspx?src=CalmView.Catalog&id=14072.

4.14 Emmwood, 'Now that we're all European, Sahib, I suppose wogs begin at Malta!', *Daily Mail*, 2 January 1973. BCA image reference number 23660, https://archive.cartoons.ac.uk/Record.aspx?src=CalmView.Catalog&id=23660.

4.15 W.K. Haselden, 'Tennis fashions for Wimbledon', *Daily Mirror*, 22 June 1925. BCA image reference number WH3686, https://archive.cartoons.ac.uk/Record.aspx?src=CalmView.Catalog&id=WH3686.

4.16 Keith Waite, 'How the heck would I know what Jim Callaghan meant?', *Sun*, 1 March 1968. BCA image reference number 13143,

4.17 Jak, 'Now give us your honest opinion!', *Evening Standard*, 23 April 1968. BCA image reference number 13317, https://archive.cartoons.ac.uk/Record.aspx?src=CalmView.Catalog&id=13317.

4.18 Stanley Franklin, 'You having another of your nightmares, Enoch?', *Daily Mirror*, 24 April 1968. BCA image reference number 13319, https://archive.cartoons.ac.uk/Record.aspx?src=CalmView.Catalog&id=13319.

4.19 Peter Brookes, no caption, *The Times*, 29 July 2010. BCA image reference number 81542, https://archive.cartoons.ac.uk/Record.aspx?src=CalmView.Catalog&id=81542.

Chapter 5 – Burqas on the beach: Muslim women in political cartoons

5.1 Peter Brookes, 'New Jane Austen £10 Note (as designed by Vince Cable)', *The Times*, 25 July 2013.

5.2 Dave Brown, no caption, *Independent*, 3 August 2005. BCA image reference number 71997, https://www.cartoons.ac.uk/record/71997.

5.3 Paul Thomas, no caption, *Daily Express*, 12 November 2001. BCA image reference number 59694, https://www.cartoons.ac.uk/record/59694.

5.4 Peter Brookes, 'Meanwhile, in downtown Kabul …', *The Times*, 16 November 2001. BCA image reference number 59652, https://www.cartoons.ac.uk/record/59652.

5.5 Peter Schrank, no caption, *Independent on Sunday*, 11 March 2012. BCA image reference number SCD0040, https://archive.cartoons.ac.uk/Record.aspx?src=CalmView.Catalog&id=SCD0040.

5.6 Matt, no caption, *Daily Telegraph*, 12 April 2011. BCA image reference number 84444, https://www.cartoons.ac.uk/record/84444.

5.7 Peter Brookes, no caption, *The Times*, 12 April 2011. BCA image reference number 84438, https://www.cartoons.ac.uk/record/84438.

5.8 Peter Schrank, no caption, *Independent*, 19 July 2010. BCA image reference number 81488, https://www.cartoons.ac.uk/record/81488.

5.9 Mac, 'Doris, love. How would you like to feel empowered?', *Daily Mail*, 20 July 2010. BCA reference 81493, https://www.cartoons.ac.uk/record/81493.

5.10 Matt, 'And don't be late tomorrow, it's the school photo …', *Daily Telegraph*, 17 September 2013. BCA image reference number 99612, https://www.cartoons.ac.uk/record/99612.

5.11 Peter Brookes, 'Silly Burka … ', *The Times*, 5 November 2013. BCA image reference number 99998, https://www.cartoons.ac.uk/record/99998.

5.12 Matt, 'Wait till I catch that cat', *Daily Telegraph*, 8 November 2013. BCA image reference number 100154, https://www.cartoons.ac.uk/record/100154.

5.13 Matt, no caption, *Daily Telegraph*, 30 August 2011. BCA image reference number 95089, https://www.cartoons.ac.uk/record/95089.

5.14 Brighty, 'Nothing to hide', *Sun*, 16 September 2013. BCA image reference number 102387, https://www.cartoons.ac.uk/record/102387.

5.15 Christian Adams, 'Trojan horse in niqab', *Daily Telegraph*, 4 May 2014. BCA image reference number 100758, https://www.cartoons.ac.uk/record/100758.

5.16 Nicholas Newman, 'Oh no! A Trojan Horse School!', *Sunday Times*, 27 July 2014. BCA image reference number 101084, https://www.cartoons.ac.uk/record/101084.

5.17 Peter Brookes, 'New UK Poll … ', *The Times*, 26 February 2015. BCA image reference number 102284, https://www.cartoons.ac.uk/record/102284.

5.18 Ben Jennings, 'This is what I'm talking about people! The "Burka" is an affront to our Christian values!', *i News*, 29 April 2017. BCA image reference number BJD0421, https://www.cartoons.ac.uk/record/BJD0421.

Chapter 6 – Beards, bombs and barbarians: Muslim men in political cartoons

6.1 Peter Schrank, no caption, *Independent*, 12 September 2001. BCA image reference number 59105, http://archives.cartoons.ac.uk/Record.aspx?src=CalmView.Catalog&id=59105.

6.2 Steve Bell, '1638-12-9-01_WORLDTRADEBURN', *Guardian*, 12 September 2001, BCA image reference number 59102, http://archives.cartoons.ac.uk/Record.aspx?src=CalmView.Catalog&id=59102.

6.3 Peter Brookes, no caption, *The Times*, 12 September 2001. BCA image reference number 59106, http://archives.cartoons.ac.uk/Record.aspx?src=CalmView.Catalog&id=59106.

6.4 Mac, 'Parasite: (Chambers English Dictionary) a creature which obtains food and physical protection from a host which never benefits from its presence', *Daily Mail*, 20 September 2001. BCA image reference number 59049, http://archives.cartoons.ac.uk/Record.aspx?src=CalmView.Catalog&id=59049.

6.5 Nicholas Garland, no caption, *Daily Telegraph*, 16 October 2001. BCA image reference number 59365, http://archives.cartoons.ac.uk/Record.aspx?src=CalmView.Catalog&id=59365.

6.6 Steve Fricker, no caption, *Daily Telegraph*, 17 September 2001. BCA image reference number 59069, https://archive.cartoons.ac.uk/record.aspx?src=CalmView.Catalog&id=59069.

6.7 David Austin, no caption, *Guardian*, 8 July 2005. BCA image reference number 86517, https://archive.cartoons.ac.uk/Record.aspx?src=CalmView.Catalog&id=86517.

6.8 Paul Thomas, no caption, *Daily Express*, 8 July 2005. BCA image reference number 71847, https://archive.cartoons.ac.uk/Record.aspx?src=CalmView.Catalog&id=71847.

6.9 Nicholas Garland, no caption, *Daily Telegraph*, 8 July 2005. BCA image reference number 71846, https://archive.cartoons.ac.uk/Record.aspx?src=CalmView.Catalog&id=71846.

6.10 Kenneth Mahood, 'Mirror, mirror, on the wall, who is the most murderous one of all?', *Daily Mail*, 8 July 2005. BCA image reference number 86519, https://archive.cartoons.ac.uk/Record.aspx?src=CalmView.Catalog&id=86519.

6.11 Morten Morland, 'Mind the Gap …', *The Times*, 11 July 2005. BCA image reference number 71866, https://archive.cartoons.ac.uk/Record.aspx?src=CalmView.Catalog&id=71866.

6.12 Nicholas Garland, 'Kicking and Screaming', *Daily Telegraph*, 21 July 2005. BCA image reference number 71922, http://archives.cartoons.ac.uk/Record.aspx?src=CalmView.Catalog&id=71922.

List of Images Cited   229

6.13 Peter Schrank, 'Back to the future', *Independent*, 20 August 2006. BCA reference 74170, http://archives.cartoons.ac.uk/Record.aspx?src=CalmView.Catalog&id=74170.

6.14 Nicholas Garland, 'Coming to a high street near you?', *Daily Telegraph*, 3 July 2007. BCA image reference number 75988, http://archives.cartoons.ac.uk/Record.aspx?src=CalmView.Catalog&id=75988.

6.15 Scott, no caption, *Daily Star*, 24 September 2006. BCA image reference number 74432, http://archives.cartoons.ac.uk/Record.aspx?src=CalmView.Catalog&id=74432.

6.16 Nicholas Garland, no caption, *Daily Telegraph*, 21 September 2006. BCA image reference number 74418, http://archives.cartoons.ac.uk/Record.aspx?src=CalmView.Catalog&id=74418.

6.17 Paul Thomas, no caption, *Daily Express*, 27 April 2004. BCA image reference number 69363, http://archives.cartoons.ac.uk/Record.aspx?src=CalmView.Catalog&id=69363.

6.18 Dave Gaskill, no caption, *Sun*, 31 January 2003. BCA image reference number 63832, http://archives.cartoons.ac.uk/Record.aspx?src=CalmView.Catalog&id=63832.

6.19 Brighty, 'I have decided it is time to integrate … ', *Sun*, 19 November 2012. BCA image reference number 97679, http://archives.cartoons.ac.uk/Record.aspx?src=CalmView.Catalog&id=97679.

6.20 Peter Brookes, 'Absolute scandal how Muslims refuse to integrate with society, eh, chaps?', *The Times*, 19 January 2016. BCA image reference number, 103642, https://archive.cartoons.ac.uk/Record.aspx?src=CalmView.Catalog&id=103642.

6.21 Christian Adams, 'Foiled', *Daily Telegraph*, 27 May 2013. BCA image reference number 98979, https://archive.cartoons.ac.uk/Record.aspx?src=CalmView.Catalog&id=98979.

6.22 Dave Brown, '"Thousands are at risk of radicalisation … " - Theresa May', *Independent*, 27 May 2013. BCA image reference number 98947, https://archive.cartoons.ac.uk/Record.aspx?src=CalmView.Catalog&id=98947.

6.23 Mac, 'This way, infidels!', *Daily Mail*, 12 August 2014. BCA image reference number 101389, http://archives.cartoons.ac.uk/Record.aspx?src=CalmView.Catalog&id=101389.

6.24 Chris Riddell, 'The second coming', *Observer*, 28 September 2014. BCA image reference number 101688, http://archives.cartoons.ac.uk/Record.aspx?src=CalmView.Catalog&id=101688.

6.25 Michael Heath, '"Where's Jihadi John?" (with apologies to Where's Wally?)', *Daily Mail*, 1 March 2015. BCA image reference number 102107, http://archives.cartoons.ac.uk/Record.aspx?src=CalmView.Catalog&id=102107.

6.26 Steve Bell, '4102-230316_INCIDENT', *Guardian*, 23 March 2017. BCA image reference number SBD1782, http://archives.cartoons.ac.uk/Record.aspx?src=CalmView.Catalog&id=SBD1782.

6.27 Ben Jennings, 'Terror Base … ', *i News*, 25 March 2017. BCA image reference number BJD0418, http://archives.cartoons.ac.uk/Record.aspx?src=CalmView.Catalog&id=BJD0418.

6.28 Christian Adams, 'Who is smaller … ?', *Evening Standard*, 23 May 2017. https://twitter.com/George_Osborne/status/866966691028361218/photo/1.

6.29 Martin Rowson, 'Enough is enough', *Guardian*, 4 June 2017. BCA image reference number MRD1033, https://archive.cartoons.ac.uk/Record.aspx?src=CalmView.Catalog&id=MRD1033.

6.30 Patrick Blower, no caption, *Daily Telegraph*, 5 June 2017. BCA image reference number 105700, https://archive.cartoons.ac.uk/Record.aspx?src=CalmView.Catalog&id=105700.

6.31 Brian Adcock, no caption, *Independent*, 5 June 2017. BCA image reference number BAD0461, https://archive.cartoons.ac.uk/Record.aspx?src=CalmView.Catalog&id=BAD0461.

6.32 Ben Jennings, 'To terror from London', *i News*, 16 September 2017. BCA image reference number BJD0437, http://archives.cartoons.ac.uk/Record.aspx?src=CalmView.Catalog&id=BJD0437.

6.33 Martin Rowson, 'Read the Sun & Daily Mail', *Guardian*, 20 June 2017. BCA image reference number MRD102, http://archives.cartoons.ac.uk/Record.aspx?src=CalmView.Catalog&id=MRD1023.

6.34 Ben Jennings, no caption, *Guardian*, 1 December 2019, https://www.theguardian.com/commentisfree/picture/2019/dec/01/ben-jennings-on-boris-johnson-and-the-london-bridge-attack-cartoon.

6.35 Morten Morland, no caption, *The Times*, 2 December 2019. https://www.thetimes.co.uk/article/morten-morland-times-cartoon-december-2-2019-0x2fggrw8.

List of Images Cited 231

Conclusion

7.1 'Breaking point, the EU has failed us all', Ukip advert. https://www.theguardian.com/politics/2016/jun/16/nigel-farage-defends-ukip-breaking-point-poster-queue-of-migrants.

7.2 Scott, 'So long, farewell, auf wiedersehen, goodbye …', *Daily Star*, 29 March 2017. BCA image reference number CLD1054, https://archive.cartoons.ac.uk/Record.aspx?src=CalmView.Catalog&id=CLD1054.

7.3 Scott, 'Commonwealth passport', *Sunday Express*, 19 February 2017. BCA image reference number CLD0984, https://archive.cartoons.ac.uk/Record.aspx?src=CalmView.Catalog&id=CLD0984.

7.4 Martin Rowson, 'Blue … ', *Guardian*, 3 April 2017. BCA image reference number MRD0992, https://archive.cartoons.ac.uk/Record.aspx?src=CalmView.Catalog&id=MRD0992.

7.5 Brian Adcock, 'Post-Brexit immigration policy revealed … ', *Independent*, 7 September 2017. BCA image reference number BAD0390, https://archive.cartoons.ac.uk/Record.aspx?src=CalmView.Catalog&id=BAD0390.

7.6 Peter Brookes, no caption, *The Times*, 20 April 2018. BCA image reference number 106732, https://archive.cartoons.ac.uk/Record.aspx?src=CalmView.Catalog&id=106732.

7.7 Christian Adams, Immigration Policy, *Evening Standard*, 17 April 2018. https://www.instagram.com/p/BhqzeythwXj/.

7.8 Martin Rowson, 'A vision of Britain, uncorrupted by the vile stain of immigration!', *Guardian*, 16 April 2018. https://twitter.com/MartinRowson/status/985791339223834624.

7.9 David Low, 'The Hard of Lot of A Cartoonist', *Evening Standard*, 13 October 1927. BCA image reference number LSE0278, https://archive.cartoons.ac.uk/Record.aspx?src=CalmView.Catalog&id=LSE0278.

7.10 Ben Jennings, 'A Week of Idiocy … ', *i News*, 10 January 2015. BCA image reference number BJD0193, https://archive.cartoons.ac.uk/Record.aspx?src=CalmView.Catalog&id=BJD0193.

Index

7/7 attacks 2005 1, 20, 36, 101, 106, 108, 109, 127, 128, 133–6, 138, 141, 145, 146, 147, 148, 150, 159
9/11 20, 101, 103, 106, 108, 112, 123, 127, 128, 129–36, 148, 153

Act of Union 1800 24
Adams, Christian 118, 141, 146, 155
Adams, Gerry 46
Adcock, Brian 146, 154
Adebolajo, Michael *see* Rigby, Lee
Adebowale, Michael *see* Rigby, Lee
Afghanistan 2, 47, 104, 106, 109–11, 118, 123, 131, 132, 134 *see also* Taliban
African 26, 39 *see also* African-Caribbean, Afro-Caribbean
African-Caribbean 98, 104, 121, 147 *see also* African, Afro-Caribbean
Afro-Caribbean 63 *see also* African, African-Caribbean
Ahmed Ali, Abdulla 136
Al Qaeda 36, 128, 129, 134, 142
Al Qaeda in the Arabian Peninsula (AQAP) 119
al-Baghdadi, Abu Bakr 129
al-Masri, Abu Hamza 139–40, 145, 155
Aliens Order 1920 63
Amrit 82, 93
Anglo-
  Caucasian 41
  Christian 41
  Irish Treaty 1922 30
  Jewish 56, 58–63, 70–1
  Saxon 17, 25, 26, 42, 58, 81, 90, 93, 99, 156
  Sikh 81–2, 91, 100
ape 26, 27–8, 40 *see also* gorilla
appeasement 66, 159
Arab 38, 60, 62, 63, 67, 69, 71, 72, 73, 105, 134, 136 *see also* Palestinian
Arab-Israeli conflict 38–9, 77, 158 *see also* Arab-Israeli war

Arab-Israeli war
  1948 68–9
  1967 71
Arafat, Yasser 72, 73, 129, 130
army
  British 32, 33–4, 37, 39, 41, 47, 59, 61
  British Indian 42, 83, 156
  Indian 93
  Israeli 72, 75
Asian 16, 19–20, 63, 86, 90, 96–7, 98, 104, 105, 128, 134, 142, 147, 153, 159, 160
  Kenyans 97–8, 100 *See also* Indian
assimilation 20, 135, 157, 160
Auschwitz 2 *see also* Shoah
Austen, Jane 107, 108
Austin, David 133–4

baby 36, 75 *see also* child
balaclava 38, 45–8, 53, 128, 129, 144, 145, 147, 158
Balfour Declaration 1917 58
Bandeau 97, 98
Bangladesh 1, 3, 128
Bank of England 107, 112
Battle of the Boyne 24, 48
BBC *see* British Broadcasting Corporation
beard 40, 81–2, 84–5, 87, 88, 90–1, 98, 106, 110–1, 118, 127, 131, 134, 136, 137, 143, 148, 153
Beaverbrook, Lord William Maxwell Aitken 66, 165
Beckett, Gilbert á 7
Beirut 72
Belfast 32, 34, 35–6, 37, 38, 43, 47
Belgium 113, 143, 152
Bell, Steve 4, 8, 48, 73–4, 76–7, 129, 145–6
Ben-Gurion, David 69, 70
Biden, Joe 51
Blair, Tony 49, 76, 132, 134, 135
Blears, Hazel 108–9
Blood 33, 62, 72, 76, 142, 143, 146
  libel 75–7, 158

Bloody Sunday 32, 34
Blower, Patrick 146, 151
bomb 1, 2, 32, 33, 45, 46, 136, 137, 142
bombings
    Air India Flight 182 1985 95
    Clerkenwell Prison 1858 25
    Docklands 1996 1
    litter 36
    London Underground 2017 146
    Manchester Arena 2017 146
    Republican campaign 1970s 42, 43
    Shankhill Road 1993 36
    See also 7/7, 9/11
Borough Market attack 2017 146
Brexit 17, 18, 50–1, 153–4, 155
Brighty 117, 141
Britannia 27
British Broadcasting Corporation 3
British Empire 4, 19, 57, 63, 82, 86, 93, 99, 100, 153, 160
British Mandate in Palestine *or* Mandated Palestine *or* Mandatory Palestine 58, 59–61, 62, 63, 67, 69, 70, 73, 160, 161 *see also* Palestine
British Nationality Act
    1948 86
    1981 44
British Union of Fascists 63
Brookes, Peter 74, 99, 107, 110, 112–13, 116, 119–20, 129–30, 141, 155
Brown, Dave 8, 49, 74–5, 76, 77, 108, 109, 141
Bull, John 48, 154
burqa 16, 19, 46, 101, 103–4, 108–9, 110–14, 116–17, 119, 120, 121, 122–4, 125, 126, 128, 129, 135, 144, 145, 148, 157, 159, 160, 161 *see also* niqab

Cable, Vince 107, 108, 112
Callaghan, Jim 97
Cameron, David 99, 141
cap *see* hat
Catholic 11, 17–18, 23, 24, 25, 30–1, 34, 35, 39, 40, 41, 48, 121, 156, 158
Celt 23, 25–6, 52, 155
Chamberlain, Neville 159
Charlie Hebdo 2, 3, 119
child 34, 35–6, 46, 66, 69, 75, 76, 104, 112, 142, 146, 162 *see also* baby

Christ 11, 32, 75, 121
Christian 11, 19, 39, 41, 44, 55, 56, 57, 75, 85, 105, 120, 121, 130, 136, 156, 157–8
Christianity *see* Christian
Churchill, Winston 107, 165
citizenship 44, 86, 97, 124–5, 139, 155
Commonwealth 8, 14, 19, 86–7, 90, 100, 104, 153, 154, 155
Commonwealth Immigrants Act
    1962 86
    1968 90, 97
Cookson, Bernard 32, 34, 35
Corbyn, Jeremy 147
counter-terrorism 108, 109
Craig, James 31
crocodile 49
Cromwell, Oliver 55
crown 47, 57
Cruikshank, George 5
Cummings, Michael 16, 39, 40, 41, 44, 45, 90, 94–5

Daesh 20, 35, 45, 52, 117, 127, 128, 129, 142–5, 147, 149, 158, 165
Danish 2, 3, 77 *see also* Posten, Jyllands
democracy 19, 27, 95, 103, 106, 107, 111, 123, 131, 135, 140, 145, 146
Democratic Unionist Party (DUP) 15, 18, 45, 51, 163
Disraeli, Benjamin 8, 57–8, 77, 78
dove 49, 73
Downing Street 95, 98, 131
Doyle, John 8
Dublin 23, 29, 32, 35
Duke of Wellington 24
DUP *see* Democratic Unionist Party
Dyer, Colonel Reginald Edward Harry 42

East Africa 90
East Pakistan *see* Bangladesh
Eastern European 20, 63
Edward I 55
EEC *see* European Economic Community
Egypt 67, 68–9, 70, 71, 97
elephant 88
Emmwood 48, 96
empire *see* British Empire
Employment Equality (Religion or Belief) Regulations 2003 91

Emwazi, Mohammed 20, 128, 144
epaulettes 117
Erdogan, Recep Tayyip 3
Erin 29, 30, 50, 161 *see also* Hibernia
EU *see* European Union
European Economic Community (EEC) 90, 92
European Union (EU) 8, 11, 17, 51, 143, 153, 154
eyes 46–7, 104, 105, 107, 112, 127, 132, 139, 140, 142, 143

face 19, 26, 43, 44, 45, 46–7, 48, 57, 68, 70, 74, 98, 103, 104, 108, 112, 113, 115–17, 121, 122, 123–4, 128, 129, 131, 132, 136, 137–8, 139, 143, 148, 158 *see also* burqa, balaclava
femininity 16, 108–9, 159, 161
Fenian Brotherhood 25, 26, 27, 28–9, 158
Finsbury Park Mosque 139, 140, 146
First World War 58, 132
Fitzgerald, William Vesey 24
'Five Ks' 82, 83, 84
    See also Kara
flag 3, 38, 47, 67, 68, 71, 76, 113, 129, 143, 152, 155
France 3, 112, 113, 115, 143, 152 *see also* Paty, Samuel, Charlie Hebdo
Franklin, Stanley 35, 41, 47, 88–9, 95, 98
free speech 3–4, 75, 103, 106, 133
Fricker, Steve 132

Gaddafi, Colonel Muammar 117, 122, 129, 130
Gandhi, Indira 93
Garda 47
Garland, Nicholas 8, 33, 35–6, 37, 43, 50, 73, 74, 132, 134, 135, 137–9, 149
Gaskill, Dave 49, 140
Gaza 70, 75
gaze 9–10, 20, 121, 125–6, 159
gender 16, 19, 26, 47, 50, 77, 84, 96, 103, 106–8, 110, 113–14, 115, 116, 121–3, 124, 148, 149, 159, 160, 163–4
George, Lloyd 29–30
Germany 64, 66, 143 *see also* Nazi
Gibbard, Leslie 32–3, 92, 112
Giles, Ronald Carl 15, 17, 40
Gillray, James 5, 6, 162, 165
Gladstone, William 58

Goering, Hermann 69
Golden Temple 93, 95
Good Friday Agreement 18, 45, 46, 47, 49, 50–1, 158
gorilla 27, 29, 45 *see also* ape
Gould, Francis Carruthers 8
Government of Ireland Act 1920 29
Greater Transjordan *see* Jordan
gun 34, 36, 45, 77, 165 *see also* pistol, rifle, revolver
Gurdwara 88, 96

Hague, William 76
hair or hairstyle 27, 43, 81–4, 85, 90, 91, 101, 103–4, 107, 143 *see also* beard, *burqa*, 'Five Ks'
Haldane, David 46
Haselden, William Kerridge 97
hat 27, 29–30, 38, 40, 42, 48, 49, 53, 87, 88, 90, 92–3, 97, 118, 128 *see also* helmet
headscarf 104, 109, 111 *see also* burqa
Heath, Edward 33, 92
Heath, Michael 144
heels 110, 113, 116, 117
helmet 91–3, 161 *see also* hat
Henry VIII 25
Hibernia 26, 27, 29, 50 *see also* Erin
Hindu 16, 82, 83, 94, 95
Hitler, Adolf 63–6
Hobbs, Jack 4
Hogarth, William 5, 7, 112, 162, 165
Holocaust *see* Shoah
House of Commons 24 *see also* Westminster
House of Lords 24, 91 *see also* Westminster
Houses of Parliament 95, 131 *see also* Westminster
Hussain, Tanvir 136
Hussein, Saddam 129, 130

Illingworth, Leslie Gilbert 60
immigrant 11, 18, 20, 43, 44, 63, 81, 86, 90, 93, 95, 96, 98, 99–100, 101, 104, 105, 113, 128, 133, 136, 141, 145, 147–8, 153, 154, 155, 156, 159, 160
Immigration Act
    1968 90, 97
    1971 44

India 1, 4, 42, 57, 81–2, 83, 85, 86, 93, 94, 95, 99–100
Indian 16, 42, 43–4, 83, 85, 90, 92, 93, 94, 95, 99 *see also* Asian
integration 19, 20, 57, 63, 81, 87, 88, 89, 96, 98, 122, 129, 133, 135, 141, 142, 145, 148, 149, 153, 156, 157, 159, 160
International Holocaust Cartoon Competition 2
Iran 2, 104, 105, 130
Iraq 47, 127, 142, 147 *see also* Daesh
Irgun (also known as Etzel) 59, 60
Irish Republican Army (IRA) 1, 15, 30, 31, 33–7, 38, 43, 45–50, 51 *see also* Real Irish Republican Army and Provisional Irish Republican Army
Islamic State of Iraq and the Levant (ISIS) *see* Daesh
Islamophobia 106, 123, 127, 133
Israel 18, 38, 55–6, 58–9, 62–3, 67–76, 77, 78–9, 134, 158 *see also* Arab-Israeli conflict, Arab-Israeli war
Israeli Defence Forces (IDF) 67, 70, 72, 77
Izzadeen, Abu 138–9

Jak 31–2, 33, 43, 44, 71–2, 96, 98
James II 24
JAS 49
jaw 25, 27, 45
Jennings, Ben 120–1, 145–7, 151, 164–5
Jerusalem 2
Jesus *see* Christ
Jewish Chronicle 57, 59, 60–1
'Jihadi John' *see* Emwazi, Mohammed
Johnson, Boris 3, 124, 141, 147, 154
Jon 32, 38–9, 49
Jordan 67, 69, 70
Jyllands-Posten 2, 4

Kara 82, 84, 164 *see also* 'Five Ks'
Kenya 37, 41, 97–8, 100 *see also* Kenyatta, Jomo, Asian Kenyan
Kenyatta, Jomo 37, 97
Khalistan 93, 95
Khalsa 82, 84, 93, 95
Khamenei, Ali 130
Khan, Imran 3
Khan, Usman 146
Khomeini, Ayatollah 105, 129, 130

King David Hotel 60
kippah 74, 160
Krauze, Andrzej 48

Laden, Osama Bin 103, 114, 117, 123, 134, 157, 161
Leech, John 6, 7, 25
Lehi, Lohamei Herut Israel *see* Stern Gang
Lenglen, Suzanne 97, 98
liquid racism 18, 56, 77, 79 *see also* racism
London 1, 14, 25, 31, 35, 43, 56, 63, 82, 86, 87, 88, 90, 96, 101, 127, 136, 138, 139, 141, 142, 144, 155
    Bridge attack 2017 146, 147
Londonderry 31, 32, 37
Low, David 4, 15, 42, 60–70, 72, 77, 78, 159, 164–5
Loyalist 18, 24, 45, 47, 48, 49, 50, 52, 53, 158 *see also* nationalist
Lynch, Jack 33

Mac 17, 34, 35–6, 41, 47, 91, 114, 131, 133, 143, 145
macho 77, 84 *see also* masculinity
Macron, Emmanuel 3
Mahood, Kenneth 43, 44, 164
Malta 96–7
Manchester
    Arena attack 2017 146, 150
    City Council 85
    region 85
    Transport Committee 85
Mandatory Palestine *see* British Mandate in Palestine
Martin, Sidney William 45
masculinity 16, 47, 50, 78, 82, 83, 84, 99, 101, 108, 161 *see also* macho
mask 23, 45, 46, 48, 52, 53, 117, 120, 128, 144–5, 158–9
Masood, Khalid 145, 146, 147
Matar, Hadi 105
Matt 112–16
May, Theresa 116, 141, 146, 154, 155, 163
meat cleaver 141, 142
Meir, Golda 77
Middle East 41, 76, 79, 104, 144 *see also* British Mandate in Palestine, Israel, Palestine
Mohamed, Mohammed Ahmed 116
Morgan, Matt 28

Morgenavisen Jyllands-Posten see Jyllands-Posten
Morland, Morten 134, 136, 147, 149
Moses 57, 70
Motor-Cycle Crash Helmets (Religious Exemption) Act 1976 93
motorcycles 82, 91–3, 100
Mowlam, Mo 48
Muhammad 2, 3, 4, 77, 103, 105, 119
Myers, David 87

nationalist 30, 31, 35, 101 *see also* loyalist
Nazis 18, 58, 59, 62, 63–4, 66, 69, 78, 132, 154, 159
  neo 165
Netanyahu, Benjamin 73–4, 76, 79
Newman, Nicholas 118
Nigeria/Nigerian 2, 142
niqab 98, 103, 104, 107, 108, 109, 112, 113, 114, 115, 116–17, 118, 119, 123, 124, 126, 135, 137, 149, 157 *see also* burqa
nose 2, 18, 27, 55, 57, 58, 78
nun 36–7, 121
Nuremberg trials 1946 69
Nuttall, Paul 121

O'Connell, Daniel 24–5
olive branch 49, 73
Osaka, Naomi 3
Oslo Peace Accords 1993 72, 73

Paddy 23, 25, 26, 27, 29, 34, 37, 40, 41
Pakistani 3, 81, 104, 105, 128
Palestine 130 *see also* British Mandate in Palestine
Palestine Liberation Organisation (PLO)72–3
Palestinian 59, 62, 68, 69, 70, 72, 73, 75, 76 *see also* Arab
Panopticon 125
paramilitary 18, 24, 35, 38, 45, 48, 52
Parnell, Charles Stewart 30
Partridge, Bernard 30, 34
passport 97, 154, 155
patriarchal 84, 96
Paty, Samuel 3
peace 36, 39, 41, 45, 46, 47, 48, 49, 68, 72–4, 75, 78, 146
perahan tunban 110, 127, 131

pistol 68 *see also* gun, rifle, revolver
Poland 64
police 25, 31–2, 40, 43, 47, 49, 88, 91, 92, 94, 98, 109, 112, 145, 147
  Services Northern Ireland (PSNI) 49
Powell, Enoch 44, 90, 98 *see also* 'Rivers of blood'
Priestley, Chris 46, 48
Prison Maze 48
prisoner 48, 67
prognathism 26, 27, 29, 52
Protestant 17, 18, 23, 24, 25, 26, 29, 36, 38, 39, 40, 41, 46, 47, 48, 156
Provisional Irish Republican Army (PIRA) 35
Pugh, Jonathan 49
Punjab 86, 93, 104

Qatar 3

Rabin, Yitzhak 72, 73, 74
race 4, 11, 16, 17, 19, 21, 26, 41–2, 43, 45, 53, 91, 98, 104, 105, 136, 156, 160, 164
Race Relations Act 1976 91
racism 21, 26, 52, 56, 77, 105 *see also* liquid racism
radicalism 20, 135, 138, 145
rape 36, 50
Raven-Hill, Leonard 30
Real Irish Republican Army (RIRA) 46, 47
Red Sea 62
refugee 63, 69–70
Reid, John 138, 139
republican 18, 24, 33, 42, 43, 47, 48, 50, 52–3 *see also* loyalist
resistance 36, 58, 59, 60, 68, 100, 123, 147, 157
revolver 78 *see also* rifle, pistol
Riddell, Chris 46, 143, 144
rifle 33, 34, 38, 46, 47, 48, 49, 67, 68 *see also* revolver, pistol
Rigby, Lee 141, 142
Rigby, Paul 33
riot 34, 35, 37, 51
'Rivers of Blood' speech 44, 90, 98 *see also* Powell, Enoch
Roman Catholic *see* Catholic
Roman Catholic Relief Act 24
Rothschild, Baron Lionel de 25, 56

Rowson, Martin 3, 146, 147, 150, 154, 155, 165
Rushdie, Salman 105, 106, 112, 131 *see also* Matar, Hadi

Sagar, G. S. S. 85
salwar kameez 16, 46, 128, 134, 135, 136, 137, 138, 141, 143, 148, 160
Sandhu, Tarsem Singh 85
Sarkozy, Nicolas 113
Sarwar, Assad 136
Satanic Verses 105, 106 *see also* Rushdie, Salman
Saudi Arabia 2, 125, 146, 163
Scarfe, Gerald 75-7
Schrank, Peter 110-1, 113-14, 129, 136-7, 149
Scott 138-9, 154
Scottish 40
Second World War 18, 55, 59, 60, 61-2, 63, 77, 85, 160
Shankhill Road 36, 41
Shard 146, 147
Sharett, Moshe 69
Sharon, Ariel 74, 75, 79
Sharp, Richard 3-4, 165
Shoah 18, 56, 63, 69, 70, 71
simian 17, 25, 26, 27, 28, 29, 40, 45, 52, 158
Sinai 67, 70
Singh, Guru Gobind 82
Singh, Manmohan 99
Singh, Sant Fateh 85
Sinn Fein 30, 35, 45, 46, 49
Six Day War *see* Arab-Israeli War 1967
social media 119, 138, 147, 151, 152
soldier 32, 33, 34, 35, 38, 39, 41, 42, 47, 49, 59, 60, 68, 71, 72, 77, 83, 92, 93, 110-1, 158 *see also* Rigby, Lee
South Asian *see* Asian
sphinx 58
Statue of Liberty 129
stereotype 2-3, 9-10, 17, 18, 20, 34, 44, 55, 58, 76, 78, 79, 108, 112, 118, 136, 142, 148, 159, 160
Stern Gang 59, 62
Stern, Avraham *see* Stern Gang
Stonehouse, John 90
Stormont 49, 50
subversion 19, 81, 88, 96, 101, 103, 118, 122, 123, 157, 161

Suez
  Canal 57
  Crisis 1956 43, 70, 71
Sunak, Rishi 51
symbol 2, 16, 19, 29, 56, 58, 75, 76, 79, 81, 87, 88, 96, 100, 123, 129, 133, 136, 144, 157, 165
Syria 69, 142, 143 *see also* Daesh

Taliban 103, 106, 107, 109-10, 111, 112, 118, 123, 131, 132, 133, 134, 135, 157
Tenniel, John 7, 27, 78
terrorist 2, 18, 20, 24, 36, 43, 48, 50, 52, 53, 59, 60, 61, 62, 68, 71, 99, 101, 107, 108, 117, 127, 128, 131, 133, 135, 138, 141, 146, 147, 149, 150, 152, 153, 158
Thatcher, Margaret 94, 95
thawb 134, 135, 148
Thomas, Paul 110, 133-4, 139-140
topi 118, 120, 128, 134, 135, 136, 141, 148
torture 33, 37
Transjordan *see* Jordan
trench coat 23, 34, 46, 52
Trimble, David 49
trog 38, 96
Trojan horse 118
Troubles 17, 32-3, 34, 46, 51
Trump, Donald 74, 146, 153
Tube
  map 146, 147
  train 134, 146
turban 2, 16, 19, 42, 44, 46, 58, 108, 112, 123, 127, 131, 138, 143, 148, 153, 157, 161, 164
Turkey 152

Uganda 38, 41
Ulster 29, 37, 39, 48
Ulster Defence Association (UDA) 38, 45, 47, 48, 51
Ulster Unionist Party (UUP) 30-1
Ulsteran/Ulstermen 26, 45
Uncle Sam 129
uniform 31, 45, 48, 49, 67, 68, 71, 85, 87, 88, 89, 91, 93
Union Jack 47, 48, 90, 110, 139, 154
United Nations (UN) 47, 66, 67, 68, 70, 72, 77
United States 67, 70, 106, 112, 136, 139

Valera, Eamon De 23, 30
values 20, 88, 89, 106, 107, 113, 114, 119, 120, 121, 122, 125, 133, 135, 139, 143, 145, 149
Victoria, Queen 57
vulture 45, 95

Waite, Keith 31–2, 36–7, 87, 88–9, 91, 97
war
    of Independence 1919–21 37
    on Terror 106, 112, 127, 132
weapon 30, 49, 67, 143, 144
West Bank 67

Westminster
    Bridge 145, 146
    Palace 131, 145, 146, 147
    UK government 18, 24, 25, 32, 51, 56, 154
White House 73
Whitelaw, William 44
William of Orange 24, 48
Williams, Serena 2–3
Windrush 154–5
wog 96, 97

Zion *see* Israel
Zionism 58, 59, 60, 62, 63, 64, 69, 71, 161

www.ingramcontent.com/pod-product-compliance
Lightning Source LLC
Chambersburg PA
CBHW071825300426

44116CB00009B/1447